GLENN CURTISS

GLENN CURTISS

PIONEER OF AVIATION

ALDEN HATCH

INTRODUCTION BY R. L. RASMUSSEN, CAPTAIN USN (RET.)
DIRECTOR, NATIONAL MUSEUM OF NAVAL AVIATION

THE LYONS PRESS
Guilford, Connecticut
An imprint of The Globe Pequot Press

The Lyons Press is an imprint of The Globe Pequot Press.

10 9 8 7 6 5 4 3 2 1

Printed in the United States of America

ISBN 978-1-59921-145-9

Library of Congress Cataloging-in-Publication Data is available on file.

WITH MUCH APPRECIATION

It seems probable that no one ever had more co-operation in gathering material for a book than I have received from the family and former associates of Glenn Curtiss. He had the ability to inspire such loyalty and devotion in all who knew him, that, even so long after his death, they blazed with enthusiasm at the mention of his name and labored for days ransacking their files and searching their memories for every scrap of information which might help me to describe him more fully. This, I realize, was in order that I might do justice to a very great American, but I am deeply appreciative of their assistance and of the honor they did me in believing that I could do the job.

One reason that they were so anxious that this book should be written was the feeling, which they all had, that the great services which Curtiss performed for aviation and for his country were being forgotten—and this feeling had a basis in fact. The memory of Glenn Curtiss has been dimmed by the prominence of the Wright brothers. They were the first men truly to fly, and no words of mine could or should dim the glory of that achievement. Nevertheless, Curtiss' contributions to aviation, though not as spectacular, were at least as important, for his inventions were in the direct line of progress. In all the world no plane ventures into the sky without the ailerons which he devised, and none rises anywhere from water that does not ride for a few vital seconds on his hydroplane step.

So much he did for aviation in general, but his services to

his own country were no less vital. Working almost alone and in the face of colossal inertia, he formed the Naval Aviation of the United States and gave it such a headstart that it has never been overtaken. The great victory of Midway, which may have given America naval supremacy in the Pacific, is directly traceable to his tireless and unselfish devotion to the cause in which he so ardently believed. This man cannot be forgotten.

Specifically, I wish to acknowledge with much gratitude the invaluable assistance of Mrs. Sayre Wheeler, the former Lena Curtiss; Harry Genung, Martha Genung, Mrs. Florence Ilig, Mr. and Mrs. Carl Adams, Sayre Wheeler, Hugh Robinson, James H. Bright, G. Leonard (Tank) Waters, Becky Havens, E. H. Ballard, and many others, including many officials of the Curtiss-Wright Company, each of whom went to endless trouble to make his contribution.

I am also greatly indebted to Clara Studer's *Sky Storming Yankee*, and to an unpublished manuscript by Richard Steele.

I offer my thanks to them in the form of this book, with the hope that they will feel that it justifies their exertion and their faith in me.

ALDEN HATCH

Somerleas, Cedarhurst, Long Island
August 15, 1942.

FOREWORD

THE STORY OF THE life of any man is difficult to construct. Even though the author may have known him well, it is most unlikely that he can cover all aspects; therefore, he necessarily must seek information from others. Whether the final character picture correctly portrays the subject depends upon the skill and judgment of the author. In this biography Alden Hatch has shown an honesty of purpose. Along with the pleasant and interesting he has taken the unpleasant and controversial. Fortunately, time has smoothed and rounded the corners of the latter.

The story of Glenn Curtiss does not follow the usual pattern of that of the traditional American who "made good." What his boyish ideals may have been I never discovered, but I know they were not riches, position or power. He seemed always to be trying to find means of doing things in a better way and thereby helping his fellowmen. He was modest and diffident to a degree which was really embarrassing to those who did not know him well, yet behind it all was a cold courage and a determination which ever drove him onward, and enabled him to hurdle obstacles which would have stopped most others.

I had the good fortune to be one of the very few who knew Glenn Curtiss well and enjoyed his confidence, from the rather early days of aviation up to his death in 1930. I never ceased to wonder at the man. He had no engineering education, yet his solution of engineering problems in a practical way stood the test of mathematical analysis. He lived a simple life rather away from the world, yet he developed a vision of the future which subsequent events proved to be astoundingly accurate. Above all, he had an abiding faith in the future of his country and strove to the end to do his share toward the fulfillment of its destiny.

REAR ADMIRAL JOHN H. TOWERS, U.S.N.
Chief of the Bureau of Aeronautics

CONTENTS

ix

INTRODUCTION

IN HIS ORIGINAL FOREWORD to the book *Glenn Curtiss: Pioneer of Naval Aviation*, Rear Admiral John H. Towers reminisced about his personal relationship with the famed aviation pioneer that began when he reported to Curtiss to learn to fly for the navy. Admiral Towers was not the first naval aviator, but he was the only one of the first few to stick with naval aviation against a tide of navy philosophy where the battleship reigned supreme. It was the genius of Glenn Curtiss that most influenced Admiral Towers in his successful crusade for the dominance of naval aviation.

Few naval aviators had the privilege of knowing him, but we all owe Glenn Curtiss a debt of gratitude. The aircraft carriers from which we flew, and their aircraft, were built upon the foundation of his successful efforts to convince naval officers of the early twentieth century of the potential of aircraft to operate at sea from the decks of ships. The naval aviators of today are similarly indebted to this man.

He constructed the TS-1, the first airplane designed as a carrier aircraft, and he designed and built the F6C Hawk, both first-generation carrier fighters, predecessors of the thousands of aircraft that covered the navy's carrier decks throughout the history of naval aviation. Indeed, Glenn Curtiss permeates the fabric of naval aviation history, his contributions woven into its enduring heritage. He greets visitors to the National Museum of Naval Aviation at every turn, from the A-1 Triad, the navy's first aircraft; to the famed Jenny that trained pilots of the Great War at home and abroad; to the NC-4 flying boat that in 1919 first bridged the Atlantic. As happened many times in aviation history, Glenn Curtiss fortuitously appeared at the right moment in history, at the threshold of the "American Century" in which the science of aviation achieved unimaginable heights. And these accomplishments were due in large part to the determination and vision of the humble genius from Hammondsport, New York. Without naval aviation, it is hard to imagine how differently the history of the navy and our country might have unfolded over the past one hundred years. But we do know that without Glenn Curtiss, history would have been far different and certainly less of a triumph of the human spirit.

R. L. Rasmussen, Captain USN (Ret.)

Director, National Museum of Naval Aviation

2007

CHAPTER ONE

CAPTAIN BALDWIN FINDS A MOTOR

THE CROWD PRESSED HARD against the ropes and tried to see beyond the bright California sunshine into the old circus tent that housed the airship. They could barely distinguish the vague outlines of its silken gas bag, which scraped gently against the top of the tent between poles set just far enough apart to clear its swollen girth.

Inside the tent "Captain" Thomas Scott Baldwin was working despairingly on the mass of ironmongery that was the best motor he could find in that summer of 1903. He was a short, thick man of forty-eight, already an ancient in the flying game. But, perhaps because in all his life he never grew up, he was driven by the dreams of youth. His was the vision, shared by a few men here and there, scoffed at by millions throughout the world, that someday man would learn to navigate the air. And now that dream was near to fulfillment, as close as the visions of Tantalus, and like them just beyond his grasp.

The captain fastened a final wire into place and vaulted over the edge of the car. Above him the great bag shivered and swayed against its restraining ropes.

He cast a quick look through the wide, high flaps of the tent. Beyond the roped-in square of ground he saw that his mechanics were talking to the crowd, quite evidently striving to allay their impatience.

"Hey, Roy!" he shouted.

3

Young Roy Knabenshue loped into the tent. "What is it, Uncle Tom?"

"How's the gate?" demanded the captain, who combined the shrewdness of a showman with the credulity of an inventor.

"Fair," Roy answered. " 'Bout a hundred and fifty dollars."

"How's the wind?"

"Flat calm."

"Call the boys," commanded his employer. "We might as well try her. She's as ready as she'll ever be."

Roy ran out shouting and the crowd raised a feeble cheer. Three other young mechanics came back with him into the tent, leaving only the veteran ticket taker on duty outside. Expertly they unhitched the ropes which shackled the pachyderm of the skies. Two on a side they slowly walked the swaying ship out into the California sunshine and set the car on waiting trestles. Then they stood holding it down.

In old scientific journals you will find the airship described in dignified but inaccurate terms: "A cigar-shaped envelope made of Japanese silk varnished to make it gasproof. . . ."

Actually the envelope was a bloated bag with unexpected bulges in the oddest places. The nose looked as though it had rammed a concrete wall and the tail drooped unhappily above the loosely attached rudder. Both ends sloped downward from the hump in the center. It was cigar-shaped, if you will; the shape of a cigar which has been dropped in the street, stamped on by a dray horse, and then rescued by a passing hobo who has endeavored to remold it to its original form.

The crowd cheered again as Captain Baldwin walked toward the airship. He was wearing a frock coat, and a semi-nautical cap was perched on his graying hair. As he climbed into the latticed girder slung beneath the gas bag, he acknowledged their shouts with a genial wave of his hand. Then he bent to prime the motor.

When that was done, one of the boys handed him a crank. He fitted it into place and began to turn her over. There were hissing noises, a half-hearted pop, and then nothing but dismal gasps as he heaved against the compression.

He put down the crank and fiddled with the carburetor. Then he primed her again and set to cranking. This time she caught. There was a single explosion and then a ragged series of reports. The car shook madly and the vanes of the propeller began to revolve. Captain Baldwin felt their grateful breeze in his face as he sprang into violent activity. He worked the throttle and spark and fingered the knobs on the carburetor. The unsilenced motor sounded like a battle between undisciplined troops, shooting at random. The engine was running as raggedly as a three-legged horse. First one cylinder cut out, then the other. Then both, and she stopped with a groan.

The captain pulled out a big bandana and wiped the sweat out of his eyes. Then he bent over the engine.

He was still at it two hours later. Nothing he could do would make that engine run. The crowd was getting ugly. They were pushing against the ropes and two of the mechanics were trying to hold them back. There were angry shouts of "Fake! Fake!" and pop bottles began to fly. The captain caught a couple and juggled them for a moment—he had learned that in the circus and it earned him a laugh.

"I'm doing my best," he shouted. "Don't shoot. I feel worse than you do."

He did, too. Not that he minded the crowd; he understood and sympathized with them, for they had paid good money to see something which couldn't be done. Not today anyway. It was the failure of his motor that discouraged him.

In all those thousands of flights he had made in free balloons, jockeying them up and down in the search for favorable slants of wind that would carry him where he wanted to go, helpless to direct a true course, he had dreamed of the day when he would drive an airship through the skies to an intended destination. He had poured out the money he made by risking his neck in parachute drops at a thousand country fairs and in tours throughout the world, on his experiments. And here he was almost back where he started. If only he could find a decent motor!

Someday there would be one. Someday man would sail through the air as familiarly as now he traversed the land or steered confidently over the oceans. But it looked as though it would be too late for Tom Baldwin.

Wearily he opened the petcocks and primed again. Then he picked up the crank. As he fitted it into its socket he paused.

There was a far vibration in the air. Off along the road he saw a trail of dust moving rapidly. The vibration resolved itself into the sound of a motor running sweetly. Over the fence he could see the head and shoulders of a man skimming along. The machine turned in at the gate and speeded expertly among the buggies and farm wagons. Captain Baldwin saw that it was a motor bicycle. He watched as the rider pulled up beside the ticket taker and jumped neatly off.

"Boys," said the captain, "hold her down. I've got to get a look at that thing."

He sprinted across the dusty ground toward the young man at the gate.

"Son," he said, "mind if I look at your machine for a moment?"

"Of course not," said its owner. "She's a beauty, isn't she?"

"She sure is," agreed the captain. He grasped the frame of the motorcycle and lifted it easily into the air. "Light too. What's the horsepower?"

"Five. She certainly does hum along."

The captain was on his knees examining the beautifully machined, little air-cooled motor.

"I see it's a Hercules," he said. "Who makes them?"

"A man called Glenn H. Curtiss of Hammondsport, New York," was the answer.

"That's the man for me," said Captain Baldwin.

From his hip pocket he whipped a greasy wallet fat with money, for the captain was no believer in banks. He selected a tattered envelope and with the stub of a pencil wrote slowly and with difficulty.

"Got to get this right," he said. "It's mighty important; more important than you'd believe. There, Glenn H. Curtiss, Hammondsport, New York."

CHAPTER TWO

THE HOUSE ON THE HILL

THE UNITED STATES NAVY leads the world, as it always has, in one vital department—naval aviation. No other country can meet the fighting planes which it launches from its great carriers, none can match the giant flying boats, the fast seaplanes, and the deadly dive bombers, which guard its ships and harry those of the enemy. This peculiar supremacy is due to the existence of a certain landlocked body of water, hundreds of miles from any ocean, and to Glenn Hammond Curtiss, who lived beside it.

Keuka is one of the Finger Lakes of upper New York State. It is surrounded by steep hills and narrow valleys and in all that region there is no piece of level ground more than a mile in length or a few hundred yards in width, no safe place to fly an aeroplane; only that fine plane of water, twenty-two miles long and one across, a perfect landing field.

The little town of Hammondsport climbs hardily up the rocky shore near the head of the lake. In 1878 it was a busy little port, which was the upstate shipping center of the Southern Tier of counties. The vineyards on the surrounding hillsides were the basis of the New World attempt to produce fine wines, and the inhabitants stoutly maintained that the local champagne compared favorably with the best vintages of France. They built great stone cellars in the cliffs in which to age their wine and they christened the post office in Pleasant

Valley, "Rheims," New York. That name was one day to echo back to them from France as their beloved fellow townsman won his greatest triumph there.

But in spite of its flourishing trade and its promising baby industry, Hammondsport might have remained forever content with purely local fame were it not for the boy born that year to Frank and Lua Andrews Curtiss.

The baby's background was as American as stars on a blue field. Behind him stood his grandfather Claudius Curtiss, who came to Hammondsport in 1865 as Methodist minister, a classic pioneer pastor, erudite, righteous, and stern. His grandmother, Ruth Curtiss, held principles as high, but she tempered them with worldly wisdom and a sense of humor. Because she had the quality of understanding and a powerful will, she managed her men, and was the real head of the family. They lived in a fine new house on the hill back of Hammondsport, with a view over the roofs of the town to the lake in one direction and down the sunny sweep of Pleasant Valley in another.

The baby's father, Frank, was not quite the son for this splendid couple, but in his way he was as native to the country. Content with his small harness business, amiable and indolent, his overfondness for the flow of the vineyards was excused by all because of his disarming charm.

On his mother's side the baby was descended from the same sort of folks. Grandfather Andrews, with his white, waist-long beard and fine aquiline nose, looked even more patriarchal than Claudius Curtiss. In Lua Andrews Curtiss an artistic and romantic strain unexpectedly predominated.

Frank had courted Lua in Hammondsport Glen, a romantic and rocky defile with appropriate cascades, pools, and grottoes, which was the favorite spooning spot of Hammondsport. It was the place in all the world she loved best, and when her son was born she said to her husband, "Frank, I've thought of a lovely name for the baby. I'm going to call him Glen, after Hammondsport Glen."

"You can't do that," Frank expostulated. "That's a thing, not a name."

Lua laughed at him affectionately. "Oh yes I can," she said. "But if you like, we'll add another *n* to make it sound more like a real name. And his middle name shall be Hammond, so that he'll always remember the lovely town he came from no matter how far away he goes. You can't say *Hammond* is a thing."

"It will make a very odd name," Frank said.

"I'm a very odd person," observed Lua. "Glenn Hammond Curtiss," she said softly. "It's a splendid name. There's a sort of sweep to it worthy of a great man. He's going to be one, you know, Frank."

"All mothers think that," said Frank Curtiss.

When Glenn was four years old, Grandfather Claudius Curtiss died. Ruth was very lonely in the big house. She liked life all around her, the pleasure of meeting its problems and having people to manage.

"Come live with me, Frank," she urged her son. "I've got to have somebody to fuss about."

"That's fine, Ma," said Frank, "if you think you can stand us."

"I've stood a lot in my time," said Ruth Curtiss.

So that summer Glenn came to live in his real home, the House on the Hill.

Frank Curtiss continued to run the harness shop on the main street down by the lake. In such a time and locality barter was the life of trade, and besides the farm products which he often accepted as payment for his wares, Frank accumulated a large assortment of parts of farm machinery and metal fittings for wagons and buggies. These oddments were piled in the back-yard until such a time as some farmer might come in needing a second-hand axle tree or a spare disk for his harrow. They made the loveliest junk pile that ever a mechanically minded little boy had to play in. To Glenn it was the same as it might be to some other child to have an island of ice cream all his own. For building things was his greatest pleasure, and he could always find a needed part in his treasure heap.

Frank Curtiss died the year after they moved to the House on the Hill, but the family still owned the now disused shop, and Glenn was free of his beloved junk pile. When he got older and went to school, he brought the other boys back to play there with him.

"Let's play football," Fred Hastings might shout, as they tore out of the door of the Union Free School.

"How about hunting rabbits?"

"I think I'll go build a sled"—from Glenn.

"What's the use, there's no snow yet?"

"There will be soon, and I've got an idea I want to try."

And because Glenn was a leader, who could make what he did seem more exciting and interesting than anything else, the discussion always ended with at least half the boys coming back to the junk pile.

That was the time before the great age of machines and, especially in a little country town, boys, who would now be building aeroplanes or tanks or automobiles, normally cared more for fishing or hunting or playing games. That the boys of Hammondsport came with Glenn gave them an interest and feel for mechanics that was a generation ahead of the times. All unconsciously he was training the men who were to help him when the great days came.

In school Glenn was less than a joy to "Prof" Cates, the Quaker schoolmaster. At arithmetic he was good, there was some sense to that; but history and English were to him just bypaths, useless trimmings of the mind, and Glenn's brain always held to its course. It was like trying to turn a gyroscope, to force it into deviations.

During summer vacations his grandmother's house was the rendezvous of all the neighboring kids. Ruth Curtiss knew how to manage boys as well as men; indeed, she had a masculine mind and sympathized with their pursuits, never interfering unless things went too far. Take, for instance, the Battle for the Cave.

That particular summer Glenn, surveying the almost vertical hillside that dropped from the terrace on which his home was built, had a great idea.

"Let's build a cave," he suggested to the gang.

"Yea! Let's!"

"Get some shovels."

"And a pick."

"And some planks to shore it up," said Glenn.

Soon they were all hard at work, digging into the black soil, rolling away the stones and boulders, worn smooth by the Great Glacier which had formed the hill.

When it was done it was no ordinary foxhole, such as boys might begin and weary of halfway through. What Glenn started he finished, and he could hold the others to his purpose. A proper cave it was, snug and dry, with a splendid view that nobody looked at. It could easily shelter the dozen boys, big and little, who had built it. But when the work was done, it left a vacant feeling. It's a pretty boring thing, just sitting around in a cave, and the problem of what to do with it, now that they had it, was urgent but unsolved. One afternoon, when the gang was sitting rather disconsolately in their shelter, that question was magnificently answered.

A group of kids from the waterfront gathered below the slope and stared enviously upward. Instantly the cave became again highly desirable, things were looking up.

"That's a pretty good cave," shouted a boy from below. "Did you build it?"

"Yes," called Glenn. "Why don't you build one farther along?"

"We like that one," said the leader of the gang.

"Well, you can't have it," shouted Fred Hastings.

"Sez who?"

"Try and take it."

"Come on fellers, let's clean the sissies out."

The boys charged furiously up the hill. But the fortress, which the cave had now become, had been unexpectedly stocked with ammunition by that friendly glacier long ago. The smooth, round stones began to fly, and the enemy retreated in a hurry.

The gang held a council of war at the foot of the hill, then streamed back to town. But it was only a repulse—not a victory. The invaders came back soon, carrying heavy armament in the shape of broken bricks, bottles, and every other lethal missile they could find.

"Surrender, if you know what's good for you," shouted the leader.

"Never!" Glenn yelled.

His eyes were bright with battle, his thin body seemed everywhere at once as he rallied his forces. Up the hill came the second charge, and the defenders were now badly out-numbered. As the enemy got closer, the air was filled with flying objects; it looked as though there might be a massacre.

But for once Ruth Curtiss abandoned her policy of non-intervention. Down from the house she charged, with black skirts flying, like an avenging Cossack. So fierce were her stern face and flashing eyes that friend and foe alike fled madly down the hill. Panting a little, with small beads of sweat starting from her face, she came to Glenn, alone in his cave.

"Why did you do that?" he asked. "We'd have beat them anyway."

"I know, Glenn," she said, "but it looked like somebody was going to get hurt. I'm sorry I had to spoil such a splendid battle."

Now that his father was dead, Glenn was pretty short of money. But he didn't think much about it, and would carelessly give or spend anything he had in his pocket. When he needed more, he gathered flowers in his grandmother's garden and went down to the pier to sell them to the people who landed from the little excursion steamer which circled the lake. It was his first business venture, but soon circumstances made him a real wage earner.

The year before her son finished grammar school, Lua Curtiss married Charles J. Adams and went to live at his home in Rock Stream on Seneca Lake. She took Glenn's little sister, Rutha, with her; but he remained with his grandmother.

Just about the time Glenn squeaked through his final exam-inations and Prof Cates wished him a delighted farewell, word came that Rutha was very sick with scarlet fever.

"Do you think she's going to die, Gran'ma?" Glenn asked. "She's awful young and pretty."

"Don't be morbid, Glenn," said Ruth Curtiss briskly. "All

children get scarlet fever. She'll be well again in a couple of weeks."

But Rutha never was quite well again, because the disease left her completely deaf. Lua decided to take her to Rochester, New York, for treatment by the great doctors there. So she uprooted Charlie Adams and dragged him to the city. Then she sent for Glenn.

"I surely hate to see you go," said Glenn's grandmother, as he stood ready with his one small suitcase.

Glenn kissed her soft cheek.

"Don't you fret," he said. "I'll be back before long."

The cost of living in Rochester and Rutha's doctors' bills put a terrific strain on the Adams' exchequer. Glenn saw that he would have to help out, and he found a job with the Eastman Kodak Company. It wasn't very interesting work, just stenciling red numbers on black rolls of paper and gluing them to the film. But it was piecework, and the faster he did it the more he got paid.

It wasn't long before Glenn was expert enough to make as much money as anybody could. But he wasn't satisfied.

"This is a silly way to attach the paper," he said to the foreman. "It's too slow."

"Huh," the Irishman snorted. "I suppose ye'll be knowin' of some other way that the boss himself hasn't heard of."

"I'll figure something out," said Glenn.

His work went badly for the next few days while his eyes had the lost look that they always wore when he "was figuring something out."

"Mind if I do this my own way?" he asked the foreman one morning.

"It's your funeral," was the answer. "But mind, if you fall too low, out you go."

So Glenn tried his scheme. The first week he doubled his earnings and the next week he trebled that. He was soon making altogether too much money for a boy of fifteen in the depression year of 1893. The big boss himself came down to see about it, and Glenn, with visions of an Oliver Optic rise from office boy to president, eagerly demonstrated his system.

"Curtiss," said the boss, "you're a bright young man, so bright that I'm afraid this company can't afford you. Thank you for your brilliant assistance, and—good-by."

So Glenn had figured himself out of a job.

His next position was less lucrative, but much more fun; he got a job with Western Union. This, too, was piecework, ten cents for every telegram delivered. Of course, if a boy owned a bicycle he could deliver four times as many messages as he could on foot. Glenn saw clearly that he was under a moral obligation to get one; he always went on the principle that to make money you must venture it boldly—sometimes too boldly. And, of course, he had been absolutely mad to own one of those beautiful shining machines ever since he had first seen them on the streets of Rochester.

Somehow he found the money to pay the exorbitant price of one hundred and twenty-five dollars which the manufacturers asked in those guileless days. Then indeed work became play, and play but an extension of his congenial work. He loved every moment that he spent in the cleverly sprung saddle of his splendid plaything. When he wasn't on duty at the Western Union office, he was busman's holidaying around town, looking for races and scorching over the asphalt.

That was the time when the bicycle was king for its brief, romantic reign. It represented the first great mechanical extension of life since the coming of the steam cars. All the world went mad on wheels. Young men clipped their trousers and pedaled madly around the cinder tracks; old men puffed methodically along on "century" runs. The ladies suddenly came out of the haremlike languor of the Victorian way and sailed prettily about on their "safeties" in sailor hats and ankle-length bloomers that caused pious folks' eyebrows to retreat permanently to the hairline.

The machines themselves bore splendid names, like the Stearns Racer, the National, and the Barnes White Flyer, while the men who rode in the great races were the apotheosis of glamour. Eddie Ball, Fred Titus, Walter Sanger and the Big Four of the New York Athletic Club were familiar figures to the whole population, and what boy did not long to emulate them? Certainly Glenn Curtiss did.

Every evening, after pedaling for miles on his rounds, he turned up for sprinting practice on the fast stretch on Alexander Street. From East Avenue to University there were no side streets, and it was the accepted meeting ground of the "speed demons."

The speed got into Glenn's blood. From then on throughout his life he wanted to go fast and ever faster, and fixed his mind, unswerving, on the problem until, more by his inventions than those of any other man, the sluggish human animal was lifted on wings that mocked the birds and made the wind seem slow.

CHAPTER THREE

"CALL ME G. H."

TANK WATERS LEANED AGAINST a post outside the drugstore on the square at Hammondsport. Above his head hung the amazingly apposite sign: J. H. SMELLIE, MEDICAL HALL. Tank was bored. He realized that he was pretty lucky to have found a job in a strange place, but it was not very interesting work, and he knew no one with whom he could talk on his favorite topic, bicycle racing. He wished that something exciting would turn up, and just then the most exciting thing that ever happened to him did.

Down the steep road, in a satisfying cloud of dust, shot a bicycle going like thunder. It swung into the square and circled it at racing speed. Tank appraised the rider with a connoisseur's eyes and found him good. He was a thin, dark young man, who rode with a style and speed that was far beyond anything the local boys could do.

After a second lap the rider eased up, and as he came around, Tank shouted tentatively, "Hi!"

The young man jumped expertly off his bicycle.

"Hello," he said.

"I like the way you ride," Tank said.

The other looked embarrassed. "Thanks, you ride yourself, I guess."

"A bit," remarked Tank. "Been in a few races. Nothing very much."

"Oh! I'm thinking of trying some racing now that I'm home. My name's Glenn Curtiss."

"I'm Tank Waters. I hit town a few months ago."

"Like to come up to my house when you get through? I've got a lot of interesting catalogues and cycling papers."

"I sure would," Tank answered.

So began a friendship that lasted out the years of life. Every evening the boys got together to talk cycling lore; every morning they arose early to practice sprinting on the half-mile race track at Stony Brook Farm. It was the only flat piece of ground in the whole valley, and Curtiss was to spend many another dawn there learning a more difficult art.

Glenn was a very busy young man those days. He was eighteen, and he had tired of working for other people. When his mother and stepfather moved back to Rock Stream, he had labored in the vineyards and then worked on some houses that Mr. Adams was building. But this was no life for Glenn Curtiss. He had mounted his precious bicycle and pedaled back to Hammondsport, where he had used his experience to get a temporary job in a photographic studio.

Now he was starting in business for himself. He rented a small shop a few hundred yards from his father's old location on the lake front and painted an imposing sign which read:

G. H. CURTISS
Dealer in Harness and Horse Furnishings
also
Bicycles and Sundries

His new friend helped him to erect the sign. It made the tiny shop look decidedly top-heavy. Then they stood off in the dusty street to admire it.

"Pretty fancy," said Tank. "Doesn't it make you feel important, Glenn?"

"I'm going to *be* important," Glenn affirmed. "Say Tank, I don't think Glenn sounds very businesslike. After this call me G. H."

Business prospered from the first, for young Curtiss would do anything from stitching up a harness to fixing doorbells. He was so handy with mechanical gadgets that when anything went wrong, people formed the habit of sending for "G. H." He fixed Seymour Hubbs' acetylene lighting plant, and while he was working on it, had one of his flashes of mechanical insight. He figured out a way to make a more efficient generator, and built it himself with the aid of a tinsmith. It worked splendidly and he put his generating plants into the shop, where they took the place of the Horse Furnishings. Glenn's heart was never in the harness business—horses were much too slow.

Meanwhile, the House on the Hill became again the meeting place of all the lads in the village. Ruth Curtiss still loved boys, and Curtiss, though he was a bustling young businessman now, was never too busy to bother with them. They adored him: he was their leader and their idol.

The most worshipful of all the boys who followed G. H. was twelve-year-old Harry Genung. He included the grand old lady in his adoration, and many an evening climbed the hill to sit and read to her, since her eyes were failing. G. H. in turn was devoted to Harry. Already he perceived the quality of the youngster's mind, the stanchness of his character.

Evenings furnished the only time G. H. had to read. All day he was tending his shop, repairing bicycles, or hurrying out to fix the neighbors' gadgets. But at night he went to his room right after dinner and got into bed. Under it and in huge piles around the floor were cycling papers, catalogues, and scientific publications from all over the world. Those in foreign languages he could not read, but he could look at the pictures and study the mechanical drawings, and thus find out what was going on in France and Germany and the other progressive countries of Europe.

Harry often came to join him, and the two would sit for hours silently reading until some item struck fire from Curtiss' brain and he would launch into excited theorizing on how this or that could be improved.

One night Genung arrived to find G. H. studying a new kind of journal.

"Harry," he exclaimed, "there's money in rabbits."

"Rabbits!" Harry was round-eyed.

"Look at this."

The boy put on his spectacles and examined the journal. It was devoted to the culture of Belgian hares. All the time he was reading, Curtiss was talking. "I've heard people discussing this business for a long time," he said, "but I never realized it was such a big thing. Why, they have shows all over the country, people come for miles, and they pay whopping prices for breeding rabbits, too. It's the easiest way to collar a little coin I ever heard of. All you have to do is to put a pair together and they multiply like—like rabbits."

"But G. H.—"

"It looks like fun. What say you and I go partners in the rabbit business?"

"Great," said Harry. "But won't it cost a lot to get started?"

"Sure it will, but you can't make money without risking it, and rabbits produce dividends by the laws of nature. Couldn't be safer. Now, first of all, we'll need a good buck. Here's one advertised for sale that seems to be the blood royal of rabbit-dom: Lord Defiance."

"Gosh, G. H., he costs a hundred dollars."

"That's right, but we've got to have the best. I'll find it somehow."

"A hundred dollars for a rabbit!" gasped Harry.

Lord Defiance came to Hammondsport; so did Lady Helen, and Princess Primrose, the Gentle Lady Anne, and the haughty Countess of Wakeham. Under G. H.'s direction Harry built fine hutches for them, each with the name of its occupant proudly displayed above the door as in the stables of blood horses. Soon the "dividends" arrived, and Harry and his senior partner began to show their stock at the county fairs and rabbit meets. On show days such a washing and brushing, currying and curling of long silky hair took place as might hardly be equaled at Madison Square Garden on a horse-show night.

Soon the hares from Hammondsport began to bring back blue ribbons; and, as their fame spread, people came for miles to see the model rabbit farm and were duly impressed by its fancy embellishments into paying enormous prices for the dividends.

So the eccentric partnership prospered, and it continued to do so for three years until it was dissolved by the departure of the junior partner to seek his fortune in the cities.

Meanwhile, Curtiss had something on his mind besides rabbits; for a little while even the bicycles took a back seat. It was, of course, a girl.

Lena Neff was a slim child of fifteen when Glenn first met her on his return from Rochester. She had fine-spun golden hair and big brown eyes, which she *would* hide behind pince-nez. Those glasses and her shyness gave her an air of austerity which was far from her real nature. She loved people and gaiety, and in this she supplied the perfect balance for Glenn's complete indifference to social life. Throughout the years, she filled his home with the grace of living in which he could relax, to go forth refreshed to his world of machines and danger and achievement.

Few people liked Lena at first meeting, but from the start Glenn seemed to feel her charm. He was shy too, painfully so, and therefore he understood her and she him.

Almost against his will he found himself deserting his beloved bedroom and the fascinating piles of papers to go calling at the Neffs'.

Together they walked on summer evenings in the glen for which he was named, and if he wasted lovely moonlight talking of mechanical things she did not understand, why that was fine with Lena, she loved him so completely that everything he did was right.

Their courting, if discussions of mechanics in the moonlight could so be called, lasted for two years. By then their relationship seemed to Glenn so natural and inevitable that when he proposed marriage he did so with the casual words: "Let's get married, Lena."

She was so astonished that her glasses fell off. As they groped for them, she said, "Why Glenn, what made you think of that?"

"I've always thought we would," he answered. "Do you love me, Lena?"

"Of course, Glenn. Do you care for me?"

"I've never thought much about love," Glenn said, "but I guess this is it, for when you're not with me I'm only half myself. Shall we, Lena?"

"Yes, Glenn. I'll tell my people tonight, and as soon—"
She stopped because his face was so dismayed.

"No Lena," he said violently. "I don't mean like that. I couldn't stand it. Having them look me over, having a big crowd at the wedding. Why, your family might make a fuss; I haven't any money at all, and people think me rather odd, I guess. Not at all the husband a man would choose for his daughter. And if they minded, it might somehow come between us and spoil things. Oh, that way won't do at all."

"How do you want it then?" asked Lena gently.

"I meant now, this afternoon. Just find a preacher and get married. You can explain things afterward."

"Well, let's go find the preacher," Lena said.

That is the way they were married. He was twenty-one and she just turned eighteen. But for all its casualness, their marriage was as enduring as though an archbishop had joined them with all the rites and ceremonies devised by God and man. For the bonds between them were stronger than laws or sacraments or golden rings, since they were founded on complete love and understanding.

After the ceremony, they walked back to her house and told her people. They too must have had a fine quality of kindly comprehension, for in spite of the young couple's nervousness, there was no fuss, only congratulations and a blessing.

Then Glenn took his bride with him to live in the House on the Hill.

CHAPTER FOUR

THE DARING YOUNG MAN ON THE FLYING MOTORCYCLE

MARRIAGE SPEEDED CURTISS UP. He was always driven by the fact that no human being could keep up with the multiplicity of ideas which his mind shot forth. He was never satisfied with an accomplished thing; it being done, others could tend it while he went on. His first reaction to marriage was a new venture.

"Look, Mr. Smellie," said G. H. "Cyclists who come in for repairs are always asking me what make of bicycle to buy next. I think I could do a pretty good business if I had some for sale."

"Why don't you get some?" asked the druggist.

"I want to," said Curtiss bluntly, "but it takes capital. That's where you come in."

"Do I now?" exclaimed Mr. Smellie.

Then he looked thoughtful, for he was not the sort of man to shut his mind against a business opportunity, and he shared the opinion of the town, that anybody who worked as hard as G. H. Curtiss must succeed.

"What is your proposition?" he asked.

"You put up the money to buy the machines and I'll sell them," said Curtiss. "We'll split the profits fifty-fifty. Furthermore, Tank and I will get advertising by winning races. How about it, Mr. Smellie?"

"It's a deal," said Smellie.

So a rack of flashily painted bicycles appeared outside the shedlike shop near the drugstore to which Curtiss had recently removed his business. Tank and G. H. clipped their trousers tighter, which is a cyclist's way of girding up his loins, and set out to do some real racing.

Every evening after supper they went out to Stony Brook Farm to pedal madly around the dirt track until sunset and exhaustion drove them to lean their precious machines against a tree and burrow into a handy haystack. There they slept until the sun's rays slid across the fields, scooping the dew off the timothy, to pry open their eyelids. Then up again in the chill sweet air, to jog around the track until cramped muscles had limbered enough for them to ride.

On Saturdays they mounted their machines and rode twenty, fifty, a hundred miles over country roads deep with dust to wherever a race might be.

And they were good. Time after time, in spite of long miles already ridden, the boys from Hammondsport finished first and second, always in the same order, G. H. leading with apparently effortless speed, Tank puffing furiously just behind.

Presently they got more ambitious and, buying themselves racing suits of the cotton sweaters and long, black, skin-tight drawers that cyclists affected, they ventured to attempt the hard, banked tracks of the bigger meets. Here they did not do so well, since their machines were comparatively low-geared for country work. But on the rough dirt tracks they were for a time supreme in the county.

Meanwhile, Curtiss was selling the bicycles well and doing a little figuring. He couldn't see how the big-name manufacturers could get one hundred and twenty-five dollars for a collection of steel and rubber that could be put together at any forge for fifteen or twenty dollars. His profits from the sale of the machines he bought were only twenty per cent; he saw a way to do better than that.

"Look, Mr. Smellie."

Mr. Smellie looked. It was G. H. again.

"What do you want to try this time?" he asked.

"I think we should make our own bicycles," Curtiss said. "I figure we could sell them for sixty dollars and still get twice as much profit."

"Go ahead and try it," said Mr. Smellie.

Curtiss designed a bicycle and found a little factory at Addison, near Corning, where they could be made for twenty dollars apiece. In the bicycle business everything was in a name. After a good deal of unaccustomed literary cogitation, he decided to call his machine "the Hercules."

The Hercules was a hit. Curtiss took in his old friend Bill Damoth as his assistant. Then he opened a branch in Bath eight miles up the valley, with Barney Feagles in charge. Next came a venture at Corning. The expanding business at Hammondsport needed more help, and young Carlton Wheeler was glad to take a part-time job at ten cents an hour. The nucleus of an organization was growing, and over the door of his Hammondsport shop Curtiss cockily hung the prophetic sign: INDUSTRIAL INCUBATOR.

Around the widening circle of his interests G. H. spun at a dizzy pace. Hammondsport, Bath, races, rabbits, Corning, races; Hammondsport again. He was never tired, and in spite of the success of his ventures, he never had any cash. A dollar didn't have time to light while it was working for G. H.

Lena only glimpsed him on the fly; his grandmother watched him flash past with approving eyes.

"Glenn will go far," she prophesied.

"I wish he wouldn't go quite *so* far," sighed Lena. "But anyhow, I have Carlton to remind me of him."

"He's certainly the very spit of his dad," agreed Ruth Curtiss, looking admiringly at the baby born earlier that year.

Then came a dismal day when Curtiss realized that in one field he was slowing up. In a meet on their own chosen type of track he and Tank were beaten by a man they could formerly have disposed of without even puffing. Soberly they discussed it as they pedaled slowly home. G. H. was acutely depressed, Tank more philosophical.

"You can't win all the time," he said.

"That's not the point," said Curtiss. "We're not as good as we were. Do you think we're getting old?"

"Could be," Tank said, "but we're only twenty-two."

It was G. H. who found the answer.

"Look, Tank, in this magazine it says cycle racers should not walk far, it does something to their riding muscles; and above all they should never, never run."

"Gosh," Tank muttered. "That's it then: jogging around the track mornings to warm up before we ride."

"Yes," said Curtiss bitterly. "We're permanently slowed up."

He faced the prospect bleakly. It was the beginning of the new century: the world seemed to be gathering itself for a great spring forward, and he was faced by a hundred years of slowing up. Then Tank saw the abstracted look glaze those hazel eyes.

"You figuring something, G. H.?" he asked.

"I've got it," said Curtiss. "We'll build us one of those new motor bicycles. We'll go faster than ever."

In that year of 1900 the first flimsy bicycles with a motor

attachment were tentatively appearing on the highways. Nobody in Hammondsport had ever seen one, but there were some catalogues. G. H. and Tank studied them feverishly until Curtiss scraped together enough money to order a motor from E. R. Thomas of Buffalo. Note that name, for in the spiral of life, which seems always to repeat the same thing in different combinations, it was a key piece.

The motor was a disappointment. It was a tiny fragile thing unsuited to the hilly terrain.

"What are you going to do?" asked Tank when they had proved the uselessness of the machine.

"I'll build a bigger motor myself," said Curtiss. "I know where I can get castings for it. That will be more fun anyway."

He ordered the castings and took them to the Kirkham boys to be machined in their water-power mill three miles up the valley.

Then G. H., Bill Damoth, Tank, and Charlie Kirkham fitted the air-cooled motor together in the back room of Smellie's drugstore. But they still needed a coil and a distributor. They got the first from Dr. Phillias Alden, who lent them the jump spark coil he used to give his patients up-to-date electrical treatments. Curtiss devised a distributor.

Then the question of a carburetor came up. The manufacturer had sent no casting for that. Curtiss got a tomato can—not a big one, the pint size. He cut off the top and fitted a gauze screen through which the gasoline vaporized. The mixture was controlled by a needle valve and passed through a pipe to the cylinder.

They mounted the engine on a specially built bicycle frame, and Curtiss worked out the transmission hook-up of a broad webbed belt running over an extra rim attached to the rear wheel. This belt could be tightened or loosened by a lever.

When it was finished, they set the motor bicycle on its stand in the roadway outside the shop. Harry Genung came tearing around the corner with his arms full of schoolbooks.

"Am I too late?" he gasped. "Have you tried it yet?"

"You're just in time," said Curtiss. "Get on there and pedal while I adjust the mixture."

Harry dropped his books in the roadway and climbed cautiously onto the machine while Tank and Bill steadied the shaky stand. Curtiss pulled the lever which tightened the belt.

"All set, Harry. Pedal away," he said.

Half an hour later they were still at it. Harry was covered with sweat and his spectacles were fogged. Tank and Bill were sitting on the ground and G. H. was patiently adjusting things.

"Want I should spell you, Harry?" Tank asked.

"No, I'll give her another whirl," the boy said doggedly.

"Pedal away," said G. H.

Harry pumped as hard as his aching legs permitted. There was a loud *Bang!* and a belch of blue smoke.

"Hurrah!"

"Yeay!"

Tank and Bill jumped to their feet cheering. Curtiss' fingers flew around the adjustments.

Bang, *bang, whee, whee,* bang, bang, BANG. The boy and the bicycle were enveloped in smoke; the back wheel was spinning furiously. Curtiss threw the lever which loosened the belt.

"Get off," he shouted above the racket.

Harry jumped down and Curtiss pushed the bicycle off its stand. He swung a long leg over the saddle and stood for an instant straddling the thundering, shaking machine. Then he pedaled forward until he had gotten up a little speed and pulled hard on the belt lever. The motor coughed once as it took the load, and then resumed its staccato chorus. Curtiss felt himself lifted effortlessly forward. Across the level square on up the Main Street hill, like a bird mounting the wind, he flew; it was the most wonderful sensation he had ever known.

At the crest of the rise he swung onto the valley road. Down the long slope he sped faster and faster, then up another hill with that splendid feel of the power beneath him. He knew he should turn and go back to the others, but his will could not command his hand to shut down the motor.

At last the engine gasped and choked, the machine rolled to a standstill, and the elation died. G. H. dismounted and took stock of the situation. He was out of gas.

He was, he admitted to himself, in a pretty fix. He was eight miles from home and his motor bicycle seemed to weigh a ton; the chances were that there wasn't a drop of gasoline this side of Hammondsport.

Just ahead lay the village of Wayne. Curtiss pedaled laboriously up to the general store.

"Got any gasoline?" he shouted to the proprietor, hoping for a miracle.

"Nope," answered the storekeeper. "Whale oil do you any good?"

"Nope," said Curtiss. "Do you know anybody who might have some?"

"They's a fella called Curtiss in Hammondsport could maybe fix you up," was the answer.

"Uh," said G. H. "It's a long way to Hammondsport."

"That's right, close to nine miles."

"Hank Cutler might have some," volunteered an interested bystander. "He's got a gasoline stove."

A curious little procession made its way to the Cutlers',

Curtiss pushing the heavy machine. Hank turned out to be a progressive fellow with the true feeling of fellowship of one innovator for another.

"All the gas I've got is right in the stove," he said, "but I'll drain it out and give it to you."

"You've saved my life," said Curtiss.

With the tank full again, Curtiss remounted. The miracle of inanimate matter coming to life thrilled him—all through his life it would—as the motor barked again. Back to Hammondsport he rode, skimming over the hills with the cool, exhilarating wind of speed in his face, and his elongated shadow pointing the way ahead.

As soon as Curtiss got back from his ride, he ordered another and bigger set of castings—more power equals more speed. A third and fourth machine followed, and when this last one proved a brilliant success, he knew he was ready to enter the mushrooming market as a manufacturer of motorcycles. What he needed, as usual, was money.

But by now the whole town was ready to accept Grandma Curtiss' opinion that Glenn was going far. Their faith in him, which stood firm through bad years and good and which he justified so brilliantly, was an unusual example of loyalty. Curtiss was one prophet who was not without honor among his own people.

Seymour Hubbs, whose acetylene plant had inspired Curtiss' earliest manufacturing venture, put up the first thousand dollars.

Others who showed their faith in him by lending him five hundred dollars each for this venture were Victor and Leo Masson, Henry Miller, Banker Pratt, and Professor Plough, principal of the high school. He acquired a little shed halfway up the hill to his house and, engaging two or three extra mechanics, moved his small staff to it. So began the G. H. Curtiss Manufacturing Company, financed by the faith of the young man's fellow townsmen.

It rapidly became evident that the judgment of G. H.'s backers was not in error. Orders began to come in. Soon he was obliged to hire a Miss Swarthout as his secretary. He tried to keep the books himself, but such routine work irked him terribly.

"I wish I could afford to hire a bookkeeper," he said to Lena one night. "That job tires me more than everything else I do put together."

"You know I'm no good at figures," she said, "but if it will relieve you, Glenn, I'll take it on myself."

"Would you, Lena?" he asked in delight.

"Of course. Maybe then I'll see something of you."

Through some miracle of love, Lena, who had never been able even to add, did the job and did it well. She was glad enough to have the work, for her baby had died before his first year of life was out, and Grandma Curtiss, too, was gone. The big house was lonely.

As soon as Curtiss was established as a manufacturer he took up the racing game, to advertise, as he said, Hercules motorcycles, but in his secret heart he knew that he would have done so whether there was a commercial advantage or not. Speed was the thing.

His first race was the Ocean Boulevard Handicap at Brooklyn, run through the streets of that city. All the makers of motorcycles in America were represented by professional riders, but Curtiss preferred to roll his own. After a spectacular trial run, the professionals got together and succeeded in having Curtiss so heavily handicapped that he did not have a chance to win. At that he took second place and won the time prize, since he covered the course faster than anyone else.

But it wasn't fast enough. During the winter Curtiss called together the Kirkham boys, Bill Damoth, and Nelson Dalton, who had helped him design a racing motor.

"We've got to have a motor with nearly twice as much horsepower," he said.

"How are you going to do it?" asked Charlie Kirkham. "That cylinder is about as big as is practical now."

"We'll put in two cylinders," answered Curtiss.

"Gosh," said Bill, "it's never been done on a motorcycle."

"Lots of people will do it next year, and we can't be left behind."

"You're going to have carburetion trouble, G. H.," warned Dalton. "It will be hard to get an equal mixture in both cylinders."

"I'll figure out something," said Curtiss. "You see, I want to win the New York Motor Cycle Club Gold Medal for the Hill Climbing Contest at Riverdale next spring, and I also want a crack at the new N. C. A.* Championship, so I've got to have power."

"Wait a minute and catch up with yourself," said Bill. "Both those races are on Decoration Day."

"I know," G. H. said, "but one is in the morning and the other in the afternoon. I can make it if I hurry a little."

"Gee whiz," said Bill Damoth.

All that winter they worked on the new engine.

On May 28, 1903, two days before the races, it was running at last, if you could call it that. It was, in fact, running like a

* National Cyclists Association.

lame camel. The carburetion trouble that Dalton had predicted was upon it. If one cylinder had the right mixture, the other got too rich a dose; and if this was leaned down, the first cylinder began to sputter. They had tried all sorts of manifolds with no better result.

"All right," said Curtiss wearily, "take it off the block and ship it."

"Not like this," objected Bill. "You'll make a fool of yourself."

"I won't do that," said G. H. "If I can't fix it I won't start, but I may get a flash."

They put the machine in the baggage car of the early train from Bath. Curtiss rode alone in the day coach, for there was no spare cash to pay the expenses of a mechanic. He was lonely and almost frantic during the long cindery ride. Around and around through his brain revolved all the expedients he might try to get the motor to run smoothly. If he could, he felt sure he would win, even though his engine had never been road-tested in the machine it was to drive. But nothing came to him except a great weariness.

Late that afternoon the motorcycle was delivered to a shed near the Riverdale hill, and Curtiss set to work. By the yellow light of a stable lantern he toiled through all the evening hours and on past midnight into the morning.

At about three o'clock he got his flash. He took a sixteenth-inch drill and bored a hole in the feed pipe to admit more air to the overrich cylinder. When he tried the engine, it ran better. There in the darkness his eyes blazed with triumph; he knew he had it. He continued boring holes and testing until the motor ran as sweetly as a kitten's purr. Then, all covered with oil and grease, he lay down beside his machine and slept.

At eight o'clock he was walking up the hill, studying the course. It was a narrow road with sharp twists in it; one corner in particular meant slowing almost to a standstill, you could never get up momentum again. If only it were banked the least little bit, or if there was a way to cut the corner. . . . He studied the steep down slope of grass in the arm of the curve, and again his eyes glinted: he had found the way.

At ten o'clock the contestants lined up for the start. Curtiss in his black leather jacket, leather boots and black cap and goggles, with his face a matching black from oil, made a somber contrast to the gaudy get-ups of the professional riders, but his engine was singing a song of victory.

The starter's flag sent them off with a noise like three or four battles being fought at once. G. H.'s inexperience allowed several riders to get the jump on him, but one by one he picked them up as the gradient rose and power began to tell. At last there was only one man ahead, and the sharp corner was close.

Curtiss saw the machine in front begin to come back to him, slowing for the corner. He twisted his throttle wider and gritted his teeth. The other rider turned a startled face.

Now! With his exact sense of timing, Curtiss jumped his machine over the gully and off the road. The steep hillside furnished a perfect bank for the turn and an instant later he regained the road with a bump that threw him half out of the saddle. The way to victory lay plain ahead, and while his nearest rival strove vainly to regain speed, Curtiss crossed the line sitting nonchalantly erect in the saddle.

That afternoon at the Empire Track he won the first N. C. A. Championship with the greatest of ease.

Those races gave Curtiss a national reputation, not only as the leading manufacturer of motorcycles, but as an utterly reckless daredevil. This latter was undeserved, for he always calculated his risks coolly in advance. Instance the time he built a machine expressly for a certain race at Coney Island and, when he arrived there, discovered that it was too long to maneuver safely around the narrow circle of the track. Instead of taking an unjustifiable risk, he scratched his entry despite the chorus of protests he was obliged to face.

But when the risk was worth while, he never hesitated to face it, and during the next few years he added trophy after trophy to his collection, and his machines set the pace for all America.

One of his greatest triumphs was at Ormond Beach in the winter of 1904, when against the toughest competition that Europe and America could furnish he established a world's record for motorcycles by making ten miles in 8 minutes 54 2/5 seconds. The old dream of mile-a-minute speed was far surpassed, and still he was not going fast enough.

Meanwhile, he did not neglect the commercial aspects of his business. He made motorcycles for every conceivable use and fancy. In the faded pages of his catalogues are single-cylinder, double-cylinder, racing motorcycles, pleasure and business machines. He designed one tremendous two-place job, with the passenger sitting in front and the driver perched far in back steering by enormously elongated handlebars. He placed his faith in two-seaters rather than sidecars, because, as he stated in a newspaper interview, "It is doubtful if the trailers and sidecars, popular in Europe, will go here because of our poor roads."

Part of his advertising campaign was directed at commercial travelers, and the arguments he instanced to induce them to use motorcycles instead of trains were evidently valid, judging

by the present use of automotive transportation for this purpose. Actually, the first motorcycle drummer was one H. A.
Smith, who testified that the use of a Hercules increased his
efficiency fourfold. Soon this enterprising gentleman had
swarms of competitors similarly mounted.

In this era of tremendous expansion, Curtiss was as hard-
pressed for cash as ever. Every cent he made went straight
back into the business, and at that there was never enough
working capital to take care of the purchase of material that
the rising volume of orders demanded. But the faith of the
townspeople helped him over the hump.

Mr. Bauder, of the Hammondsport Bank, financed him far
beyond conservative banking practice, because he felt that
G. H.'s character was better collateral than stocks and bonds.

When Banker Bauder died and the other local bank closed
its doors, Curtiss was panic-stricken.

"How am I to get financing now?" he asked.

"Why don't you try Mr. Hallock over at Bath?" suggested
Lena.

"He doesn't know me," G. H. objected.

Nevertheless, he tried and, to his surprise, found that Mr.
Hallock knew a great deal about him and was very glad to
enter into business relations with the Curtiss company.

This inability to recognize the extent of his celebrity showed
clearly when a day in 1905 found him in a mood of depression
because he had discovered that a company in California had
a prior claim to the name of Hercules and, now that he was
doing business on a national scale, they were in conflict. He
called a meeting of his confidants in the tiny office on the
second floor of the factory.

"We've got to change the name of our machine," he said.

"It seems hard luck when I have worked so hard and risked so much to build it up."

"Perhaps it's a good thing," said Lena.

"How can it be?"

"You might find a better name."

"Don't talk foolishly," said G. H. "What name could be better than the one we've advertised?"

"I see what Lena's getting at," said Bill Damoth excitedly. "She wants you to call it the 'Curtiss'!"

"My name means nothing," G. H. objected. "It's the Hercules that people know."

"You're crazy," said Bill bluntly. "Thousands of people have heard of you that don't even know there's such a thing as a Hercules motorcycle."

"Do you really think so?"

"I know it," Bill said.

"It's true, Glenn," said Lena proudly.

Curtiss grinned at them in embarrassed pleasure.

"All right," he said, "Curtiss it is. Anybody got any more bright ideas?"

"Why not put the name on in your own writing, like an autograph on every machine?" proposed Bill.

Curtiss shrugged his shoulders. "Might as well go whole hog," he said.

"Do it now," Bill urged, "and I'll get a facsimile made."

G. H. pulled a piece of paper toward him.

"Write carefully, Glenn," Lena begged. "A lot of people are going to see it."

In flowing Spencerian script G. H. wrote and finished with a scroll and flourish.

"Will that do?" he asked.

"Swell," said Bill.

"Very nice," said Lena.

More people than even she could guess throughout the crowded countries of Europe and the wide, sparse veldt of Africa, in the ancient cities of Asia and Malayan jungles, were to see and know that signature as still undreamed-of wings carried it across the world.

CHAPTER FIVE

THE NUT FROM CALIFORNIA

"LOOK AT THIS, MR. CURTISS," said Miss Swarthout, tossing a letter across the narrow space between the desks in the little upstairs office behind the plant. "Some nut in California wants you to build a motor for a balloon."

Curtiss' eyes took fire as they always did when someone suggested a new idea to him. "Well, why shouldn't we?" he demanded. "It might even fly."

He read the letter while Miss Swarthout continued opening the morning mail.

"I've heard of this fellow," he said at last. "Captain Baldwin. He invented the modern parachute. Perhaps he really has something in this dirigible balloon."

"Are you going to do it?" asked Miss Swarthout.

"I certainly am," said Curtiss. "Write to him and tell him that we accept his order. I'll figure out something for him when I get around to it."

But that was the summer of 1903, when the motorcycles were just getting going. Curtiss' mind was concentrated like a beam of light on building better and faster ones than his powerful competitors, on holding the pre-eminent place he had won by the fertility of his mind and at the risk of his neck.

Occasionally during their sessions with the morning mail, Miss Swarthout would hand him a letter saying, "It's the Nut again."

Curtiss would read it and say remorsefully, "I must do something for him. Tomorrow I'll put my mind to it."

But when winter cracked down on Hammondsport, he still had not found time to think of the problem. One day when the little stove in one corner of the office was bright red with the effort to keep it warm and the windows were opaque with frost, Miss Swarthout handed him another of those big thin sheets of paper.

"Your Captain says he's coming here to get his motor," she commented.

Curtiss glanced rapidly through the letter. "Good!" he exclaimed enthusiastically. "Now we'll have to get on with it. Write him a letter inviting him to stay with us while he's here."

The night the captain was to arrive, Lena was fluttering all over the house. Curtiss, dressed uncomfortably in his best suit, which she had forced him to put on, sat hunched over the inevitable pile of engineering magazines. Somebody banged on the front door.

"There he is," Lena said nervously. "Go let him in."

Curtiss raised eyes that were lost in abstraction.

"Who?" he asked.

"Captain Baldwin," Lena squealed. "Please go to the door, Glenn. I just can't face him right away."

Curtiss was at the door in three long strides. As he swung it open, a snowy blast propelled a short, powerfully built man across the threshold. Captain Baldwin shoved the door shut with a quick twist of his broad shoulders and, dropping a badly worn valise on the floor, removed a dark blue cap from his pepper-and-salt hair.

"Are you Mr. Glenn H. Curtiss?" he asked.

G. H. found himself looking into humorous gray eyes set in a square-cut, weather-worn face.

"I'm Mr. Curtiss," he said.

His visitor grinned amiably. "Gosh, you're young," he said. "I'm Tom Baldwin. Have you finished my motor?"

Curtiss looked a shade embarrassed. "Well, Mr. Baldwin—" he began.

"Captain, I'm called."

"Captain Baldwin, of course. Well, Captain, I haven't quite got it built yet, but I have some good ideas. You see, we've been pretty busy around here."

"I see," said the captain shrewdly, "that you haven't even started it."

"Well," said Curtiss, "that's a fact. But we'll soon build it. Look, what do you think of this idea?"

He fished some scraps of paper and a stub of pencil out of his pocket and began to sketch rapidly while the captain peered over his shoulder.

"Glenn," called Lena from the parlor, "who's out there?"

"Why, Captain Baldwin, of course," said her husband. "You said so yourself. Come here and meet him."

Lena came into the hall, her eyeglasses twinkling anxiously.

"So pleased to meet you, Captain," she said, as her small hand was engulfed by the aeronaut's calloused palm. "Hasn't Mr. Curtiss even asked you to take off your overcoat?"

"I forgot about it, too, ma'm," said the captain. "It's mighty good of you to take me into your home like this."

"I do hope you'll be comfortable," said Lena, leading the way to the parlor. "We live very simply here, not at all in the way you must be used to."

"It certainly ain't what I'm used to," said Baldwin, surveying the pleasant room with its fire and big comfortable chairs. "I've lived in the darnedest bunch of boardinghouses and cheap hotels. This is real homey and it's good to be in a home."

After dinner that night they sat again in the parlor. Curtiss thought that the captain, in his frock coat with a Thirty-third Degree Masonic emblem glittering in its lapel, and his black bow tie, looked rather like a Western senator. He was tremendously interested in the man; every moment with him made his enthusiasm mount, and Lena was plainly captivated.

"Do you really think you can navigate the air, Captain?" he asked. "Men have been trying for so long, and they haven't got anywhere."

"You're wrong there," said Baldwin. "We've gone a long way. We're just on the verge of it, any day now. Look at Santos-Dumont."

"What did he do?"

"He flew around the Eiffel Tower. Doesn't that prove something?"

"It certainly does," said Curtiss. "Do you think I can help you?"

"You're the only man in America who can," said the captain solemnly. "I've lived all my life for this one thing, and now you hold it in those clever hands of yours. You've got to give it to me."

"I want to," Curtiss said. "I'm tremendously interested."

"That's good," said Baldwin. "That's fine. Almost nobody is nowadays. Ever since Langley fell into the river in that fool flying machine of his, the whole country has turned against flying in any form. But my proposition is different. It's a real ship, a ship of the air. All it needs is the right motor and it will navigate the atmosphere as surely as ships sail on the sea."

"You've done a lot of ballooning, haven't you, Captain?" put in Lena.

"Quite a bit, ma'm," said Baldwin dryly. " 'Bout three thousand flights and a thousand jumps. That's where I got the money I've put into this dirigible of mine."

"You must have had a thrilling life," Lena said. "Tell us about it."

"It's not so much," said the captain, "but I'll tell my story. Maybe then you'll see why I have to have this motor."

"Would you like some wine first?" asked Lena. "My husband doesn't take any, but perhaps you . . ."

"Nope," said the captain. "I don't use it. No tea or coffee either. I figure they'd sort of interfere with my business. You see, I've never had much time for easy things. Right almost from the day I was born I had to keep working. At first it was just little jobs around the small town in Missouri where we lived."

Glenn and Lena sat perfectly still for an hour while the captain talked. He told them that his first job was on the Illinois Central Railroad when he was fourteen. Then he joined a circus and learned to walk a tight-rope.

"My first flying lesson," he said, "though I didn't know it then."

In 1875, when he was twenty-one, Baldwin made his first balloon ascension. From that moment he never rested until he had saved money enough to buy a gas bag of his own.

"That's how I got the handle to my name," he said. "All balloon pilots are called 'Captain.'"

"I'll never forget my first flight alone," he went on. "You'd think it wouldn't have fazed me after walking a wire at the top of a circus tent, but it did. I felt like a little child learning to walk."

"Do you have to be an acrobat to be able to fly?" asked Curtiss.

"I wouldn't say that," said Baldwin, "but you have to have gymnastic ability. Also you have a terrific struggle with physical and mental gravity—the habits gravity has imposed on mind and body."

"I guess I'd never make an aeronaut," laughed Curtiss.

"You can't tell," said Baldwin. "I've heard of some pretty fancy riding you've done on the motorbikes. You just might."

"I don't know if I want to," said Curtiss.

The captain shrugged his broad shoulders. "Along in the eighties," he resumed, "people began to get bored with balloons. The gates fell off, so I started figuring what I could do to give 'em more of a thrill. I did a bit of reading about parachutes. It seemed that this fellow Guernin had made one that worked back in the eighteenth century. It had sticks all around like a Japanese parasol, and I couldn't see what good those sticks did, so I made a couple of models without them. They were successful, so I got a full-size one built.

"I tried it out at San Francisco in 1885. I certainly got a gate that day: ten thousand people turned out to see me killed. It sort of made you wonder. Nobody was ever so scared as I when I went over the side of that basket. But she worked. I floated down just as easy as a bit of dandelion fluff.

"That made my fortune. I was the first man to jump from a balloon in the U. S. A. Everybody wanted to see me do it again. I toured all over this country and then around the world, making first jumps in Japan, China, all sorts of outlandish places. I charged a dollar a foot, but I wouldn't jump less than five hundred feet. Most people wanted me to do a thousand, which was safer, but I didn't tell 'em that.

"Other people copied my parachute, of course, and cashed in, too."

"Didn't you patent it?" asked Curtiss.

"Nope," answered Baldwin. "I don't believe in patents. What a man does to make the world progress ought to belong to all men. Besides, they didn't cut in on my market, I was the original 'Daredevil Parachute Jumper.'"

"You must have had a lot of narrow escapes," said Lena.

"Sure I did. The worst was one time when I was up about four thousand feet and the basket began to break loose from the gas bag. I tried to climb up the ropes and fix it, but I got dizzy and fell back into the basket. My one idea after that was to get out in a hurry.

"I was in such a rush that I didn't fix the parachute properly and it failed to open. I fell like a stone. I was so paralyzed with fright that I couldn't even close my mouth, and the terrific rush of air nearly strangled me. I was like to drown on air.

"Then the chute opened. My mouth snapped shut, and I bit my tongue practically in half. That was my only injury, but what I'll never know is how I managed to hang onto the trapeze of the parachute when she opened."

"You've said enough," remarked Curtiss. "No flying for me."

The captain looked distressed.

"I don't want you to get that impression," he said. "I just told a hair-raising story because Mrs. Curtiss asked for it, but, really, flying is the most wonderful thing in the world. After you've been up awhile, your mind seems suddenly released from earthly bonds; you feel a great flood of energy pouring into you. When I'm up at two miles for a few hours, I feel as though I could walk through naked space, or step from cloud to cloud like you'd cross a brook on stepping stones. And I've never had a serious accident when I felt that power in me. Not that I've tried walking on clouds, but often I'll hang my feet over the edge of the basket or lean far out just for the fun of it."

"It's hard to believe, Captain," said Curtiss.

"It's true, honest it is." Baldwin's eyes were burning with the light of conviction. "I tell you, Mr. Curtiss, that when the time comes that all men fly, it will cure half the troubles of the world. You can't think small, mean thoughts when you're way up there looking down on the gentle earth, seeing how orderly it is, how the fields of grain and the forests grow for man's delight, and how the rivers and railways and roads all make a planned pattern, connecting neighbors with each other, and villages and far-off cities, so that everyone's needs can be brought to them from the most distant places. It frees your mind like I said, and you grasp the whole wonderful designs and see that it was *meant* by some Greater Intelligence."

Lena's eyes were shining. "You make flying seem very wonderful, Captain," she said.

"It's just that, but what we have now isn't enough. It's no good unless you can go where you want to. Many a time I've sat there in the basket, spinning slowly around—balloons spin, you know, all the time—trying to figure it out. I could go up and down looking for favorable slants, but I wasn't much better off than a leaf in the wind. I'd never know if I was going to bring up in the ocean and be drowned, or light in the middle of the wilderness and starve to death. One thing though, I had plenty of time to think.

"Now I've got it. My dirigible will navigate the air if I can get the right motor, and that's up to you."

Curtiss sat slumped in his chair, his lank form all tangled up in itself. His eyes were intent with thought. Lena was leaning forward, looking from her husband to the anxious face of the old aeronaut.

"Can you do it, Glenn?" she asked softly. "I think you should."

Curtiss uncoiled himself and stood up.

"I can and I will," he said. "We'll start tomorrow."

Baldwin breathed deeply, and the tenseness went out of his big frame.

"Thanks, Glenn," he said.

"You're a great salesman, Captain Baldwin," said Curtiss.

The captain's face became one wide grin.

"Look here," he said. "If we're going to work together, we've got to drop this formality. The people I like call me Uncle Tom."

CHAPTER SIX

THE *CALIFORNIA ARROW* HITS THE MARK

THEY TOOK A TWO-CYLINDER motorcycle engine and set it up on a testing block. They called Clarence White and Bill Damoth, and the four of them stood around looking at it.

"First tell us just how she's supposed to set in this flying machine of yours," said Clarence.

"It isn't a flying machine," said the captain indignantly. "They're just crazy. It's an airship."

"Well, how's it built?"

"There's a long triangular frame with a board at the bottom," said Baldwin, "and if we block her up a bit, the vee of the motor will fit in nice and snug. It's got to be right at the center of gravity, otherwise I can't control the ship in the air. You see, I make it go up and down by moving my weight backward and forward along the car. It's a very delicate balance."

"Sounds too delicate for me," said Clarence. "What happens if your silk envelope rips and she loses all her gas?"

"Not as bad as you'd think," said the captain. "I have the silk cut in such a way that if it tears and empties, it forms itself into an enormous parachute that just eases you back to earth."

"If the motor has to be near the center of the car," said Curtiss, "the propeller must be driven by a long shaft."

"Exactly," said Baldwin.

"Well, boys, let's design that hook-up first and then see what we've got. In the meantime, Uncle Tom, you show us how to build a propeller."

They machined a light shaft and designed a reduction gear so the propeller would not revolve as fast as the engine. Uncle Tom showed them how to build a propeller with a curved wooden frame covered with canvas, like a Dutch windmill. When it was all ready, they set it up on the testing block and started the engine.

For a little while it ran perfectly. The great canvas vanes whirled madly and a small but satisfactory gale blew out behind. Then the motor slowed up and died.

Bill Damoth spit on a cylinder and it hissed like a red-hot iron.

"She's overheated," he announced unnecessarily.

"Why should it do that?" asked the captain. "The motorcycles run for hours."

"When you're going fast on a cycle," said Curtiss, "the motor gets plenty of air to cool it. But on the block this doesn't get any. How fast do you figure your airship will travel?"

"I wouldn't be surprised to see her do fifteen miles an hour," said the captain optimistically.

"Not fast enough," remarked Curtiss. "We have to figure something out."

The lines in the captain's face deepened with worry; he seemed to be up against the old stone wall. He watched Curtiss standing there, looking at the motor but quite evidently not seeing anything in his abstraction of deep thought. Then the merest flicker in the young engineer's expression promised an idea.

"That propeller now," he said slowly. "It must give a thirty forty-mile wind. Uncle Tom, do you suppose we could fix the angle of those blades so that the wind would blow against the motor?"

"Sure we could. Would that do it?"

"It might," said Curtiss. "It just might."

So eventually it did, and Curtiss set to work to build a new motor embodying the lessons learned on the testing block. It followed the general design of the five-horsepower motorcycle engine. The flywheel was a light bicycle wheel with a thick wooden rim, the cylinders were machined as thin as possible, and the carburetor was made of metal no thicker than paper.

The months had flown by, the ice was out of the lake, and the hills were bright with springtide before the motor was ready. Captain Baldwin had stayed on the job and was "Uncle Tom" to half of Hammondsport. Between him and Curtiss a friendship had grown that was to withstand a stormy future neither of them could foresee. The old aeronaut had imbued his young friend with many of his idealistic ideas, and one of them in particular, his casual attitude toward patents, was to cause one of the most violent of those future storms.

Even after the months of work and experiment, the motor still showed a tendency to overheat.

"These air-cooled motors are all like that," said Curtiss. "Someday, Uncle Tom, I'll build you a water-cooled engine that will be really good. In the meantime this is as perfect as we can make it."

"Thanks, G. H.," said the captain. "You've done a lot for me and, I believe, for the whole world. You'll hear from me. Keep your fingers crossed."

The captain's boy mechanics, Roy Knabenshue and young, red-headed Lincoln Beachey, were at the station to meet him when the overland train pulled into Oakland.

"We thought you'd never get back," said Roy.

"Have you got the motor with you?" asked Link Beachey. "Is it really good?"

"It's up in the baggage car," said the captain, "and it's a dandy. Boys, we're going to fly."

Link knocked furtively on the wooden side of a Pullman.

"That's right, knock for me, too," laughed Baldwin. "But it's true."

They chartered a one-horse express wagon and drove out to the field with the precious motor.

"How's the ship?" asked Baldwin, as their vehicle rattled over the cobblestones.

"All ready to inflate," answered Roy, "as soon as we get the motor installed."

But that was not a thing that could be done in a hurry. The balance, as Captain Baldwin had said, was very delicate. The engine had to be in exactly the right place: it was a matter of inches. For weeks they worked on the problem, not with intricate mathematical computations as such things are done today, but by the rule of thumb, by trial and error. A dozen times the length of the driveshaft had to be altered and the bearings changed. The captain would leave no single thing undone that might insure success. Someday, he knew, men would navigate the air, but this, he felt, was his last chance. His lifelong labors, his hopes, and his beliefs all hung on that "very delicate balance."

At last she is ready. Look at her well as she rests lightly on her trestles, for history is waiting on her.

The envelope is made of the finest yellow Japanese silk. It is fifty-two feet long and seventeen feet in diameter and contains eight thousand cubic feet of hydrogen gas, the lightest element on earth.* In the lower part of the envelope is an open neck through which the highly explosive gas may escape if the pressure inside becomes too great—there will be no smoking aboard and the motor is well removed, but there is always the chance of a spark. Up through this neck run two cords. One is attached to the valve through which gas may be let out for a descent; the other to the rip panel, which is designed to tear out and allow all the gas to escape in case of a forced landing.

The fat yellow bag is covered by a netting of cord from which the car is suspended. This latter is a triangular girder forty feet long made of white spruce braced with piano wire. It forms a right-hand prism, with the broad side at the bottom. Along its base runs an inch-thick plank of spruce for the aeronaut to stand on, but he must straddle the long spar which forms the top of the triangle. Attached to the sides of the car are bags of fine sand for ballast. The little five-horsepower motor is mounted just forward of the center of the gondola. By a chain-and-sprocket reduction gear it drives a seven-foot puller propeller at the end of a long shaft.

The pilot rides near the rear of the car to counterbalance the weight of the motor, which he is unable to reach, although a wire leads to its throttle. Beside him are the cords which work the only control, the long wood-and-canvas rudder suspended from the rear of the envelope.

So she stands in the hot sunshine that morning of August 3, 1904. Captain Baldwin has christened her the *California Arrow*, but she looks more like a gigantic summer squash.

The crowd begins to pour into the field early. The captain is no secretive inventor furtively testing his device, but a show-

---

* The smallest blimp today has four times this capacity and the mighty *Hindenburg* had eight hundred times as much.

man born. If success is at last to be his, it is unthinkable that
the public shall not share the moment; if failure, then the crowd
who came, he knows, to see him fail, will not be disappointed.
Fly or fall, it means a thundering good gate.

There is hardly a breath of air to sway the silken bag as the
captain in his official frock coat and peaked blue cap walks
slowly out to his ship. The crowd cheers him perfunctorily.
They know enough to expect nothing; it is merely a gesture
toward a man who, however hopeless the task, keeps on trying.
This time the captain does not give his usual cheery acknowledgment, for he has not even heard them. His mind is too
intent on what the next quarter hour will bring.

For a moment he stands beside the narrow car, which Roy
and Link and some other boys are holding down on the trestles.
His face is graver than they have ever seen it; no twinkle lights
the gray eyes that stare past them toward the horizon.

Young Knabenshue, in an agony of longing, speaks. "Why
don't you let me try her first, Uncle Tom? I'm so much
lighter than you, I'd have a better chance."

"Eh?" The captain is still deep in abstraction. "I suppose
you would."

Then he seems to come back to himself. He grins and pats
the boy's shoulder.

"You'll have your chance, Roy," he says. "But this is my
ship and, perhaps, my hour. Gangway for an old man."

Light as a monkey, he climbs into the gondola. Quickly he
primes the motor and grasps the bicycle wheel. He spins it with
a powerful heave.

The gods are kind this day, and Curtiss has built well. The
motor catches on the first whirl. It bangs unevenly at first and
then, as Baldwin makes slight adjustments, it warms to its work.
The captain pauses for a moment to listen to its steady rhythm,

while the wind from the propeller blows his coat tails out.
Then he inches aft to his place at the controls.

Once more he stops to look into the gentle sky. Then in a
voice so hoarse he hardly knows it, he calls, "Let her go, boys."

The young men lift the car shoulder high and give a slight
heave. There is a shudder through the frame, and then it is
floating free.

The captain notes his position. The dirigible is moving
slowly forward and drifting slightly in a faint gust of wind.
The bow rises too steeply. Quickly he pulls himself a little forward along his spar. That does it; the bow begins to descend.
Not too far now, half as much back and she is in equilibrium.

Baldwin looks down through the bottom braces and sees the
gaping faces of the crowd. He is straddling his pole, with one
foot hooked around the trusses and the other on the narrow
plank, not ten feet above them. The idling motor hardly gives
the airship motion; the side drift has increased. There is danger
of fouling a band of telephone wires. The captain reaches for
the scoop and ladles a spoonful of loose sand out of the box.
He sees a man in the crowd duck and rub his eyes, but the ship
is rising faster. She clears the wires and floats in the free air.

Now he has time to take his bearings. To his right are the
roofs of Oakland, the tangled railway tracks and the steep
green hills; ahead and to the left, the wide bay. The water is so
calm it looks like blue chiffon except where a steamer cuts a
white gash as it heads for the Golden Gate. San Francisco,
climbing its steep hills from the dock line, looks pure, almost
ethereal in the haze.

So far the captain has handled his ship like a free balloon.
Now is the moment come to test her as—a ship. Gingerly he
pulls on the throttle wire. The motor answers him with a
quickened beat and the great canvas blades ahead turn faster.

The bow lifts and, as he inches forward to correct it, he opens the throttle more. Soon the motor is going as fast as he dares run it and the light car is shaking to its vibrations.

The captain, watching the ground, sees it begin to move faster underneath; his ship is gathering way. Delighted, he estimates his speed at ten miles an hour, perhaps more. But still he is not going where he wishes, the time has come for the crucial test.

He decides to go out over the bay against the light wind so it will be easier coming back. Pull then on the left rudder line: it takes strength to haul the canvas fin against the wind of his progress. Anxiously he watches the bow; slowly it begins to swing. It is pointed at San Pablo Bay. Now it comes on around toward the Gate, and then it is notched on the city itself. Straighten her now, hard on the right rudder line.

The bow stops turning. It points straight as the arrow for which it is named at the heart of the city.

The captain pulls out his bandana and wipes the moisture from his face. This is his answer, and it is yes. Come storm or disaster, though the motor fail or a wind come up to blow him helplessly away, he knows now that man can navigate the air. It remains to prove it to those others on the ground.

Steadily the ship moves forward. Over his shoulder the captain can barely see the field, and the waiting crowd is a dark blur against the green. He is over the water and a railroad ferry underneath salutes him. He sees the wisp of white steam at her stack and hears the friendly roar of her whistle. The people on her deck are aflutter with hats and handkerchiefs.

Then he judges that it is time to turn back; not to tempt the fates too far. This time he pulls the right rudder cord. Slowly the bow swings back, past the Golden Gate, past the far-off hills, round it comes until it points for Oakland.

With the breeze astern, he comes back fast. The ferry slips slide underneath, then the city and the field beyond. Jockeying the rudder lines, he passes right over it and hears the crowd cheering like a sighing of the wind above the noise of his motor. Now one more turn. The captain gives her left rudder. Skidding down the wind she comes slowly about. When the airship is headed right, he catches her expertly—he is learning fast. Then, as she plows back toward the field, he moves forward slightly. The bow goes down and she comes in on a long, slow slant.

The airship clears the wires nicely and the captain edges forward and valves gas. She settles quickly and he tosses over the landing lines. They uncoil snakily and hit the ground. The ship bounces upward, but Roy and Link are running hard for the dangling ropes. They are almost out of reach, but Link gets one with a flying leap. Captain Baldwin shuts off the motor.

While his men are dragging him down and the crowd is racing over the field, while their hands are grasping the edges of the car and their voices are yelling at the crowd to keep off, all through the hysterical frenzy of that landing the captain stands motionless on his narrow plank. He looks like some quaint figure in a waxworks, with his old-fashioned frock coat and his funny peaked cap, and his impassive face from which the gray eyes look out at the future. He is an oddly ancient figure to be the harbinger of a new age.

Actually he is dazed, trying to realize what has been done this day. For a dream, dreamed by thousands through generations long gone by, has been realized. At long last a man has taken the air, sailed a determined course, and then returned to the place from which he started. It is hard to believe that it has really happened. It is impossible for the old aeronaut to realize that it is he who has made the dream come true.

CHAPTER SEVEN

LOST: ONE AIRSHIP

CAPTAIN BALDWIN DID NOT long remain in his daze. He knew he had something and his showman instinct took charge.

"Now boys," he said, "we're going to make some money."

"We sure need it," grinned Link Beachey. "When do we start?"

"At the Louisiana Purchase Exposition," answered Tom Baldwin.

There were other dirigibles behind the thirty-foot-high wind screen that sheltered the Airship Concourse at the St. Louis Exposition. But after looking them over, the captain decided that the $25,000 Grand Prize was, so to speak, in his gas bag.

At first, things went smoothly. The envelope was inflated and Knabenshue made a short flight which qualified for entry in the Grand Prize contest. But two days later black disaster struck.

Roy again started on a flight, this time over the city. At an altitude of one thousand feet above the gaping crowds in the streets, the faithful little engine quit for the first time. So far there was nothing serious in that.

Roy, maneuvering as a free balloon, went a mile high and down again, searching for a favorable slant to drive him back to the field. It was not in the cards, so he drifted across the broad brown river and landed gently on a level field in Indiana.

Captain Baldwin arrived in a wheezy automobile and a state of mind. But when he found his young friend was safe and his dirigible undamaged he beamed again.

"Shall I deflate her," asked Roy, "and haul her back?"

The captain considered.

"That's an awful waste of gas," he said. "I think we can tow her back behind a cart."

They hired a wagon from one of the farmers who had crowded up to the scene. The bow rope of the *Arrow* was fastened under the driver's seat and the stern rope to the wagon's tailboard. The captain took the reins and, with the little airship floating oddly over his head, started slowly back to the fair.

It was black night before they crossed the river. Through back streets they made their slow progress accompanied by a curious crowd on foot. The air was chilly but dead still. It was, thought Baldwin, going to be easy.

"Wires ahead!" shouted Beachey.

The captain pulled up his team.

"Is there any way around?" he shouted to a man in the crowd.

"Nope," was the answer. "That telephone line runs for miles in both directions."

"Then I guess we'll have to maneuver over it," the captain announced. "Roy, you unhitch the bow line; and Link, you take the stern. Tow her up to the wires and then Roy will let go of his rope. We'll work that over and then pull the stern after it."

The maneuver began precisely as planned. The airship was walked up to the wire and, with half a hundred people shouting encouragement and advice, Roy let the bow line go. It swung up and across the wires and dangled just out of reach. Baldwin drove the wagon under it and Roy stood up on the seat.

"I've got it," he shouted, as his fingers touched the rope. Link Beachey excitedly let go of the stern line and the dirigible jerked upward. The bow line slithered through Roy's fingers.

For one awful moment the airship hung poised above them, reflecting the yellow gaslight like a great golden moon. Then silently it rose, diminishing swiftly until it was lost in the darkness of the sky.

Jacob Wipke locked the door of his saloon and hitched up the buggy. There was just enough light in the eastern sky to make it needless to light the lamps. He clucked to his horse and started at a smart trot for St. Louis.

It was a cold gray morning and Wipke snuggled his chin in his muffler and paid no heed to the familiar farms and woods he passed. So he didn't notice the thing until he was almost upon it. Gleaming yellow against the gray sky and brown fields, it looked almost like a piece of sun fallen to earth. It was as exotic an object in that prosaic landscape as a live dinosaur on Broadway. It was an anachronism. It couldn't be.

Wipke whipped up his horse and drew rapidly closer. There, nestled confidingly against a tree, was a little airship, completely intact and as inexplicable as an empty ship with all sails set.

Wipke was a practical man. In a situation that had all the qualities of a bad dream, he did the commonplace, the sensible thing. He jumped out of his buggy and walked over to the airship. Grabbing one of its trailing ropes, he led it gently across the fields and hitched it firmly to a shock of corn.

Then he drove as fast as he could to St. Louis and reported his adventure.

The rejoicing of the Biblical shepherd over the return of his lost lamb was as nothing to the joy in Baldwin's camp over the reappearance of their errant airship. It seemed to all of them a veritable miracle, and a portent for the future.

Nor was the omen false. Three days later Roy Knabenshue redeemed himself by a brilliant flight over the city and back, which beyond doubt or peradventure won the $25,000 Grand Prize and established Captain Baldwin as the leading airship designer of his era.

CHAPTER EIGHT

GLENN CURTISS TAKES THE AIR

BACK IN HAMMONDSPORT, CURTISS was delighted by the success of his motor—he still thought of it more in that way than of the airship itself. The news that his engine had won first prize at the Lewis and Clark Exposition in the spring of 1905 fired him still further. He set to work designing a power plant that would be really spectacular. It was to be a V8 air-cooled motor, delivering no less than forty horsepower.

In designing it he had the invaluable assistance of a new addition to his force. Henry Kleckler as an engineer was a natural in the true sense of the word. He was a lanky man who hardly ever emerged from beneath the thick coat of grease which covered his hands and face, his clothes and even his hair. Formal education had he none, but practical experience combined with a special sense for metal made him in time the greatest engineer Curtiss ever employed.

They say that Henry could take a piece of baling wire and make a motor out of it. Whenever a difficult piece of design stumped the others they called for Henry.

Kleckler would come up grinning, listen intently to what was required and invariably say, "I fix him."

Fix him he did, and if at times the elaborateness of his device made it look like something from the brain of Rube Goldberg, it always worked. The rest was merely a matter of simplification.

In the fall of 1905 Captain Baldwin came again to Hammondsport. Curtiss greeted him affectionately.

"Uncle Tom," he said, "what you have done was beyond my wildest expectations."

"We've just begun," said Captain Baldwin. "What have you been doing, G. H.?"

"Nothing that I'm very proud of," Curtiss answered. "Come and look."

He led the way to the machine shop. There on the testing block stood the shining motor. Baldwin's eyes lighted as he looked at the serried cylinders.

"It's beautiful," he said. "Is it any good?"

"It's the best engine in the world," Curtiss told him, "for exactly three minutes."

"And then?"

"It heats up and freezes."

"You can lick that," said the captain confidently.

Curtiss shook his head. "I've tried everything," he answered. "Been experimenting all summer, and it's no go."

"Nothing you can do with it?"

Curtiss grinned, half triumphant, half sheepish.

"I've a notion to break the world's speed record at Ormond Beach," he said.

"What with?"

"That—in a motorcycle."

The captain dropped his eyebrows. "Give me a nice safe airship!"

"Maybe you're right, but think of the advertising."

"It's your neck," Baldwin said. "Like me to come with you?"

"I'd like nothing better."

The Curtiss Works turned out a special motorcycle frame

in a hurry. It was so long that a man had to lie almost flat to reach the built-out handlebars. A small automobile wheel was at the rear and a big motorcycle wheel in front. The thing was grotesque. Nobody knew if it could even be ridden, and there was no time to find out. They shipped it to Florida as it stood.

Curtiss, the captain, and Tank Waters were to follow it next day, but before they left they had to attend the gala ceremony which Hammondsport was determined to tender to Captain Baldwin as the first real aeronaut, the Columbus of the Atmosphere. Tank had materially aided this determination, for fired by enthusiasm for his beloved G. H.'s distinguished guest, he had personally canvassed the entire town, extracting from every man but one a dollar to defray the expense. That one was John Cameron, a pious Scot, who didn't believe it was true that men could fly, because "It doesn't say so in the Bible."

But even in the early winter of 1906, Hammondsport was air-minded. John Cameron was almost the only resident absent from the crowd that stood before the flag-draped platform from which the captain was to speak. They cheered him as he came upon the dais; they shouted wildly as Glenn and Lena stood beside him. They listened respectfully as Mr. Matterly, the beloved Dutchman who had been chosen as master of ceremonies, stepped forward to make his introductory speech.

In spite of their enthusiasm, Mr. Matterly was not happy. He had forgotten his speech and lost control of his precarious English. The silence of the great crowd was matched only by the silence of Mr. Matterly as he stood forlornly looking out at that collection of friendly faces. Finally he produced the most remarkable tribute in the whole history of aviation.

"Ladies and shentlemen," he said. "This is Captain Baldwin, the mudder of all airships."

That night the three friends were on the train to Ormond. When they arrived, Captain Baldwin put up at the Breakers; but G. H. and Tank could afford no such luxury. They took up their quarters in the hotel garage where they lived and slept beside the motorcycles.

On the hard, flat sand of Ormond Beach, they were holding the Annual Speed Carnival. There were gas automobiles and steamers, and motorcycles in droves, all of them bent on traveling that minutely measured mile in the least number of seconds.

Curtiss, with two conventional machines, neatly clipped some fractions of time off the records he already held for light and heavy motorcycles, thus maintaining his position at the head of the industry. But his pleasure in the feat was mitigated by the thought of the monstrosity in his tent. He began to regard it as a sort of inanimate Frankenstein's monster, and his nerves were in nowise soothed when a Stanley Steamer blew its boiler into the ocean and its owner into the hospital.

But his determination was not shaken. With Tank Waters and Uncle Tom he wheeled his enormity to the starting point. It took two of them to hold it erect, and there was no guarantee that it would stay that way while moving. Curtiss hoisted his long legs over the saddle and assumed the necessary monkey crouch. His two friends began to push.

"For Heaven's sake keep me straight," Curtiss begged.

Wobbling badly, the machine proceeded down the beach by manpower—Curtiss simply couldn't make up his mind to start the engine. He wished he was at home and that internal-combustion engines had never been invented.

"Throw in the clutch," gasped the captain.

Automatically Curtiss obeyed. There was an instantaneous

roar and the machine almost shot out from under him. He settled himself in the saddle and experimentally twisted the throttle control. The machine seemed to soar forward. That splendid surge of power was the most exhilarating feeling in the world.

His fears forgotten, his nerves singing with elation, Curtiss opened her wide and drove for the starting line. The flags flashed past, the crowd was a swift blur. At the end of the long brown lane of sand were the flags that marked the finish. You did not steer at this speed. Curtiss *aimed* himself at the gap between those far-off flags. The wind tore at his clothes with steely talons, it pressed against head and shoulders with crushing force. In those swift seconds his mind registered the resistant power of air.

The flags leaped past him and he closed the throttle. As though braked, the motorcycle slowed quickly; then, as the pressure lifted, it rolled on and on with the momentum of its weight. Curtiss had not thought how to dismount without being crushed by the weight of his machine. He was now confronted by the necessity.

He figured there was only one thing to do, and as the motorcycle slowed to the point of wobble, he leaped clear, leaving it to crash on the sand. It had, after all, run its course; it remained to be seen whether it had fulfilled its destiny.

When the timers' figures went up they showed that Curtiss had done a mile in 26 2/5 seconds at a speed of 136.47 miles an hour. It was a record that stood for many years.

There followed a tremendous dispute about classification. The motorcycle people indignantly denied that his machine was a motorcycle; it was too big, they said. The automobile men shrugged their shoulders and remarked that it was certainly not an automobile. But no one could take from Curtiss the fact that on his whatisit he had traveled the fastest mile ever made by man until that time.

The fame of Glenn Curtiss as a builder of reliable light engines spread like lightning in that spring of 1906. "The Fastest Mile" was ballyhooed by the press throughout the land. Orders poured through in a flood that overwhelmed the little factory. Lena, who was still keeping the books, became lost in the vast tangle of figures; Miss Swarthout was on the verge of a nervous breakdown; Curtiss drove himself all day and most of the night, doing everything from planning new motors to working beside the men who made them. But the great tide threatened to submerge them all. Something had to be done to channel and control it.

At this point Curtiss thought of Harry Genung, his young partner of the rabbit business. Even then the boy had shown business ability and the great qualities of loyalty and integrity. Curtiss had watched these traits develop as Harry grew from a boy into a youth.

"I've got the solution of all our troubles, Lena," he said to his wife. "I'm going to get Harry Genung to straighten us out."

"That's a wonderful idea, Glenn," said Lena. "But do you think he'll come? I hear he is doing so well in that optical business in Elmira."

"I am sure that Harry will come with me," said Glenn.

The next day he went to Elmira. Harry Genung, he found, though still under twenty, was a prosperous young businessman. But he yet retained the devotion for his boyhood idol, which through long years never weakened.

"Will you come back to Hammondsport and be my office manager?" Curtiss asked.

Harry thought of his brilliant prospects, and of a certain girl in Elmira, but he hesitated no more than a fraction of a second.

"Of course, G. H.," he said. "How soon do you need me?"

There was never a word about salary. To both of these men money was always an afterthought.

So Harry came to live at the House on the Hill and the organization for the great years ahead was nearly complete. A little later in the summer the faithful Miss Swarthout was taken ill and resigned.

"What am I to do for a secretary?" Curtiss demanded of his new manager. "I'll never get another like her."

"I know a girl in Elmira," said Harry slyly, "who is a crackerjack."

"Get her," said Curtiss.

Martha Gregory Burch arrived in Hammondsport late one summer afternoon, hot and dirty from the long ride in the cinder-showered cars. Harry met her and drove her straight to the factory, where G. H. was waiting to get off some letters. At the door of the office Martha stopped, appalled; it was the most barren place she had ever seen. The hot afternoon sun glared through unshaded windows on a bare, dusty floor. In the only chair, a long lean man, with a thin eager face and a small dark mustache, sat sketching at a littered desk. As they entered, he looked up and she met for the first time the impact of those glowing hazel eyes.

"This is Mrs. Burch, G. H.," said Harry.

"Glad to have you with us," said Curtiss. "We're awfully busy. Could you take some letters now?"

Martha looked wildly around the room. On another desk, dripping with papers, stood a worn typewriter.

"Am I supposed to do them standing up?" she asked.

"No, of course not," Harry said. "I'll find another chair."

He bustled out and Curtiss said, "You'll find us rather badly equipped, I'm afraid, Mrs. Burch. We never seem to have time or money to get the things we need."

"I don't mind," Martha said cheerfully.

Curtiss grinned. "I can't think what happened to the chair Miss Swarthout used," he said.

"Here we are." Harry entered triumphantly carrying a battered kitchen chair with one rung broken. "I found it out in the shop."

Martha took off her hat and laid it on the floor. Then she sat down at the machine and blew the dust off it.

"To Linden Brothers, Rochester, New York," Curtiss began. "Gentlemen: In regard to the shipment of khaki—do you know how to spell khaki, Mrs. Burch?"

"Yes," said Martha.

"That's good," Curtiss remarked, "that's fine, because I don't."

Whatever Harry's partiality may have been, he had not exaggerated Martha's ability. In a few days she had the office cleaned up and the mass of loose papers neatly filed. Among them she found dozens of memoranda of amounts due the Curtiss Company ranging from a few cents to hundreds of dollars. True to her training, on the first of the next month, she sent neatly typed bills to all the debtors. Early the next morning Leo Masson arrived in a towering rage.

"What do you mean by sending me this bill?" he demanded.

"Why not?" asked Martha. "It's three years old."

"G. H. doesn't expect me to pay till I get ready," stormed Masson.

"All right, I'll take it up with Mr. Curtiss when he comes in."

"If you're going to act that way," said Masson, madder than ever, "I'll pay it now."

He flung a wad of currency on the table and marched out. When Martha told Curtiss of the incident, he shouted with laughter. "I guess Leo was pretty surprised," he said, "but no more than I am at getting paid. Don't press 'em too hard though, Mrs. Burch. They're mostly good friends of mine."

Another sort of business was growing in the Curtiss company that year. To the success of the *California Arrow* and the winning of the highest award at the Lewis and Clark Exposition the speed record at Ormond had added the final word. Those visionaries who believed that men could fly came from all over the world begging for the motors that would make their dreams come true. Hammondsport began to assume the aspect, of which it afterward boasted so proudly, of the aircraft capital of the world.

Among the first to settle there was Captain Baldwin. The old *Arrow* and two newer ships, *The City of Portland* and *The City of Los Angeles* had burned up in a disastrous fire; his attempt to start The Baldwin Airship Company, with a capital of $3,000,000—there was nothing small about the captain—had failed, owing to the acumen of the prospective shareholders; an eccentric, styled "Professor" Montgomery, had made his life miserable by falsely but vociferously accusing him of stealing his ideas, but the captain was undaunted. He could navigate the air and nothing else mattered.

As soon as he had built himself an airship hangar in Hammondsport, the captain set to work on a new *California Arrow*. Curtiss, chastened by the glorious failure of the V8 engine, began designing a power plant for it on a more modest scale. It was a four-cylinder inline, air-cooled motor rated at fifteen horsepower. Both he and the captain worried a good deal about propeller torque.

"With powerful engines like these," Curtiss said, "the action of the blades is apt to pull you right around in a circle."

The captain agreed and tried to imagine some aerodynamic device to offset it. It was Curtiss, however, who solved the problem with one of those brilliant flashes of his inventive mind which were so often avidly seized upon and utilized in fields far removed from the original application.

His plan consisted in driving two propellers in opposite directions by means of a shaft within a hollow shaft, each geared differently to the same engine. It was a daring conception, and eventually it worked. But it took a year to perfect it.

In the spring of 1907 they tried the new *Arrow* at Stony Brook Farm. In spite of unexpected gusts of wind that blew through the rifts in the hills in all directions, the airship performed brilliantly. So easily did the captain maneuver about that Curtiss felt a strange hankering grow within him.

As the airship came to earth, he was surprised to hear himself say, "Look, Uncle Tom, I'd kinda like to try that thing myself."

Baldwin's eyes gleamed with Machiavellian delight. This was what he had long hoped for. It was his firm conviction that no man who had ever been up would thereafter be content to be earth-bound. Now Curtiss would be completely involved in the conquest of the air to which he had so far given but part of his attention. It mattered not that he might wreck the ship; the captain was always generously careless of his property.

"Go ahead, G. H."

Not so enthusiastic were Curtiss' stanch friends and employees. As he climbed into the ship, the air was filled with their lamentations and warnings.

"Don't do it, G. H. You'll break your neck sure."

"Don't be a damn fool!"

"Please, G. H. You don't know how to run it."

"I'll never learn any other way," Curtiss replied.

He had very little faith in the practical application of airships. The car in which he stood was coupled so close to the gas bag that he was forced to bend his neck. With his head pressing into the unpleasant softness of its belly, he was acutely uncomfortable both in mind and body. He wished he had not given way to that vagrant impulse, and quite agreed with his mechanic's estimate of his intelligence. But having started something, his nature imposed the necessity of finishing it.

"Let go!" he called to the men with the ropes.

The airship rose slowly, drifting dangerously toward some trees. There was a babble of shouts from underneath and Curtiss stepped backward and opened the throttle. Up went the nose, and the ship climbed to safety.

After that there was nothing to it. Curtiss felt little of the exhilaration the captain had promised, but he had no difficulty in handling the airship. It was so easy that it was not at all exciting. All its reactions were extremely sluggish—you had time to make a mistake and rectify it a dozen times before anything could happen; not like motorcycles, where you had to make up your mind in a split second—and if you were wrong you were through. Bumbling lazily about in the air seemed somehow futile.

When Curtiss landed, the captain rushed up beaming.

"How did you like it?" he demanded. "Isn't it the greatest fun in the world?"

"Yes, it's fun," said Curtiss, "and I think it offers a lot of possibilities, but it's too slow for me."

The captain was pretty disappointed at his protégé's casual-

ness. He had definitely failed to make a convert. Curtiss
doubted if he would ever fly again.

The new *Arrow* was so superior to anything which had gone
before that even the United States Army stirred in its enormous
lethargy and showed a faint quiver of interest. On a lovely
June afternoon an impressive array of gentlemen in fine blue
broadcloth uniforms, golden shoulder straps, and brass hats
stood in the little valley and watched Captain Baldwin perform
amazing evolutions with his ship. As the papers put it, he "con-
cluded his demonstrations by making a magnificent advance
at fifteen miles an hour against the wind."

The impressive gentlemen were themselves impressed.
Eventually they induced the War Department to order a dirigible from Baldwin and Curtiss. But they were careful not to
let their enthusiasm run away with them; they hedged the
order with such specifications as to make it appear impossible
to execute. Nevertheless, Baldwin and Curtiss determined to
try.

All through the summer of 1907 the captain worked out his
plans, and Curtiss, motorcycles almost forgotten except for the
revenue they brought to his use, thought and sketched and
sketched and thought about the new engine, which would be
light enough and yet run for the impossible length of time that
the government specifications demanded. No air-cooled motor
could be relied upon to keep going for two hours without a
break. It must be water-cooled, then, but to make up for the
added weight of radiator and water, everything else must be
lightened. The carburetor now. Those in general use weighed
an appalling amount. Why not try that new metal, aluminum?
Then the cylinders. How thin could the walls be made and
yet withstand the strain? How light the cylinder heads and
not blow off?

Here Henry Kleckler was invaluable. The man could pick up a piece of steel and judge its tensile strength almost by instinct. In those days, when everything was done by guess and by golly and there was none of that intricate calculation of stresses to which even the meanest rivet on a modern bomber is subjected, this gift of Henry's was heaven-sent.

The motor slowly took shape. One night while he was working on it in his home, Curtiss sensed that someone had come into the room. Slowly he raised abstracted eyes to see Harry Genung waiting patiently for his attention.

"What is it, Harry?" he asked. "And whatever it is, decide it yourself. Your business judgment is far better than mine."

"This isn't business," said Harry. "I'm sorry to disturb you, G. H., but"—he hesitated and then burst out with a shout—"Martha's promised to marry me!"

Curtiss dropped everything and jumped to his feet.

"That's grand news, Harry," he exclaimed. "She's a great girl. I always knew you had a weakness for her. Bringing her all the way from Elmira. Hey, Lena! Harry's going to marry Martha."

Lena came into the room, followed by Martha, who looked unaccustomedly shy, but radiantly happy.

"I've known it for some time," said Lena.

"So have I," admitted Martha.

"Well, nobody told me until tonight," Harry said.

Curtiss laughed delightedly. Then his face clouded. "But you're not going to take her away from me, are you, Harry? I couldn't do a thing without her."

"No," said Harry. "She wouldn't like that, would you, Martha?"

"Certainly not," said Martha. "We're all in this thing to-gether. We'll get a little house close by, and—"

"That won't do," said Curtiss. "Suppose I wake up in the middle of the night, like I so often do, with a good idea I've got to talk over with Harry. I can't go running all over town in my pajamas, looking for him. They've got to live here, haven't they, Lena?"

"I thought of that, too, Glenn," said Lena. "They can have the whole back wing and an entrance of their own."

"Will that be all right, Martha? Harry?" asked Curtiss anxiously.

Harry looked at Martha and she nodded slightly.

"Yes, G. H.," said Harry, "if that's the way you want it."

Meanwhile, work on the new government dirigible went on, until, in the summer of 1908, it was ready for trial. The airship they finally evolved was as far in advance of the little *Arrow* as a clipper ship was beyond the *Santa María*. Her envelope, made of a silk and rubber fabric devised by Baldwin, contained twenty thousand cubic feet of gas. It was not loose and shapeless, but trim and seemingly rigid, kept so by an interior bag or ballonet of air, which could be pumped up or deflated as the gas expanded or shrank. The long car was suspended from the envelope by steel cables. It contained Curtiss' first great contribution to aeronautics, a four-cylinder twenty-four-horsepower *water-cooled* engine capable of running indefinitely without overheating.

No longer was it necessary for the aeronaut to race up and down the car to balance his ship. Two box-kite stabilizers were attached on either side of the car, while a cruciform tail provided both horizontal and vertical control. The dirigible had a total lift of 1360 pounds and a disposable margin of 500 pounds.

On August 12, 1908, at Fort Myer, Virginia, with Curtiss

sitting near the bow nursing the engine and whirling the centrifugal air pump that filled the ballonet, and Captain Baldwin at the stern piloting, the airship flew for two hours at a speed of sixteen miles per hour. It had triumphantly met the impossible specifications and was accepted by the government. Designated the SC-1, it was the first vessel of that great and ever-growing aerial fleet on which the safety of our country now depends.

Significant as was the accomplishment of the SC-1 it had, before ever it left the ground, become a mere sideshow to Curtiss. For the course of aerial events had been unbelievably rapid, and the man, who had thought in 1907 that he would never go up again, was now committed, heart and soul and brain, to the advancement of true, of winged flight.

CHAPTER NINE

THE BIRTHDAY OF THE NEW WORLD

(A necessary flashback into history)

IN 1887, PROFESSOR SAMUEL PIERPONT LANGLEY, Secretary of the Smithsonian Institution at Washington, began building model aeroplanes. This did not indicate senility on the part of the professor, though ninety-nine per cent of his fellow countrymen would have said that it did. It simply meant that Langley had, contrary to orthodox opinion, become convinced that winged flight was possible to man.

For seven years he labored, calculating, experimenting, and building model aeroplanes powered by rubber bands. They were not very good models—for twenty-five cents you can get better ones in any cigar store today. The longest flight any of them made was seventy-five feet; nevertheless, they flew.

The professor proceeded with the utmost scientific exactitude. Each tiny machine which he built was weighed and measured and photographed; every flight was recorded and studied, for the professor was exploring an element hitherto virtually unknown. It seems incredible that, breathing, weighed upon, supported by, and living only by the grace of air, man should have been so completely ignorant of its nature, but it is a fact that the atmosphere was almost as unknown as was the western hemisphere before Columbus sailed from Spain.

At the end of seven years, Professor Langley produced a

quarter-size model of what was to be his man-carrying "aero-drome." It was a beautiful little machine, powered by a tiny steam engine so exquisitely constructed that, complete with water in the boiler, the power plant weighed less than eleven pounds and delivered 1 ½ horsepower. The total weight of the model was thirty pounds, its wings, set one pair behind the other, measured twelve feet, and its length overall was fifteen feet. In 1896 this machine was launched from a houseboat on the Potomac River and made a level flight of 4,200 feet, remaining in the air for 1 minute 49 seconds.

This, Professor Langley thought, conclusively proved the possibility of flight, but virtually nobody paid any attention. Langley's brilliant self-justification fell into a pool of willful disbelief.

However, the Board of Ordnance of the War Department was sufficiently impressed to allot the professor fifty thousand dollars to build a full-size machine. For seven long years more he labored (like Jacob) to earn his bride, the air. In October 1903 the first trial was made, but a failure of the launching device made it inconclusive.

On December 8, 1903, the final trial was held. On the broad Potomac off Arsenal Point floated a brilliant assemblage of generals, admirals, reporters, scientists and politicians headed by the Secretary of War, while the whole people of America waited for news with a feeling of tense uneasiness.

The spectators could see the wide white wings of the aero-drome perched insecurely on top of the specially built house-boat or "ark." The machine was an almost exact enlargement of the successful model. The wings were arranged in tandem, with the engine and pilot placed between them. Vertical control was provided by the clumsy-looking dihedral tail, and the machine was steered by a small rudder placed below the afterwings. The motor was a magnificent piece of engineering. Professor Langley and his ardent young assistant, Professor Charles M. Manly, had scoured the world for a twelve-horsepower engine which weighed no more than one hundred and twenty pounds—ten pounds per horsepower. Unable to find one, they designed and built a five-cylinder radial, water-cooled motor which weighed but one hundred and twenty-five pounds and delivered 52.4 horsepower. The like of it was not seen again for nearly ten years. Complete with Professor Manly aboard, the aerodrome weighed only eight hundred and thirty pounds.

Professor Langley had decided, foolishly as later developments proved, that the machine could only be launched by catapult from a considerable height. To this end the ark had been built and equipped with a trolley on rails propelled by extremely powerful springs.

The spectators on yachts, excursion steamers, sailboats and skiffs were all there long before noon and, like all witnesses of early aviation events, they had a long wait. It was nearly dusk before they saw Professor Manly climb into his seat between the tandem wings.

Just why the attempt was made at all that day is something of a mystery. Conditions were anything but good, for, though the weather was brilliantly clear, there was a flukey wind varying from twelve to eighteen miles per hour. It would seem that, having waited so long, the two professors could have spared one more day. Manly said afterward that their money, the fifty thousand from the Board of Ordnance and twenty thousand more from the Smithsonian, had all run out and that they could not afford the delay. But it almost seems as though the nervous strain had upset the equilibrium of the Olympian scientists. So long had they labored that now, with the moment at hand, they were seized by a fatal impatience.

From the Smithsonian tugs, which at the end of long cables were holding the ark into the wind, spectators saw through powerful fieldglasses that men were cranking the motor, then the wide propellers on either side of the fuselage began to revolve. Faster they turned until they looked like the sails of a demented windmill. At last Professor Manly raised his hand and a mechanic pulled the trigger of the catapult.

Down the deck of the ark rushed the frail machine and there, before ever it took the air, catastrophe occurred. Whether the afterwings struck a stanchion, or whether a sudden side gust of wind imposed a transverse strain, which the wings, bound still to earth, were not designed to support, no one will ever know. But a moan went up from the spectators as they saw the whole rear part of the aerodrome collapse.

The machine kept going; nothing could stop it now, and Manly was unaware of the accident. It shot off the roof of the houseboat and its nose pointed upward. So light was it and so powerful the motor that for interminable seconds it hovered with its bedraggled wings trailing uselessly below, its nose pointed straight at the sky, supported by its propellers like a helicopter. Then slowly it flopped over on its back and crashed into the river.

The whole country yelled with demoniac glee. "If Langley can't do it, nobody can," was the gist of that thunderous shout. "That settles it—man will never fly!"

Humorous press dispatches, angry editorials, professedly unbiased scientific articles, based on abstruse mathematical calculations, echoed and re-echoed the cry in a rising tirade of invective that before two years had passed drove Professor Langley to his grave. He was utterly discredited and so was the very idea of flight.

A few courageous voices, like that of Alexander Graham Bell, were raised in defense of Langley, and were drowned out by the thunder of the storm.

So terrible, so cruel a public reaction can be explained only by the vast sense of relief which sprang up at the news of the failure. Passionately, fanatically, man did not *want* to fly. It almost seems as though by some strange prescience the people of America saw beyond that frail little aerodrome the cruel, million-winged, man-devouring monster of the Luftwaffe, and in their subconscious souls cried out to God to stay his hand.

And yet—

While the presses were still roaring out the vindictive editorials, while the reporters were making their wisecracks, while the scientists were engaged in their irrefutable calculations, while the whole country screamed in triumph, "Man will never fly!" on December 17, 1903, just nine brief winter days after the crash in the Potomac, on a lonely beach at Kitty Hawk, North Carolina, an aeroplane flew 852 feet carrying a man. It was the birthday of the New World.

Why the Wrights succeeded where Langley failed is something which can only be explained by the word genius. The odds were heavily weighted in favor of the Secretary of the Smithsonian. He had the highest scientific education; the brothers from Dayton never even went to college. Langley had the resources of a great institution at his command and the backing of the United States Government; the Wrights had nothing but a bicycle shop and financed their experiments out of the profits of their business. But beyond the obvious and material things lies a great imponderable, a sort of divine flash which lights the minds of certain men and is as careless where it strikes as the thunderbolts of Jove.

This is not intended to imply that the Wrights were not true scientists. What they lacked in formal education, they made up by intensive study. Theirs was no hit-or-miss approach, but as carefully worked out, though in a simpler, shorter fashion, as Langley's. In many respects they were far more thorough than he. Their wind-pressure tables, however crude the means by which they were compiled, proved to be infinitely more accurate, and they took the sensible precaution of learning to fly on gliders before they attempted their final objective.

The fact that the Wright aeroplane staggered through the uneasy air above the dunes for those few hundred feet was the most important single piece of news of the twentieth century. It was printed in banner headlines in the *Virginian-Pilot* of December 18, 1903. And the whole world unanimously refused to believe it. Fantastic as it may seem, four and a half years elapsed before the news that man could really fly became public.

During that time hundreds of people saw Wright machines in the air. At Dayton, where they continued their experiments, the sight of the white-winged plane, clacking through the air with a sound like a McCormick reaper, was familiar to half the farmers in the county.

But still the world stopped up its ears.

This extraordinary hiatus between the event of flight and its public recognition was due to a peculiar combination of circumstance. First, was the overwhelming desire of the public not to believe. Second, was the fact that after Langley's failure every newspaper, magazine, editor, publisher, and almost every scientist in the country was absolutely committed to the position that "man can never fly." They simply couldn't afford to acknowledge the fact of flight. Their attitude toward the news in the *Virginian-Pilot* was, "They can't do this to us." So every

channel for disseminating news in the country determinedly
ignored the dispatch about those brash young men who had
dared to do the impossible.

The final factor in this conspiracy of silence was the Wrights
themselves. They had the intense secretiveness of the true inventor, and, on a higher plane, they feared the effect of pre-
mature disclosure of their invention. They wanted only to be
left in peace to perfect their marvelous machine, and to spring
it, in all its wonder, on an astonished world.

CHAPTER TEN

AERIAL EXPERIMENT

A TALL, ROBUST OLD gentleman with magnificent white whiskers was making a stately progress through the New York Aero Show of 1906. He walked with a slow but firm stride, and on every hand he was greeted with the deference due a great man. For Dr. Alexander Graham Bell was already a legendary figure, and the telephone, which he had invented over twenty-five years before, was now an accepted commonplace of life; and even to him that time seemed like a dream. But he remembered very well how people used to look at him with a half-humorous, half-pitying attitude toward a man who believed that the human voice could travel over wires.

It was only on the surface that Doctor Bell's slow movement through the hall seemed ponderous. Actually his ever-youthful brain was darting like a barn swallow from exhibit to exhibit, sampling the ideas each presented and, in the main, rejecting them. These men, he felt, were all on the wrong track.

There were only a few winged machines on view, and these were the highly improbable creations of fantastic minds with a strong bias toward the ornithopter, or flapping wing. Most of the exhibits were of lighter-than-air machines; for the failure of Langley and the success of Baldwin had decided the vast majority of men that in these alone lay the hope of aerial navigation.

Doctor Bell was ruggedly convinced that fifty million Americans could be wrong. With his own eyes he had seen the small Langley model soar over the Potomac that October afternoon ten years ago, and he had been convinced. An accident at the launching of the man-carrying machine was no reason to alter that conviction. He had been a regent of the Smithsonian when Langley was its secretary; he had known the discredited inventor well and been righteously indignant at the public ridicule and invective which had broken his friend's heart. Now he was preparing to carry on Langley's work, and had already made certain experiments at his summer home, Beinn Breagh, at Baddeck, Nova Scotia.

So it was with carefully concealed disappointment that he observed the emphasis laid on gas bags at the show.

Only once did real interest bring his progress to an abrupt halt. He was standing before a dais on which were arranged a number of shining motors. Most of them were small, two-cylinder affairs, but one was a V-8 engine that looked like business. Doctor Bell read the sign at the back of the booth: G. H. CURTISS MANUFACTURING COMPANY.

A tall young man moved reluctantly from behind the motors. He had a keen, thin face with a heavy mustache and intense hazel eyes; in spite of the extreme diffidence of his manner, Doctor Bell registered the impact of a personality.

"Are you interested in my motors, Doctor Bell?" asked the young man.

The doctor was accustomed to being recognized. "I am," he said. "Extremely. You are, I suppose, Mr. Curtiss?"

"Yes sir," was the answer.

"I have heard of your work with Captain Baldwin," said Doctor Bell. "You seem to have developed some excellent power plants."

"They're pretty fair," said Curtiss, with a shy grin. Then his eyes lighted with real enthusiasm. "By next year I hope to show one that is really good."

"At some future time, when we are both ready for it, I should like to have a long talk with you," said Doctor Bell.

That momentous talk took place the following year. In the spring of 1907 Curtiss was in Washington on the matter of the proposed military dirigible. He discovered that Doctor Bell was also in the capital and decided to pay a call—there was always the chance of making a sale. G. H. made his sale, an order for two lightweight four-cylinder motors, and was in turn sold a bill of goods. For Doctor Bell mounted the hobby of his present enthusiasm and talked for three hours on the subject of winged flight. G. H., listening with deepening interest, heard of many things of which he, like most people, had been ignorant. He learned about working drawings for a flying machine made by Leonardo da Vinci when the Renaissance was breaking down the bonds of prejudice and freeing the minds of men for intellectual adventure. He heard the well-authenticated stories of seventeenth-century pioneers, who strapped wings to their arms and soared from high towers.

Coming down to more modern times, Doctor Bell described Sir Hiram Maxim's tremendous three-hundred-horsepower steam aerodrome with four thousand square feet of lifting surface which, running under restraining rails, had actually raised its enormous weight of over eight thousand pounds off the ground. Then he sketched the successful flights of Lilienthal's batlike glider and Octave Chanute's double-decker. He gave a detailed description of the Langley experiments and affirmed the conclusive proof they furnished that flight was possible to man.

"The big machine would have flown," he said, "if it had not broken in the launching."

"Are you really certain of that?" asked Curtiss.

"Absolutely positive," said Doctor Bell, "and I hope that someday the machine will be rebuilt and flown to vindicate Langley's memory.

"Furthermore," he added, "although no one has seen them, I believe that the Wright brothers have actually flown."

"Whew!" exclaimed Curtiss. "Then the flying machine is really practical."

Doctor Bell's eyes shone with excitement and his whiskers waved with his vehemence. "Young man," he said, "the day is coming soon when you will be able to pick up a thousand pounds of bricks and fly away with them."

Doctor Bell had another important interview before he left Washington. Lieutenant Thomas Selfridge, of the United States Army, paid him a visit, and the doctor was surprised to find that the young lieutenant knew more about the history of aeronautics than he did. Selfridge was an unusual young man, who can perhaps best be described in Doctor Bell's own words, written after he became a tragic "first":

"In reply to my first query," wrote Bell, "I was informed that Lieutenant Selfridge 'is a chivalrous gentleman, fond of such society as comes in his way.' We found the report correct. . . . One's abiding impression of him was his gentleness and stillness in rest coupled with a sense of underlying strength and immovable determination. . . ."

With extraordinary foresight Tom Selfridge had become convinced that mankind was poised like a fledgling on a twig just about to take off. He realized the terrible military significance of aviation and resolved that when it came the United

States Army should have at least one officer who knew something about it. By the time he met Doctor Bell, he had mastered his subject so far as was possible in that elementary age.

The doctor appreciated the quality of Lieutenant Selfridge at their first meeting.

"I should like you to come to Baddeck to observe our experiments," he said as Selfridge rose to go.

"That is my dearest wish," said the young officer.

"Will the authorities give you leave?" asked Doctor Bell.

"I believe so," said Selfridge. "But," he added boyishly, "there is one way to make sure."

"What is the way?"

"If you should write to the President requesting it."

"I'll do it tonight," said Doctor Bell.

The next day Doctor Bell returned to Nova Scotia to continue his experiments with what he called tetrahedral kites.

These extraordinary structures were the doctor's method of meeting the basic difficulty which must be overcome if man was to fly, and fly safely—the problem of maintaining stability in the uncertain air. The kites were made of hundreds of small cells, each having four triangular surfaces. The two lower surfaces of each were covered with red Chinese silk, thus making two tiny red wings with their tips pointing upward. Each cell was aerodynamically stable, and any number of them together were equally stable. Another advantage was that, since the cells were self-sufficient in strength, they could be joined together in any quantity without material additional bracing. Thus the lifting surface of the whole could be indefinitely increased while maintaining the same ratio of weight to lift.

Doctor Bell had been flying his tetrahedral kites for several years, scientifically recording the results of his observation as to lift, drag, wind velocity, and so forth. Now he was ready to construct a man-carrying machine. But though scientifically the doctor was daring in the extreme, he placed a high value on human life, and he did not feel that he should risk anything so precious on his unaided knowledge of engineering. Nor was his laboratory superintendent, Mr. William F. Bedwin, sufficiently conversant with the problems of stress.

At this point young J. A. D. McCurdy came to stay with his father, Doctor Bell's old friend and neighbor, Arthur N. McCurdy. Douglas brought with him his college friend, F. W. (Casey) Baldwin, the son of Robert Baldwin, who had been Premier of Canada. Both of these young men had just been graduated from the Engineering School of Toronto University; they were filled with intellectual curiosity, technical knowledge and tremendous enthusiasm. In addition Casey Baldwin was a great athlete. They seemed to Doctor Bell to be a present to him from a kindly Providence.

The two young engineers joined with enthusiasm in this fascinating scientific game. Tom Selfridge arrived from Washington and there began the happiest time of all their lives. They all stayed at Beinn Breagh, Doctor Bell's big house on the thickly forested hillside which ran down to the lake. Also staying in the house were Doctor Bell's two daughters, his son-in-law, David E. Fairchild, and a couple of grandchildren. Perhaps the most amazing person of them all was the lady of the house.

Mabel Gardiner Bell had been stone deaf ever since she was six years old. It was her husband's desire to help her through electrical devices that had led to his invention of the telephone. In spite of her deafness, Mrs. Bell was, if possible, more intellectually eager than her husband, and, since she was adept at lip reading, she played her full part in the rousing scientific discussions that took place every evening before the great log fire in the hall of Beinn Breagh.

The young men played as hard as they worked, and often in the morning the big wooden veranda resounded with the stamp of feet and the clash of steel as Casey and Douglas, with mask and foil, tried to best the superb swordsmanship of Tom Selfridge. All the time, the construction of the man-carrying kite went forward. Since it was to contain no fewer than 3,690 tetrahedral cells, it was slow work.

Meanwhile, Curtiss was equally busy in Hammondsport. In addition to the motors for Bell, and work on the SC-1, the motorcycle business was booming, and airship men were arriving from all over the world to get motors to drive their gas bags. Some of them settled in Hammondsport, and the uneasy air above the valley was frequently full of curiously shaped monstrosities.

In the midst of these activities Curtiss found time to rig up what he called a "wind wagon" for the purpose of testing propellers. It was a platform mounted on three bicycle wheels powered by a two-cylinder airship motor driving a propeller. The first time he tried it, he went sailing down the valley road at thirty-five miles an hour. His progress, in a cloud of dust and blue smoke shattered by violent explosions, resembled the trail of a tornado, and the farmers were hunting up their horses for the next three days.

The first motor was shipped to Baddeck in midsummer, but without G. H.'s personal presence to soothe its eccentricities, it proved something of a disappointment. So Doctor Bell wrote to Curtiss requesting him to deliver the second motor in person, and offering to compensate him for his services.

Curtiss showed Lena the letter. "How can I find time to go up into the backwoods to talk aeronautics?" he asked.

"You must, Glenn," she answered. "Doctor Bell is counting

on you. After all, he invented the telephone and something great may come of this too."

So G. H. packed his small valise, put the second motor in the baggage car, and started off for Baddeck. After innumerable changes of cars he was set down at a little wooden station around which clustered a few frame buildings. Two bronzed young men, dressed in old flannel trousers and khaki shirts, came forward to greet him.

"I'm Jack McCurdy," said the first, "and this is Casey Baldwin. We're all glad you've come."

Curtiss shook hands with them, and sniffed the warm pine-scented air. "I'm glad to be here," he said.

"Have you got the motor with you?" asked Casey.

"It's in the baggage car."

"Come on Douglas, let's get it."

"I thought your name was Jack," said G. H.

"It's Douglas, too," said McCurdy, "but I like Jack better."

Helped by the old Scotch-Canadian porter, they hauled the crated motor out and carried it down a rickety pier to where the small steamer, *Blue Hill*, floated on the deep blue water of the Gauldrie. As soon as they boarded her, she set off across the lake.

After a run of perhaps half an hour, the *Blue Hill* approached a pier that jutted out from the pine woods into the lake. High on the hillside above it Curtiss could see through the trees the windows and gables of a great rambling house. The steamer touched the pier and a workman in overalls caught her hawser.

"They'll take care of your motor," said Casey Baldwin. "Come on up to the house."

As they climbed the path, deep in the pine needles, Curtiss looked over the details of Doctor Bell's establishment. The long sheds of the laboratory were close behind the boat house, and he saw several small shacks that stood apart under the tall trees.

"Do you sleep in those cabins?" he asked.

The two young men laughed.

"No," said Casey, "we all live up at the house. Those are to go and think in."

They crossed the wide veranda of the house and walked into a great hall furnished with comfortable, shabby divans and big easychairs. At one end, near a huge stone fireplace, a woman was sitting reading. She did not look up as they came in and McCurdy said, "That's Mrs. Bell. She's completely deaf, you know."

He moved so that his shadow crossed her light and she looked up. Then she dropped her book and came forward swiftly. As she crossed the hall, Curtiss saw that she was tall and had a long face and a rather large nose on which were perched rimless glasses. His first thought was, "How plain she is," and then, as she began to speak, he swiftly revised his estimate to, "How utterly charming."

She greeted him with unmistakable pleasure, and said to Casey, "Go tell Doctor Bell that Mr. Curtiss is here at last."

Then she called, "Tom, he's come!"

An extraordinarily handsome young man hurried out of the library and was introduced as Lieutenant Selfridge. As he and Curtiss were shaking hands, there was a clatter in the hall above and Doctor Bell came tearing down the stairs.

"My dear Mr. Curtiss," he exclaimed. "It's wonderful you are here. I've been so impatient. Welcome! Welcome to Beinn Breagh."

That evening for the first of many times, they all gathered in front of the fireplace in the hall. Now was the group complete that was to write so brilliant a chapter in the history of aviation. Curtiss' practical engineering experience, his wonderfully ingenious mind, and his ability to drive single-purposed to a definite end supplied the element needed to synthesize these men into a working body and to bring out the best in them all.

The talk was fast and furious that night, so rapid that at one time Mrs. Bell lost the thread. G. H. noticed her unhappy expression. Because his own sister was deaf, he had learned the language of hands, and now his swift fingers spelled the missing words.

Her eyes lighted with pleasure and gratitude and her hands signaled, "God bless you."

The days went by too swiftly, working in the laboratory, flying the smaller kites for further data, lying under the pine trees talking about the wings of the future. Occasionally they took time off to practice at the rifle range, and when the day was done they gathered in the hall to play with the children and drink hot tea. In the evenings there was good talk and boisterous games of billiards. On Wednesday nights shop talk was taboo, and the time was devoted to telling stories and roaring out their favorite songs.

When necessity demanded it, Curtiss found it terribly hard to leave. He came back to Lena blazing with a new enthusiasm.

"I see you had a good time, Glenn," she said, happily regarding his sun-tanned skin and shining eyes.

"It was the grandest experience of my life," said Glenn. "I'm going back in September."

"Good for you," said Lena.

So at the end of September Curtiss was back at Beinn Breagh. The first evening, when they gathered in the hall, Doctor Bell rose to his feet. It was a formality which suggested that something of unusual import was afoot.

"Gentlemen," he said, "Mrs. Bell has made a suggestion to me of which I think most highly. We have discussed it together at length and she has asked me to lay it before you.

"She has been much struck by the possibilities in the combination of an elderly man of considerable experience, like myself, with a group of young men of brilliant ability. She thinks that we should form ourselves into an association for the advancement of aeronautics. Since the association will require funds, Mrs. Bell has with the utmost generosity offered to present it with a piece of real estate she owns in Washington—it is virtually the only property of hers which I did not give her—which is worth twenty-five thousand dollars. This sum should suffice to finance the experiments of the association for a year. Our primary object would be to get into the air by hook or crook. I would like you gentlemen to consider the idea and tell me what you think of it."

When Doctor Bell finished speaking there was silence for a moment, while each of his listeners tried to realize the wonderful prospect he had opened to them. Then the hall rang with their shouts of assent, and upstairs a baby woke and added its wails to the din.

Tom Selfridge jumped to his feet and, going over to Mrs. Bell, kissed her hand. "You are magnificent," he said.

At eleven o'clock in the morning of October 1, 1907, all the members of the group met at the Halifax Hotel, in Halifax, to sign the articles of agreement which constituted the charter of the Aerial Experiment Association.

The charter read in part:

"Whereas it has been thought advisable that the undersigned should work together as an association in which all have equal interest, the above named gentlemen giving the benefit of their assistance in carrying out the ideas of the said Alex-

ander Graham Bell, said Alexander Graham Bell giving his
assistance to these gentlemen in carrying out their own independent ideas relating to aerial locomotion, and all working
together individually and conjointly in pursuance of their com-
mon aim 'to get into the air'. . . ."

The agreement further stated that all ideas, patents, and devices, contributed by individual members of the association,
should belong to each and all of them jointly and severally.

As a legal document the agreement was as full of holes as a
colander; in it was material for as fine a collection of lawsuits
as ever gummed up the courts. But as an expression of the purpose and spirit of these men it was magnificent. The Three
Musketeers' slogan, which has become trite and thin through
usage, like an old coin, was still pure gold to them: "One for
all and all for one" was their intention, and that spirit was kept
inviolate. Though the members of the A. E. A. fought other
people most of their lives, there was never a disagreement between them, and, because they honored the spirit of their bond,
its legal inadequacies never had to be tested.

On October 2, still in Halifax, the association met to elect
officers. Doctor Bell was made chairman, Curtiss was appointed
chief executive and director of experiments, and Baldwin was
chief engineer.

The next day the matter of salaries came up. These young
men were not financially independent—they must have something to live on.

Baldwin and McCurdy were voted one thousand dollars a
year each. Then, since Curtiss must neglect his business, he
was voted five thousand dollars a year.

"Hold on," said G. H. after the vote had gone through. "I
want to propose an amendment to that. As I will be away part

of the time, I want it to read that only half pay shall be given me when I am not actually working with you."

Doctor Bell expressed keen appreciation of Curtiss' attitude, and it was so voted.

On December 7, 1907, the man-carrying kite was ready for flight. Each of those thousands of tiny cells had been painstakingly completed by skillful hands; it was an exquisite piece of workmanship. They christened her *Cygnet* and took her out on the lake to try.

It was a brilliant winter morning. The breeze was light, but it came straight off the ice fields to the northward and seemed to pierce the warmest clothing. The little waves on the ultramarine surface of the Gauldrie looked as cold and sharp as blue diamonds.

When the *Blue Hill*, towing the flat boat on which the towering structure was precariously balanced, was well clear of the shore, Tom Selfridge, who had been voted the honor of the first flight, climbed into his place on the framework behind the winged cells. His cheeks were bright red from the cold and his eyes were blazing with excitement. The others adjusted the ropes, and the steamer was headed up into the wind.

Gradually her speed increased and, as she surged ahead, the great kite shivered on its float. Then as softly as a dandelion fluff it floated into the air.

They all watched tensely as it climbed steadily up the wind. There was, they noted, no bucking or veering, the huge structure rode the uneasy atmosphere as serenely as an ocean liner in a landlocked sound; it looked like a great scarlet honeycomb floating on edge in the sky.

One hundred and sixty-eight feet of altitude they reckoned it, before they neared the end of their run. Then the engine of the steamer slowed. The great kite settled so gently that Tom Selfridge, riding behind the screen of cells, did not even know when it touched the water and so failed to slip the tow rope. Catastrophe ensued.

Before they could stop the *Blue Hill*, the kite was dragged under water. The delicate cells crumpled like a wet butterfly's wing, and the whole great structure collapsed. They hauled Tom unhurt, though with chattering teeth, from the ice-cold water, but *Cygnet* was a total wreck.

In spite of the accident, and the long months of work that rebuilding would entail, Doctor Bell was in high spirits when they met that evening before the fire.

"The accident was unimportant," he said, "though it will set us back many months in our experiments. The vital thing is that we have proved the inherent stability of tetrahedral structures. I have given orders to start building ten thousand more cells immediately."

They unanimously approved the doctor's conclusions and his dauntless spirit. Then Tom Selfridge spoke.

"As Doctor Bell has observed," he said, "our work here will be delayed for a long time by the wreck of *Cygnet*. In the meantime, the world may get ahead of us. The Wrights are doing wonderful things, and in France, Mr. Henry Farman has flown eight hundred yards. While the *Cygnet* is rebuilding, I should like our association to try their hands at building an aerodrome."

"Just what Douglas and I have been wanting to do," Casey said.

"It suits me," said G. H.

"The ayes seem to have it," said Doctor Bell. "Will you put your proposal in the form of a motion, Tom?"

This was done, and then McCurdy spoke, "We should build a glider, too, to practice on."

"Assuredly," agreed Doctor Bell. "I don't want you boys flying off with no experience at all. Make the motion."

It was carried unanimously and then Curtiss untelescoped his length from a low chair.

"Since the laboratory here will be occupied in rebuilding *Cygnet*," he said, "I would like to move that the association conducts its experiments in—in aerodromics at Hammondsport. All the resources of my factory there will be placed at your disposal, and the balloonatics have taught us a good deal about building light, strong frames."

They all looked at Doctor Bell to see if he would object to leaving his comfortable home and familiar place of work. But there was no rigidity of age about the doctor.

"I think Mr. Curtiss' generous offer should be accepted," he said.

It was done by acclamation.

"That's fine," said Curtiss. "You are, of course, all invited to stay at my house. Now I think I'll go up and pack. I'll catch the early-morning train and be in Hammondsport day after tomorrow. The work can begin at once. If this is a race to get into the air, we shall not lose a day."

CHAPTER ELEVEN

THE FLEDGLINGS

THE INHABITANTS OF HAMMONDSPORT were used to strange shapes in the sky, but the sight of a pair of small white wings fluttering down from the hills with the dark body of a man slung beneath them was enormously exciting. Airships were interesting, but to them, as to the whole world, the idea of soaring on wings was vastly more appealing. Word spread that G. H. had decided to build a flying machine, and his loyal fellow townsmen said, "Now, at last, it will be done."

The glider, which was not designed to prove anything new, but merely for the purpose of gaining experience, was copied after the successful machines of Octave Chanute, who unselfishly supplied the new association with the data he had compiled. It was a tiny biplane, with a small horizontal stabilizing plane in front. The pilot was suspended by his arms through a hole in the center section of the lower plane. To launch it, he ran down a hillside in the teeth of the wind and jumped into the air. Once air-borne his only method of control was to swing the lower part of his body forward or back, to left or right, according to the exigencies of the machine's attitude.

Even before the arrival of Baldwin, McCurdy and Selfridge, Curtiss, with the enthusiastic assistance of Tod Shriver and Henry Kleckler, had the glider nearly ready. The young men came early in January 1908, and two days later Doctor and Mrs. Bell arrived, bringing Mr. Bedwin with them.

Lena was absolutely panic-stricken at the thought of lodging so famous a scientist as Doctor Bell.

"What shall I do, Glenn?" she said. "He's used to so many things we haven't got."

"Remember how scared you were when the captain was coming?" asked Glenn.

"But Uncle Tom's different, he's just folks."

"So are Doctor and Mrs. Bell. You'll love them both, Lena."

And so she did. The House on the Hill was not quite capacious enough to accommodate the entire A. E. A., so the younger members lodged in the village.

It did not take long for the enthusiastic fledglings to wear out the first glider, but before it completely collapsed each had had some valuable minutes in the air and had acquired numerous chromatic contusions.

With the final dissolution of the glider, discussion of the next step was in order.

"I think we should build one more glider," said Tom Selfridge.

"The more experience you gain, the safer you'll be when the time comes to fly," agreed Doctor Bell.

"Meanwhile, the world beats us to it," said McCurdy. "I'm for starting work on a real aerodrome."

"I agree with Douglas," said Casey. "We've learned what we can from kites."

They all looked at Curtiss.

"I'm an impatient sort of person," said G. H. "I've wanted to get on with it for weeks."

So it was voted to build Drome No. 1. In order to avoid the confusion of divided counsels, the association decided that each member in turn should be in charge of the building of a machine and have the final word as to what went into it. Since Tom Selfridge had risked his neck in *Cygnet*, he was voted the responsibility for Drome No. 1, though Casey Baldwin did more of the actual designing while Mr. Bedwin was in charge of construction. But every member of the association had his part in it, and others capable of giving advice were free to drop in and offer suggestions. Henry Kleckler was usually there, for Curtiss always discussed every new idea with him, relying on Henry's logical mind to catalyze his thoughts. So was Captain Baldwin, who, though busily engaged on the SC-1, often came around to offer valuable suggestions from his long experience with aerodynamics.

It was decided to follow the general design of the Farman-Voisin machine. The Wright aeroplanes were indubitably better, but nobody knew anything about the details of their construction. However, Drome No. 1 differed greatly from the French machine. The latter depended for lateral stability on boxed-in wings with vertical planes at intervals between them. Casey had a better idea than that. He called it concavo-convex wings, and it provided that the upper and lower planes should not be straight, but should curve toward each other at the tips, making a sort of double bow open at the ends.

G. H. studied his design with interest. "It looks good," he said, "but don't you think we should also provide some positive way of correcting tipping? Possibly lateral rudders of some sort. . . ."

"I don't think we need 'em," said Casey. "If one wing drops, the curve in my design will provide more lifting surface and automatically bring it up. Furthermore, the double curve will tend to prevent skidding on the corners."

"I still think the operator should be able to take an active hand in the game," said G. H.

"What about it, Tom?" Casey asked.

"I don't think we should give the pilot any more things to do than we have to," said Selfridge. "It will be confusing enough, handling the vertical control and the rudder. Let's try Casey's way first."

Since, by agreement, it was his machine, Tom had the last word.

Work on the aerodrome proceeded with astonishing rapidity. In the aerodrome shed, which had been added to the factory, the wings were growing daily, and soon they were ready to be covered with the fine quality red silk which had been brought down from Baddeck. When he first saw a finished section, Doctor Bell had one of his happy inspirations of nomenclature.

"We'll call her *Red Wing*," he said.

Right in the middle of the work J. Newton Williams, the typewriter manufacturer, arrived with a model helicopter, powered by rubber bands, that really flew. The A. E. A. was always open to new ideas, and they took time out to help the old inventor design a full-scale machine. Curtiss provided a motor, and one winter day they tried the strange aircraft. It consisted of a traylike base in which the motor was installed. From this a shaft extended upward at the top of which two large screw-shaped wings, or rotors, were driven in opposite directions.

Mr. Williams, dressed in a citified black overcoat with a black fez on his bald head and his big white mustachios bristling with excitement, took his place in the tray. The engine was started, and the wings began to revolve, blowing a cold draft on the little old man. But though the machine trembled and swayed, it would not lift.

Finally Mr. Williams got out and young Byron Brown, who weighed only 110 pounds, took his place. The engine was started again, the revolving wings clawed at the atmosphere and—she lifted.

Only three feet to the end of a restraining rope, but it was, as far as the records show, the first ascent ever made by a helicopter.

Meanwhile, only seven weeks from its inception, Selfridge's *Red Wing* was ready to fly. Her wings spread 43 feet 4 inches and the chord of them was 6 feet 3 inches. Their total supporting surface was 385.5 square feet of finest Chinese silk.

The pilot sat in front of the lower plane in a spindle-shaped nacelle made of bamboo outriggers covered with silk. His feet stuck out in front of him, and at the end of the bamboo poles was placed the "elevating rudder," a flat surface 8 feet by 2 feet which he could move up and down by a yoke rope control. A lever worked the four-foot square vertical rudder for steering, which was carried at the end of more bamboo outriggers extending ten feet out behind. The outriggers and main planes were all guyed with piano wire. The aerodrome was mounted on short steel runners.

Curtiss had been working on the engine ever since his return from Baddeck. It was a variation of his V-8 air-cooled job that made the "fastest mile," and suffered from the same inability to run for more than three minutes without overheating. The flywheel was a bicycle wheel with a hardwood rim. Vanes were attached to the spokes in an effort to supply a cooling draft. To make sure of maximum performance, G. H. put a carburetor on each cylinder—adjusting the mixture was an eightfold job. This motor was rated at forty horsepower, though in practice it turned the prop only at one thousand revolutions per minute, delivering but twenty horsepower. The engine complete weighed 185 pounds, and the total weight of *Red Wing* with Casey at the bat was 570 pounds.

March 12, 1908, was the day she was finally completed. Before that, Mrs. Bell, to the intense distress of the whole A. E. A. and all her new friends in Hammondsport, had been taken ill and her husband had carried her off to Washington for treatment. Tom Selfridge, too, was absent, having been called for duty in the capital, so only McCurdy, Baldwin, and Curtiss remained.

They hated to try the new machine in the absence of its sponsor, but the ice on Lake Keuka would not wait. Already their fine landing field was dissolving, and three miles of open water stretched between them and the ice. It looked like then or never.

That afternoon the inhabitants of Hammondsport saw a peculiar procession pass down the icy street. With her wings askew in a large cart, *Red Wing* was towed down the hill to the lakefront. Pulling the wagon were the three A. E. A. members and Henry Kleckler, Captain Baldwin, Mr. Bedwin, Harry Genung, and Tank Waters, assisted by workmen from the factory. Small boys ran circles around the slow parade, shouting with excitement, and though the three young men tried to march in dignity, they felt like shouting, too.

Amid agonized yells and frantic directions, *Red Wing* was loaded on a small steamer, which headed out into the lake toward the rim of the ice. Unloading at its treacherous edge was even more of a trick, but at last the aerodrome stood safely on its runners supported by the frozen floor.

Against the dark gray of the ice and the steel gray of the sky her bright wings made a vivid promise of hope; curving in a double cupid's bow they were the shape of a young girl's carmine lips.

G. H. and Casey and Jack McCurdy ceremoniously drew straws for the honor of the first flight, and Casey won. He crawled into the sledlike nacelle, and a dozen hands headed *Red Wing* to the wind. Curtiss climbed aboard to adjust the motor, and Henry Kleckler swung the prop.

The tension was too much for Tank Waters. He ran in circles, yipping like an excited puppy, and fell through a hole in the ice. They suspended operations to fish him out. Wrapped in blankets he was confined to the warm oblivion of the steamer's engine room.

Then they were finally ready. Kleckler swung the prop once, twice, three times.

"Wait a second," yelled G. H.

He swiftly adjusted the coil.

"Try her again."

Kleckler swung, and the motor roared its answer. While men strained against the throbbing wings, Curtiss' fingers flew about the carburetors and the uneven rhythm of the engine smoothed and the pitch of sound rose to its peak of power. Then Curtiss jumped down. Casey Baldwin raised his arm, held it there for one tense second, and dropped it. The men sprang away from the wing tips, and *Red Wing* slid slowly forward.

They all ran after her for a little and then, as she gathered speed, stopped in their tracks to watch. Swiftly now she gained momentum. Her wings tipped back and the miracle happened: she rose air-borne. At first there were but inches of daylight between her runners and the ice, then five feet, ten, fifteen!

"She's flying," Curtiss said in strangled tones.

"She's flying," echoed twenty hysterical voices.

Tank's head shot up through the engine-room hatch and his Comanchee yell echoed back from the hills.

For what seemed at once an eternity and the flash of a split second, the scarlet wings hung like an exotic bird against the sullen sky. Then they settled slowly and bumped on the ice. *Red Wing* skidded to a stop.

Slipping and sliding, shouting their exaltation, the men ran toward her. Casey, his face lighted by a look of ecstasy, rare on earth or even in heaven, stepped from the machine. He was almost knocked off his feet by the rush, deafened by exuberant congratulations and excited questions.

McCurdy produced the surveyor's tape, brought in the hope it might be needed, and like true scientists they measured off the distance—how minutely did they measure! From the last faint scratch of the lightening runners to the deep gash where *Red Wing* hit again it was 318 feet 11 inches.

On St. Patrick's Day they tried *Red Wing* again. This time she got off in less than the two hundred feet she used on her first hop, but then things went wrong. She staggered in the air, her nose tipped skyward. Casey wildly worked the rudders, but without lateral controls he never had a chance. The aerodrome tilted to the left, slid off on a wing, and crashed.

With icy hearts the others searched in that tangle of scarlet silk for Casey—and found him quite unscratched. But *Red Wing* was broken beyond repair, and only the motor salvaged.

That evening the association met, undaunted, and formally voted to construct Drome No. 2.

In honor of Casey's flight he was voted the sponsorship of this machine, but Curtiss was determined that it should have some positive means of lateral control, and Baldwin, after his crack-up, heartily concurred. The means was suggested in a long and thoughtful letter from Doctor Bell in which he urged using "shifting movable surfaces at the ends of each wing piece." There was the germ of the aileron!

Doctor Bell added that, since so much was expected of the aviator, it would be helpful if his instinct to lean toward the high side in a machine which was tipping could be utilized by means of a lever to operate these movable surfaces.

Drome No. 2 was named Baldwin's *White Wing*. Since the A. E. A. had run out of red silk and could not afford to buy any more, the wings were covered with white nainsook. As this porous material let the air through and so destroyed the lift, it was "doped" with the Chanute varnish. This mixture was of such a violent nature that it is a wonder that men were hardy enough even to approach a machine on which it was used, let alone venturing into the sky in one. The recipe was as follows:

> 60 grams guncotton
> 1 liter alcohol
> 3 liters sulphuric acid
> 20 grams castor oil
> 10 grams Canadian Balsam
> To be applied thinly with a flat brush.

One hopes they applied it very thinly.

In the evolution of the aeroplane, *White Wing* is a sort of missing link. Her career was brief and not particularly glorious, but her importance is far beyond her ability to fly; it lies in the fact that in her design appeared for the first time, though in rudimentary form, one thing which is basic in every aeroplane built today, and others which played a vital role in the progress of aviation, some of which are still in use. They are:

1. The aileron. Following Doctor Bell's suggestion Curtiss designed hinged tips at the extremities of the wings.

2. The shoulder yoke control. This consisted of two arms at the level of the aviator's shoulders, so that by leaning to one side or the other he could work the ailerons to correct tipping. This system of control was used on all Curtiss planes until 1914.

3. The tricycle landing gear. This type of landing gear was abandoned after 1914 only to reappear as the last word in aeronautics in the fast pursuit ships and flying fortresses of the present day.

4. The laminated-wood propeller.

5. Streamlined struts. This represented the first attempt on record to cut down the head resistance of an aeroplane.

It was May before *White Wing* was finished. Doctor and Mrs. Bell and Tom Selfridge had all returned from Washington, so the association was once more complete and in tearing high spirits. On May 13, defying superstition, the machine was taken to the race-course for her first trial. The wings would not clear the sides of the track, so they tried her in the grass plot in the center. Tom Selfridge was given the honor of piloting to make up to him for being absent from *Red Wing's* trials. He settled himself in the pilot's seat, with high hopes which were quite literally dashed to earth immediately. For as soon as *White Wing* began to move, her frail landing gear collapsed from the roughness of the field.

They strengthened it that night, and in the morning they worked feverishly to widen the race-course, plowing up the turf and rolling it. That afternoon they tried again, but the contrary machine kept running off the track, because at slow initial speed the rudder could not hold it straight.

Curtiss solved that problem by setting the front wheel in a

bicycle fork, and providing a short tiller by which the aviator could steer when on the ground.

On May 18, with Casey once more at the bat, *White Wing* had her third trial. Blowing a great cloud of dust back in the faces of the onlookers, she lumbered off. True to her course she held while her speed increased. Soon she was going twenty-five miles an hour, nearly flying speed. The wheels bounced once, twice, then, spinning, left the ground, and for the first time in America an aeroplane had taken off from wheels. Doctor Bell and his young friends stared anxiously after her. They saw with horror that the trailing edges of the wings were far too flexible. Under the pressure of the air they curled upward and fouled the big, square-ended propeller. It tore into the flimsy wood and cotton like a buzz saw, and *White Wing* staggered back to earth. But she had flown ninety-five yards.

Working at night again, they strengthened the wings and the next day Tom Selfridge made two flights, landing from the second undamaged in a plowed field.

Then, on May 22, came Curtiss' turn to take the air for the first time in winged flight. He wrote an exact account of that experience for the records of the A. E. A. As befits a scientific document, it contains no hint of the emotions that swept through him as for the first time he handled the controls he had designed. But, as much by what it leaves unsaid as by the words themselves, it gives a clear picture of the moment and the man.

His first attempt to rise was unsuccessful, as the motor had not been properly oiled. He describes the second as follows:

"After oiling the engine we tried again. Upon being released she started down the track faster than before and raised with the front control in the normal position. She glided for a short distance, gradually raising to a height of twelve feet and then seemed inclined to settle to the ground. I pulled back on the steering wheel, raising the front controlling plane slightly when the machine immediately rose and would probably have gone on to an indefinite height had I not reversed the plane again and brought it down, but as is usual in any balancing act, the novice overdoes matters, and I came down too far.

"As soon as I realized this, I again raised the controls slightly. I afterward learned that she touched ground on this dip. By this time I realized that vertical control was a very delicate thing, and although I did my best to keep on a constant level, there was more or less hitching up and down through the entire distance.

"In the meantime I had steered slightly to the left in order to make sure of clearing a vineyard which had been worrying us. When I found myself clear of the vineyard I again turned to the right. There seemed to be no trouble in steering this direction.

"When the machine first raised, the right side began to tilt down, which was easily corrected by the use of the adjustable tips, which were operated by leaning to the high side and engaging a lever with the shoulder. This control seemed to work very well indeed.

"I don't know just why I landed but I found myself so close to the ground that a landing seemed inevitable. I shut off the engine, raised the front control to the limit, grasped the tiller of the front steering wheel with my hand, and steered straight ahead out into the plowed field until the machine came to a standstill."

There you have the stark facts of the flight, complete, but like a blueprint, without the body of description or the color of emotion. G. H. gives no hint of his elation at feeling the rising surge of his wings and seeing the ground drop away from the crosspieces beneath his feet. There is never a word of the thrill of having the machine answer swiftly to the righting ailerons, nor of the terror mixed with pride which he felt as the aerodrome shot swiftly upward at the raising of the front control. Finally, there is no explanation of that perfect three-point landing, as to whether it was instinct or intelligence—it could not have been experience—which, combined with his perfect sense of timing, made him pull the front control full back at the precise moment of landing, as now on many a training field nerve-racked instructors try and try again to teach neophytes to do.

As soon as he landed, he tried to telephone Doctor Bell, who had not come out; but there was no answer. Again and again he tried, pleading with the operator to get him through. But in the end he had to give up and hurry back to tell the news himself.

Four-fifths of the A. E. A. burst riotously through the door interrupting the white-haired doctor in an abstruse mathematical calculation as to the possibility of building an aerodrome wing of tetrahedral cells.

"I flew the greatest distance yet," G. H. blurted out.

"A thousand and seventeen feet," added McCurdy.

"She flew like a bird," said Casey, prideful of his machine.

Doctor Bell jumped to his feet, his eyes dancing, his whiskers waving.

"Hurrah!" he shouted. "How I wish I had been there."

"I tried to telephone you," said Curtiss. "Didn't you hear it ring?"

The doctor was suddenly sobered, and his honest eyes seemed a bit shifty.

"It didn't ring," he said shortly.

Casey Baldwin was examining the telephone on the wall.

"What's this?" he asked, pulling wads of crumpled paper from around the bell.

A flush like sunset showed beneath the doctor's whiskers and spread up the dome of his head, and down his neck while even his ears glowed red. He made a sheepish gesture toward the phone and said, "I never thought when I invented that darn thing that it would annoy the life out of me every time I tried to do anything important."

White Wing's lifespan was hardly longer than a May fly's. The next day Jack McCurdy took her up, and Jack's luck was way out. The plane rose fast, then tipped to the left. Jack leaned to correct it, but his shoulder missed the aileron control, and the right wing went up and up until he could see blue sky between the planes. Then she crashed sideways to the ground.

White Wing was no more, but men being more durable than the machines of those days, Jack escaped with minor injuries.

Without even a discussion, the A. E. A. voted that evening to build Drome No. 3.

CHAPTER TWELVE

AS A JUNE BUG FLIES

CURTISS WAS THE LOGICAL choice for sponsor of Drome No. 3. She was very much like her predecessor, even having parts of the same wings, but there were a number of improvements, one of which was of vital importance. This was the position of the movable wing tips. In *White Wing* they were set so that when not in use they were inclined at the same positive angle of incidence as the wings. The result of this was that when they were moved, one assumed a greater angle of incidence and the other a lesser and the increased drag on one side pulled the plane off its course unless the rudder was used to counteract this effect. In the new aerodrome Curtiss placed the tips at a neutral angle. Thus, when one was raised and the other lowered, they had identical angles of incidence; there was no differential in drag and the turning tendency disappeared, so there was no need for the corrective use of the rudder. In them the true double-acting aileron appeared for the first time in history.

Curtiss was well aware of its mechanical importance, but he had no notion of the vast role which this tiny adjustment was to play in his own personal life during the troubled years ahead.

Apart from this tremendous trifle, the new aerodrome was a better machine in every way. The lower wing was greatly strengthened, and both wings were made so that they were easily detachable from the center section. Switch and spark controls were placed on the steering wheel so that the aviator now had more control over his motor. The propeller was cut down from 6 feet 2 inches to 5 feet 11 inches, resulting in a tremendous increase in the horsepower actually delivered.

While they were working on Drome No. 3, the nightly conferences continued. One evening there was a hot discussion as to how air acted when passing over airfoil sections.

"If we could only see it," exclaimed Doctor Bell. "How much we could learn!"

"Perhaps I can figure something out," remarked G. H.

A few days later an object that looked like a coffin on legs was sent up from the shop. At one end was an electric fan and at the other a radiator from an automobile.

G. H. explained its working to the delighted A. E. A.

"First we hang our model in the box," he said, "and then start the fan which draws a swift current of air through. The radiator is to comb out the air as it enters, and we can watch the behavior of the model through this glass window in the top."

"Wonderful!" exclaimed Doctor Bell. "Now if we could only think of some way to see the airflow. . . ."

"That's where Harry comes in," said G. H. grinning. "Light your pipe, Harry."

Genung, who was the only heavy smoker present, obediently lighted up.

"Now puff smoke in front of the radiator," directed the director of experiments.

Harry bent down and produced clouds of smoke which were sucked into the machine. With their heads jammed together over the window, the five A. E. A. members watched fascinated as it flowed over the little wings in the box.

"Gosh," said Casey. "Look at the eddy at the wing tips. I'll bet we could smooth it out by changing their shape."

"We can certainly learn a lot from this," said Tom Selfridge. "The government ought to build a big one. Someday it will, too, if I have anything to say."

"It's an enormous contribution to aeronautics," Doctor Bell declared.

Throughout the evening they played with their fascinating new toy, trying airfoil after airfoil, watching enthralled as the telltale smoke, flowing smoothly or boiling in ugly eddies, made plain their relative efficiency. Toward the end Harry was notably silent. Finally he made a funny choking noise.

"I'm sorry, G. H.," he gasped, "I can't go on."

They looked at him then. His face was the color of old chartreuse, and great beads of sweat rolled down his forehead into his eyes.

"Why Harry, what's the matter?" G. H. asked.

"I feel awful sick," moaned Harry. "I don't—awk."

Clutching his mouth, he fled toward the bathroom.

Harry's seizure made it necessary to substitute some other method of seeing air. Finally, Curtiss hit on the idea of using little threads of scarlet silk and these served very well in that first wind tunnel.

Often their discussions turned on the possibility of winning the *Scientific American* Trophy with the new machine. This was a trophy donated by that magazine to be the permanent possession of whoever should win it three times. To gain the first leg, it was necessary to make a public flight of one kilometer under the auspices of the Aero Club of America. Though it had been offered more than a year before, no one so far had attempted to win it.

"It would be a wonderful thing for the association if we could pull it off," said Doctor Bell one evening, "for it would give people a chance to see for themselves that flight is possible. So great an impetus to the progress of aviation would justify all our labors."

"Somebody will probably beat us to it," said Casey gloomily. "The best we've done so far is less than a third of the distance."

"It's up to Number Three all right," said Selfridge.

G. H. had been listening with determination growing in his eyes. Now he spoke.

"Number Three will do it," he said.

A little over three weeks after the wreck of *White Wing*, the new aerodrome was complete, but before they tried her they all knocked off to go to Casey Baldwin's wedding in Toronto. The young engineer had been borrowing motorcycles from the Curtiss Company all that spring to carry on his long-distance wooing. A courtship by motorcycle delighted G. H., and not even his precious aerodrome could keep him away from its consummation.

On June 21 they were all back in Hammondsport, including the bride and groom. They took No. 3 out to the race track accompanied by an unusually large crowd; for all Hammondsport knew that this machine was G. H.'s own baby and they weren't going to miss seeing her maiden flight. Even Captain Baldwin knocked off work on the SC-1 to watch the trial.

The aerodrome was placed in the usual starting position in the back stretch, which they used regardless of wind direction because it was the only place in the valley from which a straight flight could be made. Curtiss started the motor himself and got it running perfectly. Then, quickly before the engine should overheat, he scrambled into the seat and took his place at the controls of the first plane which bore his name.

With a wave of his hand to the men holding the tail, he started down the race course. The aerodrome rose more quickly than he expected—afterward they calculated her take-off speed as twenty-three miles per hour against *White Wing's* twenty-eight. She flew steadily for a little, and G. H. had time to note with a surge of pride how sensitive she was to the controls, how well the new ailerons worked.

Then suddenly the aerodrome bucked like a mustang, and shot upward. Curtiss cut the motor and pancaked to a landing.

When the others came running up through the dust, he was standing looking at the machine with a puzzled expression.

"Did the motor quit?" asked Henry Kleckler.

"No, I cut it."

"What happened?" demanded Casey. "You seemed to be going fine."

"I don't know," said G. H. "She just suddenly started up and I couldn't get her down."

Captain Baldwin arrived, puffing, in time to hear this last remark.

"The air is as full of waves as the ocean," he said. "You built her to go up, didn't you? You might have some kick coming if she'd dropped."

"That's right," said G. H. "Next time I'll just let her rip."

They pushed the aerodrome back to the starting point, and by the time she got there the engine had cooled enough for another trial. Then start the motor and off again. G. H. felt the delicious change from the roughness of earth-bound speed to silken smoothness as she became air-borne. He watched the wheels beneath him, still spinning—five, ten feet above the dusty track. At precisely the same place as before the aerodrome shot madly upward.

G. H. gritted his teeth and rode it out. The ground seemed to drop from under him, the barns and houses and trees shrank away and the horizon widened swiftly. He could see down the whole length of the lake to where its furthest tip glittered between the crowding hills. It's like a map, he thought. And then, I must be fearfully high. He steadied the machine with gentle strength as a jockey holds a thoroughbred to the course. It leveled out, then dipped and rose again. The meadow drifted underneath, and then a vineyard; another field and at its far edge more vineyards: beyond them were tall trees.

G. H. held to his course until he reached the edge of the farthest vineyard. The stakes and wires used to support the vines looked most unpleasant, and there was no place to land beyond. He turned the wheel, and the aerodrome answered her rudder. She came around in a flat half turn and, skidding, lost flying speed to settle gently in the field 1,266 feet from where she had taken off.

Doctor Bell, standing on the race track, had watched the machine dipping and rising across the valley while distance lessened the motor noise from a roar to an angry buzz. When he saw it alight safely, he turned in delight to the men beside him.

"She flies like a June bug," he exclaimed. "You know they have fixed wings with smaller rotating wings beneath. That's what we'll call her: *June Bug*."

The trials held two days later were disappointing; the wing covering began to leak air, which destroyed the lift. So Curtiss, aided by Captain Baldwin, who knew just how to make material air-proof, developed a comparatively safe, yellow varnish. Resplendent with her new golden wings, Curtiss' *June Bug* surpassed herself, and Doctor Bell, who had left for a trip through Canada to Baddeck, received the following triumphant telegram:

HAMMONDSPORT, N. Y.   6-26-08

ALEXANDER GRAHAM BELL

PRESCOTT, ONT. OR KINGSTON

CARE OF STEAMBOAT TORONTO OF R O LINE OR IF TOO LATE REPEAT TO WINDSOR HOTEL, MONTREAL, QUE.

CURTISS FLEW ELEVEN HUNDRED AND FORTY YARDS, THREE THOUSAND FOUR HUNDRED AND TWENTY FEET IN SIXTY SECONDS THIS EVENING ABOUT 7:30. WE HAVE TELEPHONED SECRETARY AERO CLUB OF AMERICA THAT WE ARE NOW READY TO TRY FOR SCIENTIFIC AMERICAN CUP. HURRAH!

                                                    SELFRIDGE

CHAPTER THIRTEEN

SCIENTIFIC AMERICAN

THE AERO CLUB OF AMERICA was, paradoxically, a rather conservative organization in 1908. Many of its prominent members were noted free balloon pilots, and the emphasis was all on gas bags. However, certain recent events had shaken them out of their shells.

In May rumors concerning the feats of those queer Wrights of Dayton had become uncomfortably persistent, and a group of New York editors had decided to scotch them once and for all. Orders went out from the city rooms, and a little band of crack reporters made their grumbling way through the swamps of North Carolina to a sand dune overlooking the beach at Kitty Hawk, where the Wrights, after four years of absence, were once more encamped.

The reporters lay unhappily behind a sand dune watching through their binoculars the camp they dared not approach because of the Wrights' ferocious attitude toward the press. But eventually they saw more than they dared to report. Those hard-boiled newspapermen watched in awe-stricken wonder as the white plane rose high in the air and circled as easily as the gulls which fled, screaming, before that tremendous apparition.

So the smokescreen of secrecy was blown away at last by the full blast of publicity from a hysterical press. Overnight the obscure brothers from Dayton became the heroes of America and the wonder of the world.

But even a month later the public had not seen an aeroplane fly, and they were fairly screaming for the chance. In spite of this, the Aero Club received the Aerial Experiment Association's announcement that they were ready to make the public trial for the *Scientific American* Cup with something less than enthusiasm. The proposed date, July 4, was inconveniently near; Hammondsport was away out in the backwoods. Nobody was very keen to take the long uncomfortable train ride to see a problematical plane make an improbable flight. What was the Aerial Experiment Association anyway? Doctor Bell, they knew, of course, but this Curtiss and the other young squirts sounded like a bunch of crackpots.

"We'll just be going up there to make fools of ourselves and bring flying into disrepute," was their reaction. "If it were the Wrights now. . . ."

Nevertheless, the Aero Club decided that, however dubious the prospect, it must be done. Grudgingly they accepted the entry.

From the moment the date was set Curtiss practiced unceasingly with his *June Bug*. Several times he almost made the full distance, but never quite. At dawn on July 3 he was out at Stony Brook Farm determined to do it once before the official trial. He took off, but the machine seemed unaccountably balky. Fighting the controls Curtiss flew thirteen hundred yards and then attempted the usual turn to avoid the vineyard. A puff of wind struck the machine and it slipped in, wrecking one wing and the front control. It looked as though all their hopes were blasted.

The other members of the association came sprinting up with faces a mile long.

"Well, that's that," said Casey.

"What shall we do?" groaned McCurdy.

"Shall I telephone the Aero Club?" asked Tom.

"You fellows are wasting time," said G. H. "We've got to rebuild her quick. Can we do it, Henry?"

Henry Kleckler examined the wreckage and turned with his slow grin.

"I fix him," he said.

With everyone working as only Curtiss could make him, *June Bug* was rebuilt in a day, and by seven o'clock that evening she took the air again. Somehow she seemed to have been improved by the wreck—perhaps it was because lack of material had forced them to make a smaller elevating rudder. In any event she handled perfectly, though still the full kilometer was not flown.

By the early morning train of July 4, the representatives of the Aero Club and the *Scientific American*, the reporters and the curious arrived. Allan R. Hawley, acting president and Charles M. Manly, who had been with Langley, represented the Aero Club, and Stanley Beach the *Scientific American*. Others who came were Ernest L. Jones, editor of the *American Journal of Aeronautics*, Augustus Post, Simon Lake, the submarine inventor, Karl Dienst, representing the Imperial German Government, and Augustus M. Herring, an eccentric individual who had been associated with Octave Chanute and claimed to have helped the Wright brothers in their early experiments. If ever there was a fish of ill omen, it was this same Herring.

From the first it became apparent that though the others had open, if somewhat skeptical, minds, Herring and Beach had come to see a failure. Nor did the weather improve their dispositions. Gusts of wind tore round the corners of the hills, and heavy clouds loosed shower after shower to dampen already drooping spirits.

During the morning Manly and Hawley tramped uncomplainingly about in the rain, through the high wet grass and the muddy vineyards, minutely measuring the distance with a surveyor's tape. At the finish they set up a red flag on a pole.

Shortly after noon the Pleasant Valley Wine Company came to the rescue of the bedraggled aeronauts. A fine buffet lunch was served to all in their great stone cellar, and the bubbling flow of the vineyards put everyone in a better temper.

In the afternoon the crowds began to arrive. Some came on special trains and in putt-putting automobiles and motorcycles. But most of them arrived in buggies and farm wagons. The whole countryside turned out to see G. H. conquer the air.

But for a while it looked as though they would be disappointed. The showers continued, and in spite of audible asides from Messrs. Beach and Herring, Curtiss would not budge. The crowd seemed to understand his reasons and were surprisingly patient and sympathetic.

At half-past five a bit of light blue showed on the western horizon. The gray line of the clouds rolled up the sky like a curtain rising on history, and as though some invisible hand had switched on the footlights, the slanting yellow rays of the afternoon sun swept across the valley. The stage was set at last.

Curtiss ordered the *June Bug* brought out of the tent, where it had waited shrouded in mystery. They wheeled her through the wet grass and placed her in her familiar position on the muddy track. The crowd pressed close around, and Henry Kleckler and the mechanics had trouble clearing a narrow lane for the take-off.

When all was ready Curtiss started the motor and scrambled for his seat. The *June Bug* bumbled down the track and took the air. But it was immediately apparent to those who knew her that something was wrong. She flew with her nose cocked up, her tail drooping. Before she had covered half a mile she sagged back to earth.

Everyone was bitterly disappointed except Herring and Beach, who rushed around saying, "I told you so."

June Bug was hauled by the tail back to the starting point, and her rear stabilizer, which had slipped into a negative angle was adjusted. Then the motor was given an extra heavy dose of oil.

Once more a lane was cleared through the crowd, and *June Bug* started down the course. She roared into the air leaving a trail of smoke like a locomotive as the excess oil burned off. But this time she flew better than ever she had before.

Swooping and rising she buzzed on, her golden wings flashing in the warm sunlight, while everyone held his breath. She passed the half-mile mark and Lena Curtiss, balancing on a log, cried out, "Oh, why does he fly so high? Do you think he'll make it?"

Then the red flag was just ahead. Triumphantly *June Bug* soared over it and winged on down the valley while the pent-up breaths went out in a great roar of cheering.

And still Curtiss held on. Distance diminished *June Bug* until she seemed no larger than the insect whose name she bore. Her wings glinted as she curved gracefully around to avoid bad country, and at last, a few feet less than a mile from her starting point, she alighted gently in a field.

The crowd was frantic, and even the dignified officials of the Aero Club joined in the cross-country race to congratulate Curtiss.

Mrs. Fairchild wrote of it to her father, who was kept in Baddeck by the renewed illness of Mrs. Bell:

"We all lost our heads and David shouted and I cried and

everyone cheered and clapped and engines tooted. . . .

"David and Mrs. Curtiss and I chose our stand on an old log at the far side of the potato patch. The first flight had raised excitement to boiling point, and as Mr. Curtiss flew over the red flag that marked the finish and way on toward the trees, I don't think that any of us quite knew what we were doing. One lady was so absorbed as not to hear a coming train and was struck by the engine and had two ribs broken.

"Mr. Masson took me right into town to telegraph the grand news to you and it was about half-past nine when the last of the party straggled in."

G. H., too, wrote to Doctor Bell in his usual matter-of-fact style, though his delight at confounding the doubters does creep in:

Hammondsport, July 7, 1908

"The affair of July fourth went off very nicely. There seemed to be some question, especially with the Scientific American representatives, if we could fly the kilometer; and when we fell short on the first trial Mr. B——seemed to be pleased rather than disappointed. . . .

"After making the adjustment on the tail, she flew like a real June bug; and just on account of Mr. B——, who was standing at the finish with a camera to photograph the machine in case I fell short on the distance, I flew the machine as far as the field would permit, regardless of fences, ditches, etc.

"We gave the Committee and the Aero Club members a little outing on the Lake on Sunday with the local band in attendance. . . ."

What a lovely day that Sunday, July 5, was. The little steamer puffed slowly around the irregular green shore of Lake Keuka; the brass band played "Daisy Bell" hilariously out of tune; the distinguished visitors and G. H.'s friends from Hammondsport ate the delicious lunch and drank quantities of Pleasant Valley champagne; and the hot sun shone down out of a gentle sky in which there was no cloud even as big as a bomber's wing.

Lena Curtiss was the gayest of them all, her shyness forgotten in her pride over her husband's achievement. Harry and Martha Genung were bubbling with delighted hospitality, and the young Casey Baldwins thought of the glorious years of achievement and happiness ahead and how lucky they were to be born into such a beautiful world.

G. H. needed no champagne to make him gay as he cracked outrageous puns to benevolent bigwigs, or talked technicalities with Mr. Herring, who had quite changed his mind and was full of pleasant flattery.

Tom Selfridge, dreaming of the brilliant career ahead of him and how well he might now serve his country, thought how good it was to be alive.

They landed late in the afternoon and made the pilgrimage again to Stony Brook Farm. Curtiss ordered the *June Bug* out, and just to prove it wasn't an accident, he flew the course again, this time completing his flight with a banked 188° turn, "rather awkward, but he got around and headed back toward his starting point."

That night the visiting aeronauts climbed aboard the sleeper, weary but pleasantly conscious of great things achieved. For the first time in the history of America a heavier-than-air machine had been flown on a scheduled date before a great concourse of people. Aviation had passed from the stage of mystery and uncertainty to the era of public participation and practicality. The gentlemen from New York felt secure in their belief that it had been a great day for civilization.

CHAPTER FOURTEEN

WRECKAGE

THE AERIAL EXPERIMENT ASSOCIATION wasted no time sitting around congratulating themselves. Though their original object had been accomplished, they all felt that this was not final achievement, but the first hour of the morning. There were great things to be done, and Monday found them up and doing.

It was Jack McCurdy's turn to sponsor a machine, and he was bursting with ideas to make Drome No. 4 the best yet. Curtiss was convinced that they had gone as far as they could with a motor which would run for only three minutes, and his mind was already full of blueprints for a V-8 water-cooled engine which would run as long as the fuel held out.

With Doctor Bell's concurrence they decided that Jack and Tom should remain for the present with G. H. in Hammondsport, while Casey Baldwin went to Baddeck to help construct the huge motor-driven tetrahedral machine and conduct experiments with hydroplane boats.

All the members of the association agreed that the purely experimental stage had been passed and that an effort should now be made toward commercial development. The first step was plainly to take out patents. Curtiss was a babe in the legal jungle, but Doctor Bell was an old woodsman, who had guided his telephone company through some very tough going. Immediately after the *Scientific American* flight, the doctor requested his patent attorneys to go to Hammondsport, and wired Curtiss begging him not to risk wrecking *June Bug* until the lawyers had seen her.

But G. H. was not interested in financial matters. He cared only for the thing itself and had no thought for money so long as enough came in to enable him to continue his work. Already he was visualizing the wings of the future, and he had the hardihood to put his prophecies on paper. In the first of the Aerial Experiment Association's Monthly Bulletins, which contain a complete record of the work of the association and the aeronautical thoughts of its members, Curtiss wrote that:

1. "The aerial flyers of the future will make higher speeds than is now accomplished on land."

2. "They may furl and reef their surfaces like a ship's sails." (This is now accomplished by the use of flaps.)

3. "Balloons and dirigibles have been of vast service, but within the next five or six years the heavier-than-air machines will have nearly replaced them."

4. "The airships, which within ten years will carry men and freight from place to place, will be a natural evolution of the aerodromes of today."

All this after one little hop of less than a mile at an average speed of twenty-five miles per hour.

G. H. was impatient to get on with the business of building those airships of the future, so, in spite of Doctor Bell's warning, he continued to fly *June Bug*. There was so much to be learned. Fortunately there were no bad wrecks and the patent men came and analyzed and made their preliminary report.

So while Curtiss dreamed of aerial transports and worked on his new motor and studied flying the hard way, the lines began to form for the great Battle of the Patents which was to bewilder and embitter so much of his life. The first faint opening gun was a letter he received from Orville Wright in July. In it Mr. Wright discussed the "movable surfaces at the tips of the wings of your '*June Bug*,'" and referred him to Patent No. 821,393. This patent, Wright said, broadly covered the combination of sustaining surfaces adjustable to different angles with a rudder adjustable to correct the turning movement caused by inequalities in the resistance of the differently adjusted wings. He further stated that it was their (the Wrights') belief that it would be very difficult to develop a successful machine without the use of some of the features covered in their patent.

When Doctor Bell saw this letter he made the definite statement that, if the adoption of the movable wing tips was due to his suggestion in the letter to Casey Baldwin, then, "this suggestion was made by me without any knowledge on my part of anything the Wright brothers may have done. They had kept the details of the construction of their machine secret and I was ignorant of anything contained in their patent."

Nevertheless, the Aerial Experiment Association were on notice that the Wrights would fight any attempt to exploit their machines commercially.

A little later Doctor Bell made a detailed analysis of the difference between the Wright machine and the *June Bug* based on a careful study of the Wright patent. The integrity of his character and his own unhappy experiences with patent thieves made him the last man on earth to attempt to use some other inventor's ideas without paying royalties, so the conclusion he reached must be treated as his sincere belief.

"The wings of the Wright machine are flexible: ours rigid," he wrote. "To correct tipping the Wrights warp both wings, this increases the drag on one side and reduces it on the other making the machine turn. The Wright patent provides for conjoint use of the rudder to correct this turning tendency.

"In our Hammondsport machine the movable tips are not

part of the supporting surface so they can be turned at a negative angle. In operation the rear of one is raised and the rear of the other lowered at precisely the same angle to the line of advance. No turning effect is produced and the use of the rudder is not necessary."

Doctor Bell winds up with the unequivocal statement:

"I am decidedly of the opinion that our invention is not covered by the Wright patent.

"ALEXANDER GRAHAM BELL."

Curtiss accepted this statement as settling the matter, and stopped thinking about it. Not that he had worried much before, for in addition to his lack of concern about money, he had adopted Captain Baldwin's attitude toward inventions, that they belonged to the world. Never in all his life did he sue anyone for infringing his patents.

Both at Hammondsport and Baddeck, work proceeded slowly during the summer of 1908. The thousands of cells for *Cygnet II* were a long time building, and while that work went on Casey conducted some highly informative tests on hydroplanes with an airscrew-driven boat whimsically named the *Dhonnas Beag*.

At Hammondsport McCurdy's Drome No. 4, now become the *Silver Dart*, because her wings were covered with the rubber and silk material which Captain Baldwin had devised for the SC-1, waited on the new motor which was giving Curtiss plenty of trouble.

Meanwhile, G. H. continued to use *June Bug* as a test tube. He strove to improve the system of oiling her motor because, as he said, it was really an oil-cooled engine. Then, at the suggestion of Professor Robert W. Wood of Johns Hopkins, who came to Hammondsport, he tried packing the cylinders with absorbent cotton soaked in water. This lengthened the running time of the engine somewhat, but Curtiss was not satisfied.

"Now that we have got beyond the seconds and minutes stage and are going on to hours," he said, "we must have a water-cooled engine."

Professor Wood was not the only distinguished visitor to Hammondsport that summer. Scientists came from all over the country, and the gentlemen of the Aero Club formed the habit of running up there to see what was going on. In August, Doctor Bell came for a brief stay and, with Augustus Post, Ernest Jones, and Mr. Means, of the *Aeronautical Annual*, who had dropped by, tried to work out a sensible vocabulary for aeronautics. Doctor Bell's pet phobia was the word "aeroplane."

"It means a supporting surface," he said, "and a flat one at that. Aerodrome, which in Greek means air runner, is much more accurate."

"I'll use it in the *Journal of Aeronautics*," agreed Jones, "but it's getting confusing. What with people calling the aerial garage an aerodrome as well as the field you fly in, we might get the sentence, 'The doors of the aerodrome were opened and the aerodrome was wheeled out on the aerodrome.'"

"That's true," laughed Bell. "But try sticking to it just the same."

But while the efforts of science could conquer the air, they could not control the tongues of men, and though aerodrome was accepted for a while, especially as applied to the Hammondsport machines, aeroplane was eventually the choice of the people.

Early in September, Curtiss went to stay with the Fairchilds in Washington to witness what was scheduled to be a tremendous triumph for aviation. For the Wrights had come out of their seclusion at last and were to make a public demonstration of their aeroplane at Fort Myer for the approval of the War Department.

G. H. found Tom Selfridge already there and in exuberant spirits.

"They're going to carry a military observer," he said excitedly. "And the Army have designated me to represent them."

"That's great," said Curtiss. "I know what it means to you."

"It means just everything," said Tom. "All I've worked for, all I've dreamed of is coming true. I think I'm the luckiest man in the world."

Curtiss could hardly contain his curiosity to see the mystery machine at last unveiled. He hurried out to the fort soon after his arrival, with the greatest anticipation. There he met Orville Wright for the first time and was permitted to examine the famous plane. In a letter to Doctor Bell he recorded his impressions:

"I had some talk with Mr. Wright and nothing was said about his patents on adjustable surfaces. He has nothing startling about his machine and no secrets. . . . The surfaces have a plain curve like a segment of a circle. . . . No attempt is made anywhere on the machine to reduce resistance."

Nevertheless, that aeroplane could fly. On September 11 Orville Wright gave a spectacular demonstration of its ability which evoked the generous admiration of the A. E. A. members. Doctor Bell expressed their sentiments in a telegram:

MR. ORVILLE WRIGHT

FORT MYER, WASHINGTON, D. C.

ON BEHALF OF THE AERIAL EXPERIMENT ASSOCIATION ALLOW ME TO CONGRATULATE YOU ON YOUR MAGNIFICENT SUCCESS. AN HOUR IN THE AIR MARKS AN HISTORICAL OCCASION.

ALEXANDER GRAHAM BELL

After witnessing this great flight, Curtiss went back to Hammondsport. But Tom Selfridge remained in Washington for his hour of destiny.

The date when he should represent the United States as its first military aviator was set for September 17, 1908. On that day the crowds gathered again on the parade ground at Fort Myer. They cheered as the white-winged biplane was carried out of its tent and set down near its tower and car. They cheered again as Orville Wright walked slowly toward it surrounded by glittering generals and top-hatted statesmen. Then they cheered his passenger, that curly-headed young lieutenant, who looked so handsome in his blue and gold uniform.

The plane was lifted to its monorail car, and a squad of soldiers hoisted the weight up the tower and attached the rope to the car. The engine was started and the propellers began to turn with that unique clacking sound. Mr. Wright took his place at the controls and Lieutenant Selfridge climbed to the seat beside him. Sitting erect with his arms folded, he looked very cool and soldierly, but inside he was near to bursting with joyous excitement. This was the moment of his great adventure; in his own person he was the Army Air Force of the United States. It was all he could do to keep a broad grin from ruining the military sternness of his face.

Orville Wright raised his arm; the weight dropped down the tower and the car shot forward. A little heavily, like an overburdened pelican, the white wings took the air. They climbed slowly upward, then banked gracefully for the first turn.

Back down the field came the aeroplane. The spectators could see Wright working the controls and Selfridge still sitting very erect. But since he was too high for them to discern his features, he needed no longer to pretend, and his face was illumined by a smile of pure delight.

The clacking sound of the propellers went steadily on, the plane was halfway down the field again, when suddenly its rhythm was interrupted by a sharp crack. A propeller had broken and fouled a wing.

The plane swooped madly downward and Wright instinctively pulled up the elevating rudder. The machine answered, shooting upward higher than before. There it hung poised for a dreadful second, its nose pointing toward the sky, its remaining propeller whirling wildly.

No one there or for years to come knew enough to know what happened then, but from their accounts we can determine that the plane lost flying speed and stalled. The nose dropped and it began the fatal spin. There was space for but half a turn before it hit the ground with a dreadful crashing and ripping noise.

As the dust rolled away it revealed the tangle of wires and canvas, the broken wings and broken bodies. Orville Wright was dragged from the wreckage groaning with the pain of his injuries. Lieutenant Selfridge did not groan. He lay quite still on the grass with the dust and blood spoiling his smart uniform, but his face still happily serene.

The Army ambulance came galloping up to take Orville Wright to the hospital, but they couldn't take Tom Selfridge anywhere. He had gone on ahead to show the way to the thousands of gallant young officers who in peace and war were to follow where he led.

CHAPTER FIFTEEN

ASSOCIATION ENDED

G. H., LIKE ALL the other members of the A. E. A., was heart-broken at the loss of his best-loved associate. Sadly they gathered in Washington to pay their last tributes to Tom Selfridge. Each had his offering of happy memories and special appreciation to bring. Mrs. Bell, who was too ill to come, wrote them a letter which so perfectly expressed their feelings that they ordered it printed in the next bulletin of the association:

"I can't get over Tom's being taken. Isn't it heart-breaking? Yet and yet it is better for him, than to die as poor Langley did. He was so happy to the very end. I know he would have said he was having the time of his life. I miss the thought of him so. Nobody ever did so many little things for me as he.

"I am so sorry for you in the breaking of your beautiful association. But it was beautiful and the memory of it will endure: 'Bell, Curtiss, Baldwin, Selfridge and McCurdy.' It was indeed a 'brilliant coterie.'

"Give my love to them all and let's hold tight together, all the tighter for the one that's gone. Casey called me the 'Little Mother of us all,' and so I want to be. I love all our boys and there can't be any others just the same.

"MABEL G. BELL."

With the final volley ringing in their ears, the A. E. A. came back from Arlington to meet and plan a future which seemed

bleak to them all. Tom Selfridge's father was invited to attend
and formally given his son's place and interests in the association. A resolution paying the highest possible tribute to Tom
was the first order of business. Then a resolution was voted
expressing the sympathy of the association for Orville Wright
in his terrible grief at the death of his passenger. It ended by
expressing the hope that "Mr. Wright will soon recover . . .
and continue in conjunction with his brother, Mr. Wilbur
Wright, his splendid demonstration to the world of the great
possibilities of aerial flight."

The year for which the A. E. A. had been chartered was
drawing to a close, but all the members felt that, though their
accomplishments were beyond their wildest hopes, there remained many things for them to do. So it was decided to
continue for another six months. Mrs. Bell scraped the bottom
of her pocket to provide ten thousand dollars more, and the
members returned to Hammondsport and Baddeck to push
the work forward.

Back in August Curtiss had begun to plan to fly from water.
The confines of the valley were growing too small for his
expanding wings, and temptingly before his eyes stretched
Lake Keuka's splendid plain. To the fluttering land planes it
was nothing but a hazard, but to a machine which could rise
from its surface, it would be one great field where a landing
could safely be made at any time.

Looking at it Curtiss thought of the tens of thousands of
lakes and rivers of America, of her thousands of miles of coast
with all the sheltered bays and sounds. If man could fly from
water, then the range and usefulness of aviation would be
extended infinitely, and with a landing field underneath all the
way, its dangers would be greatly lessened.

Curtiss' imagination took fire at the thought, and he pictured to himself the sport planes and naval planes of the future, and the great flying ships which would carry passengers and freight across all the oceans of the world at ten times the speed of the fastest liner. Always after that he strove primarily to perfect flying from water, and though he built many land machines, his heart was ever on the airways of the sea.

His first step toward accomplishing his purpose was to redesign the *June Bug* as a seaplane. Rechristened the *Loon*, she finally appeared with the V-8 water-cooled engine from the *Silver Dart* and two canoe-shaped pontoons under her center section.

On a fine afternoon early in January 1909, Curtiss took her down to the lake, which was not yet frozen. Darkness fell before she was quite ready, but a full moon swung up over the hills that were dusted with snow. The whole long valley was filled with silver light.

"We'll try her by moonlight," said Curtiss.

He climbed carefully up to his seat, while the *Loon* wobbled on her floats. Henry Kleckler started the engine and G. H. set out to learn about handling a plane on water.

Surprisingly soon he mastered the art sufficiently to attempt a flight. He opened the motor wide and roared off down the lake with the pontoons plowing two white furrows in its dark surface.

As the *Loon* attained a speed which G. H. estimated by the wind in his face to be twenty-five miles per hour, he pulled back the elevating rudder and tried to take off. But although he was going faster than *June Bug's* normal take-off speed, those pontoons stuck to the water as if it were glue. Though he rocked her and jerked her, he couldn't break her loose.

Bearing its dejected pilot, the *Loon* waddled back to the dock.

"Those hydroplanes of yours begin to look pretty good to us," G. H. wrote to Casey Baldwin, who on the Gauldrie had succeeded in getting the *Dhonnas Beag* to skim along on her sticklike hydroplanes almost clear of the surface. In a trial a few days later one of her pontoons was ripped by a snag and the *Loon* wearily sank. Although she was recovered, this and the freezing of the lake ended experiments for the winter.

Meanwhile McCurdy's *Silver Dart* was flying well with the new motor back in place, and an even more exciting event had occurred. William F. Whitehouse, Hudson Maxim, Peter Cooper Hewitt, Stanley Beach, and other younger members of the Aero Club decided to take a more active interest in heavier-than-air flying, and banded themselves together as the Aeronautical Society of New York. They tried to build a plane themselves, but it was a failure, so they empowered one of their members, Mr. Burridge, to go to Hammondsport and order one from Curtiss.

After considerable bargaining G. H. agreed to build a machine for them in the spring. The price set was five thousand dollars, and the Aeronautical Society sent Curtiss a check for five hundred dollars to bind the bargain. This was the first plane to be ordered and built for sale in America. That we were already falling behind Europe in developing the commercial possibilities of our great contribution to civilization is shown by the fact that in January 1909 no less than twenty-eight planes were ordered at the Paris Aero Show to be built in France under Wright designs.

Late in January the *Silver Dart* was shipped to Baddeck and the members of the association and their wives gathered at Beinn Breagh for the trials of *Cygnet II*. This tremendous kite, powered with another Curtiss V-8 engine, was put on runners and tried from the ice. Doctor Bell was terribly disappointed by the results, for *Cygnet II* showed little inclination to take the air. The tetrahedral principle was so dear to the doctor's heart that after the dissolution of the A. E. A. he built a third machine at his own expense. In 1910 *Cygnet III* actually got into the air, but by that time the aeroplane was definitely established in the heavier-than-air field.

In spite of the failure of *Cygnet II* it seemed like old times that February at Beinn Breagh. The Curtisses, the Baldwins, Jack McCurdy and his sister Mabel, who acted as secretary for the association, and the whole Bell family were so gay and harmonious a group that nothing could long dampen their high spirits. Even their sadness at the absence of Tom Selfridge was tempered by happy memories.

In the evening they discussed their theories and the exciting news of the progress of aviation throughout the world. Wilbur Wright had flown 124 kilometers in 2 hours 20 minutes 23 seconds at Le Mans in France; the Russian government had set aside one million dollars for military aviation. In Washington the House and Senate had passed a five-hundred-thousand-dollar appropriation for Army aviation. An Aeronautics Congress was to meet in Paris to establish rules for aerial navigation, for the air was already getting crowded.

Plans for the first aviation meet in history at Rheims, France, were going forward.

"Gosh, I'd like to take a crack at those prizes," said Jack McCurdy.

"I don't think we're up to it yet," said Curtiss. "Anyhow, the Wrights are sure to be chosen to represent America."

Daytimes, G. H. particularly loved to drive the powerful motor-powered iceboat, which, in imitation of his "wind wagon," had been constructed to test propeller efficiency.

Skimming over the ice at fifty or sixty miles an hour, with the runners singing their song of speed and the icy wind cutting his face, was as near to perfect happiness as he could get.

The iceboat required two men to work it: one to steer and another to run the engine. One evening G. H. and Casey were racing homeward at tremendous speed over the frozen Gauldrie. Curtiss at the wheel steered for the boathouse. When he judged the moment right he shouted, "Cut the engine!"

The wind snatched the words from his mouth and Casey never heard them.

At full throttle the iceboat roared straight for the shed. It leaped onto the platform and smashed into the wooden building.

Why they weren't both killed is past imagining. G. H. was hurled into the iron steering gear which was bent double by his body; Casey shot clear of the boat. He was unhurt, but Curtiss' chin was torn half off.

They carried him up to the house while Jack McCurdy jumped into a sailing iceboat and scudded down the lake to fetch Doctor McIver from Baddeck.

McIver must have been a skillful man, for he stitched G. H.'s chin on again so prettily that in time the scar hardly showed, though for a while Curtiss wore a tuft of whiskers to conceal the injury.

It was the only serious accident which ever befell him in the whole adventurous course of his life. His invulnerability must be attributed not only to perfectly stupendous luck, but also to the foresight with which he always calculated the chances he took in advance, and to his amazing sense of timing and the coolness which never deserted him no matter how desperate things looked. As Harry Genung said, "We never worried much about G. H. He always came through."

Many of the discussions at Beinn Breagh turned on the question of commercial development. Curtiss felt very strongly that in the interests of aviation the time had come to attempt to attract capital and push forward in a practical way. He was greatly impressed by the military significance of aviation and felt that this country must not lose the advantage of being first in the field by backwardness in beginning large-scale manufacture.

Casey Baldwin, too, was fearfully concerned lest this terrible new weapon be neglected by the British Empire. In a lecture before the University of Toronto on February 27, 1909, Baldwin said: "London could be destroyed and the combined navies of the world could not prevent it. A military training is hardly necessary to see that our bulwarks must be extended upward and our aerial fleet maintained at least on a two-power basis."

It was agreed that the Aerial Experiment Association could not, by its very nature, embark on commercial enterprises, but plans were considered to form a separate company to build the aerodromes developed by its members.

Curtiss urged this course on his associates, pointing out that so far practically every flying machine in existence had been built for experimental purposes, but that now government contracts and exhibitions seemed promising sources of revenue.

Doctor Bell, who had had patent trouble enough in his time, was very nervous about starting anything, and so these proposals had come to nothing at the time Curtiss left for New York, where, misled by his ideals and enthusiasm, he embarked on a business venture whose unhappy consequences were to follow him to his very deathbed.

Curtiss reached New York on March 3 and sped like a homing pigeon to the Aero Club on Forty-first Street and

Madison Avenue. There he was greeted with enthusiasm by its new president, Cortlandt Field Bishop, and many of his old friends like Augustus Post and Allan Hawley. Everyone wanted to know how things were going at Baddeck and what he was doing about the Aeronautical Society's plane.

Augustus Herring sidled up to the group around him and entered into the conversation.

"You two men should get together," said Bishop. "Herring here has a contract with the War Department for a forty-thousand-dollar plane and a lot of bright ideas. You've got an order, too, and plenty of practical experience, and a factory. Why don't you combine?"

"It's worth thinking about," said G. H.

"I'd like nothing better," said Herring. "Let's all go up to my apartment and talk things over."

They adjourned to Mr. Herring's apartment in the Alpha Delta Phi Club, and there he put on a sales talk that would have sold aeroplanes to a seagull. Enthusiasm was unbounded. Bishop, Hawley, Cooper Hewitt, and others were ready to put up money.

"Doctor Bell thinks we'll have trouble with the Wright patents," Curtiss warned them.

"Say, I've got patents that antedate the Wrights'," said Herring. "We won't have to worry about that. And let me tell you on this automatic stability thing. . . ."

Before the evening was over Curtiss was in a haze of facts, figures, and magnificent fancies. Then and there, with typical disregard of financial prudence, he signed away his brainright, and his precious G. H. Curtiss Manufacturing Company, for what turned out to be not even a good mess of pottage.

There was one thing, though, about which he was careful.

"The rights of the A. E. A. must be safeguarded," he said,

"if they decide to form a commercial company my allegiance is to them."

"Sure," said Herring. "But an even better idea would be to get them to come in with us. Write to them and urge them to get aboard on the ground floor."

So Curtiss wrote excitedly to his friends in Baddeck describing his brilliant prospects. "I would not be surprised," he said, "if Herring's patents would not pretty well control the use of the gyroscope in obtaining automatic stability. This seems about the only road to success in securing stability in an aeroplane.

"I will be manager of the new company and everything will go on just as it has (sic) except that we will have Mr. Herring's devices on our machines."

Then he went on to urge his friends to come into the company. With remarkable acumen the members of the A. E. A. politely declined the offer.

Cortlandt Field Bishop triumphantly announced the formation of the new company at the Aero Club on March 15. The papers went wild over the business and published sensational stories to the effect that the Herring-Curtiss Company planned to manufacture one hundred aerodromes a week.

Bell's son, Gardiner, commented dubiously in the A. E. A. Bulletin: "It probably means that Mr. Herring has some more convincing arguments than he has ever made public. Or is it the Curtiss Company with Mr. Herring's patents to flourish in the eyes of the bewildered capitalist?

"All of which revives interest in Herring's machine for the War Department."

The final papers were signed on March 29. Two days later the A. E. A. came to an end by time limitation. The six months' extension had passed, experiments were ended. Doctor Bell wrote sadly in the final bulletin:

"It was a pathetic little group that gathered around the fire-place in the great hall at Beinn Breagh and watched the clock go round. Only three members were present, Messrs. Bell, McCurdy, and Baldwin; with Mrs. Baldwin, Miss Mabel Mc-Curdy and Mr. Charles R. Cox present by invitation.

"The vote to adjourn sine die was hardly put when the first stroke of midnight was heard and . . . exeunt omnes."

Though he did not hear it, that deep melodious boom of the old hall clock at Beinn Breagh marked the end of the happy days for Curtiss. Great triumphs awaited him and desperate trouble, and in the far future much money and lasting fame, but the things he had loved, the experiments, the excited discussions, the good companionship belonged to a youthful phase of aeronautics which passed into limbo with that solemn note. Bell, Curtiss, Baldwin, Selfridge, and McCurdy—the harmonious band of happy scientists—had served their ardent purpose and now moved on to make way for a more complex world.

CHAPTER SIXTEEN

GOLD BUG

THE HERRING-CURTISS COMPANY started off with a bang. Its first plane, the *Gold Bug*, was an enormous success. The little golden-winged machine was the prototype of all those Curtiss planes which made history during the first great years of man's conquest of the air.

Gold Bug was much smaller than *June Bug:* Curtiss wanted more speed. Her wings spread but twenty feet and their chord was only four. She was powered by a four-cylinder twenty-four horsepower water-cooled engine driving a laminated-wood propeller.

Curtiss had abandoned Casey's concavo-convex wings because he did not think they did any good. The flat ailerons were placed between the short, straight wings which were covered with a natural linen fabric doped with the yellow Curtiss varnish. The rudder and single-surface stabilizer were carried in back on a bamboo outrigger, and more bamboo poles carried the small biplane elevating rudder in front. The only thing Herring contributed to the design, the only one of his vaunted devices which ever appeared on a Curtiss plane, was a small triangular fin in this elevating rudder, which was supposed to improve horizontal stability. In practice it reduced maneuverability and was discarded in later models.

Gold Bug was delivered to the Aeronautical Society at Morris Park Race Track in New York City on Memorial Day,

1909. The society had once before tried to hold a meet with its own machines and had provided the public with nothing but a good laugh. This time they were determined to give a good show.

Gold Bug was housed by itself under one side of the grandstand, and beneath the other was a weird collection of the freak aircraft of the day. There were ornithopters, helicopters, biplanes, triplanes, and multiplanes. One machine looked like a bicycle with parasols above it, which whirled feverishly but futilely when the operator pedaled. Other machines had flashes of the coming light.

May 30 was a fine but windy day. Early in the afternoon the public began to pour through the gates of Morris Park, the first of those great crowds, who during the next three years were to pay millions of dollars to watch aeroplane shows. For hours there was nothing for them to do but gape at the exhibits. Then, as the wind died somewhat, Captain Baldwin, who had one of his little one-man airships in a tent at the end of the field, went up and maneuvered around the track. The puffs of wind and cross-currents caused him to do some fancy acrobatics trying to balance his flying trapeze.

As the dusk began to gather, the crowd got very impatient. The shouts of "Fake!" which were to become familiar to wind-bound aviators at a thousand country fairs, resounded from the packed stands.

At last *Gold Bug* was brought out on the track. Curtiss took his place at the controls and Henry Kleckler started the engine —happily it went off on the first try. G. H. looked down the broad brown homestretch. It was empty except for one elegant young man who was standing absorbed in watching the smoke from his cigarette.

With a grin G. H. opened the throttle and signaled his men.

Gold Bug hurtled forward and whirred into the air like a startled partridge, neatly clearing the young élégant, who dropped flat on his face in the dust.

Half as high as the grandstand Curtiss leveled off. But he couldn't stay level. Those wind currents from the roofs of the buildings were like a choppy sea in the Channel. Down the course he went, buckety-buckety. He caught a glimpse of the blue Hudson beyond the roofs of Harlem. Then the sharp turn was on him and he banked steeply.

As he straightened out on the backstretch he saw one of the freak aircraft, cluttering the ground. Instantly he calculated and declined the risk of flying over it, and cutting his engine, brought *Gold Bug* abruptly to earth.

That was the end of the great flying exhibition at Morris Park. But New Yorkers had seen an aeroplane in the air, and the Aeronautical Society at last had a plane which would fly. Honor was satisfied.

Part of Curtiss' contract with the Aeronautical Society was to teach its members to fly. This was not so dangerous as it was to become after his invention of dual controls. For the present, with a plane that could just stagger into the air carrying one person, all instruction was confined to giving good advice. Once the student left the ground it was strictly up to him.

Charles F. Willard was G. H.'s first pupil, and a very apt one. That is to say, he got up and got back down without wrecking the machine. The next candidate made the earliest attempt on record to mix alcohol and flying. The result confirmed Curtiss' opinion of that combination. The machine was almost demolished, though the pilot had apparently achieved alcoholic indestructibility.

Before this, however, *Gold Bug* had her brief moment of glory. The *Scientific American* announced that its trophy award for 1909 would be made to the first person who flew twenty-five kilometers around a circular course. Twenty-five times the requirements of a year before measured the fantastic progress of aviation. G. H. decided to get another leg on the cup and borrowed *Gold Bug* from the willing Aeronautical Society. Morris Park was suggested for the trial, but G. H. thought about those vicious cross drafts and firmly turned it down. Long Island, he figured, was about the flattest place anywhere around, and motored off to scout for a good flying field. When he reached the Hempstead Plains he knew that he had found it.

With never a fence or tree the plains stretched for miles without a break. From an esthetic point of view that barren piece of country could scarcely have been uglier, but to an aviator it was the most beautiful sight in the world.

The *Scientific American* agreed to Curtiss' choice of a place and Charles M. Manly, Wilber R. Kimball, and Carl Dienstbach were appointed judges and timekeeper. On the edge of the plains, near Mineola, three fishpoles with flags at their tops were set up to make a triangular course a little over a mile in circumference.

Before dawn on the morning of July 17 great crowds poured out of New York to stand in the gathering light on the bleak plains. Captain Baldwin looked them over, a gleam in his showman's eyes.

"G. H.," he said, "if you can get this many people out of nice warm beds at this ungodly hour, you've got the greatest show business of all time. There are millions in it."

"I don't want it to be a show," said Curtiss. "I want to make aerodromes practical, not just toys."

Before the dew was off the grass, Curtiss started on his
trophy flight. It was almost too easy. The motor functioned
perfectly, the air was as smooth as cream. Round and round
went the *Gold Bug*, steadily down the straightways, banking
steeply at the corners. The twelfth and final lap was just like
any of the others except that as Curtiss passed the finish line,
he saw the great crowd tossing like a white-capped ocean as
hands and hats and handkerchiefs waved violently and the
roar of cheering sounded dimly above the motor like heavy
surf on the beaches.

But he didn't stop at that, it was ever his way to give good
measure—miles for kilometers. He made nineteen laps—24.7
miles. Then a wind sprang up and he landed, thinking himself
almost out of gas.

Before the first of the crowd reached him, he had examined
the gas tank.

"Darn it," he said to the first arrival, "I could have gone
another mile. There's nearly a quart left."

So Curtiss won the second leg on the trophy he had marked
for his own. Before a year elapsed he was to win it for the third
and conclusive time, by a flight so spectacular that at this point
even his imagination would have rejected the possibility.

CHAPTER SEVENTEEN

COUPE INTERNATIONALE D'AVIATION

WHILE CURTISS WAS THRILLING America by his flight at Mineola, far greater things were toward in France. Already on the field of Béthany outside Rheims workmen were building stands, tribunes they called them, to seat fifty thousand people. A special railway line was creeping out toward the field and a temporary station was going up. Aerodromes were rising, great sheds with rounded roofs to house the aeroplanes. For on August 22 to 29 the first race meet of heavier-than-air machines was to be held. There were to be prizes for altitude and for endurance, for distance covered, and for daily contests of speed. The climax of the meeting was to be the *Coupe Internationale d'Aviation* for a purse of five thousand dollars and a magnificent silver trophy presented by James Gordon Bennett as a companion prize to his already famous Gordon Bennett Cup for an annual free balloon race.

It is almost impossible to recall the frenzy of anticipation the meet aroused. It seemed that everyone in Europe with the price of a ticket was going to Rheims, and many Americans were on their way. The little ancient city had suddenly become the capital of the New World of the Air.

It was boiling with excitement. The price of a small suite at a hotel was five hundred dollars for the week; mere closets rented for ten dollars a day. Dozens of special trains were scheduled to run from Paris, and Paris itself was crowded by the fans of this new sport.

All the crack aviators of Europe were to compete. Blériot, who had just accomplished the tremendous feat of flying the English Channel; Latham, Farman; the skillful but unlucky Delagrange, Cockburn, Lefébvre; Louis Paulhan, lovingly nicknamed "Le Petit Meccano" because he had been a dirigible mechanic. All these and a dozen more, who were worshiped by their admirers more fervently than movie stars today, had been preparing for months for the *Grande Semaine d'Aviation*. Only America, where man had first risen on wings, had no one to represent her.

The president of the Aero Club of America was frantic. Mr. Bishop had gone to Paris to arrange for the entrance of the Wrights, the logical contenders, and now the famous brothers would not fly. They didn't like certain of the rules, and Bishop got the rules altered. Still they refused. The truth was that the Wrights regarded themselves as scientists engaged in research of vital importance to mankind. And so they were. They did not hold with exhibitions and stunts; no good, they felt, could come of them at this experimental stage—only harm if people got killed unnecessarily. They were truly conservative scientists, ready for any risk that seemed essential to their purpose, unwilling to take a single chance for mere glory.

Meanwhile Mr. Bishop tore his hair. He was in the very maelstrom of the excitement, and it seemed incredible to him that no American should fly at Rheims. Into the blackness of his despair seeped a little light. News came of Curtiss' flights near New York. Twenty-five miles was nothing compared with what the Wrights could do, but there was still a chance for America. Mr. Bishop did not think much of it, but he was in no state to quibble. He cabled Curtiss. Then he began to repace his room.

The answer came back promptly: "No." Curtiss might not

be so conservative as the Wrights, but he was no fool. With careful economy of words he pointed out that he was not "a professional aviator," that he would have little chance against the great flyers of Europe and, finally, that his one finished machine was not built for speed.

Bishop agreed with everything in the cable, but he was desperate. In a magnificent burst of patriotism he cabled Curtiss guaranteeing his expenses, and he directed the gentlemen of the Aero Club to talk to the man from Hammondsport.

The president's generosity plus the pressure of his old friends from the club were too much for G. H. Strongly against his judgment he cabled "Yes." Then he rushed back to Hammondsport. He had an ace in the hole.

When Curtiss hurried into his factory straight from the New York train, the men working there felt the electric thrill, the sudden flow of enthusiasm they always knew when G. H. came home. He called them to him.

"I'm going to Rheims," he said abruptly.

While they were still babbling amazed congratulations, he asked, "How's the new plane coming along?"

"She's nearly half finished," said Kleckler. "But I don't believe there's time to get her ready."

"She's got to be ready," said Curtiss.

In the aerodrome shed was the hope of America. There were the skeletons of some wing panels, the beginning of a frame. It looked like a pretty forlorn hope.

The *Golden Flyer*, as it was then called—though it was known ever after as the "Rheims Machine"—was to embody the priceless lessons learned from the experiences with the *Gold Bug* and other experimental changes. More especially it was designed to carry the most powerful engine Curtiss had ever built. The motor was nearing completion in the machine shop. It was the V-8 water-cooled design, and Curtiss was sure that it would develop fifty horsepower. It would, he believed, drive the new plane at a speed never yet equaled in the air—that is, if it did not shake it to pieces. If America was to have even an outside chance in the Gordon Bennett Cup, this plane must go to France.

During those few precious weeks before the last possible boat sailed, Curtiss drove his men and drove himself yet harder. From early morning to night he went from the machine shop to the aerodrome shed and back again, sketching out ideas for his foremen to follow on scraps of paper or the walls of the shop—working, as always, beside his men.

He had the supreme gift of inspiring loyalty. All those now living, who worked for him then, still love and reverence his memory. If his name is mentioned, their eyes light up and they launch forth on tales of their great chief. So when he called on them, his men labored as they never would have for money or even the hope of fame.

Somehow they got the plane finished. There was no time to try her. The wings were crated and put aboard the waiting train. The shining motor was mounted on the testing block and the new seven-foot propeller bolted into place. Curtiss and Kleckler and Tod Shriver fussed over it, while the others gathered around and listened expertly to its melodious roar.

All that last day they ran it on the testing block, making adjustments on the carburetor, changing the wiring and the timing. At last they had it running perfectly: the song of the cylinders was sweet and true. The great propeller drove a hurricane of wind behind it, lifting a funnel cloud of dust that drifted down the valley. Full fifty horsepower they gave it, and Curtiss said that it would do.

"Pack it up and put it on the car," he told Kleckler. "We've no time to waste."

So without ever having been bolted to the plane it was to drive, the great motor and the two new propellers were boxed for shipment. For the third time Curtiss was taking an untried machine to compete in a great event. Twice before, luck had been with him and he had pulled it off. He wondered if the third time would be once too many.

Though he was the executive head of a three-hundred-sixty-thousand-dollar corporation, G. H. felt that he could not afford to take more than two men with him to France. This was not the company's business, but a private venture. The most he felt he could require of the corporation was the loan of the aeroplane. It would be amply repaid by the publicity he gained.

As his companions on his exciting venture, he chose two comparative newcomers to the organization, Tod Shriver and Ward Fisher. Henry Kleckler was ready to give his best gold-filled tooth to go, but G. H. felt that he had no right to deprive the company of its best engineer's services.

Tod Shriver was practically a gift to Curtiss from Captain Baldwin. He was a tough character who could swing a mean strut when it came to driving unruly crowds back from an exhibition plane.

The captain had discovered him roustabouting at Madison Square Garden. Tod had confided his great ambition to get into the flying game. Baldwin liked him and, foreseeing the possible use of a first-rate bodyguard for Curtiss, had suggested to Harry Genung that he be hired.

For all his toughness, and his occasional sprees, Tod proved a most valuable man. He turned into a first-rate mechanic, and nobody could put a broken wing together with a piece of baling wire quicker than he.

Ward Fisher, though less picturesque, was an old motor-cycling friend and a good mechanic.

Nevertheless, as he drove down to the pier with Lena and the Genungs, who had come to see him off, Curtiss was nervous. He was going alone, except for two mechanics, to uphold the honor of America against all of Europe, alone with an untried plane and a single motor against men who for a year had planned and worked for this occasion, and who were at home with unlimited resources to back them. Well might he be nervous.

But as the horse trotted over the cobblestones toward the pier, and the high sides of *La Savoie*—her great stacks and tall masts flying gay flags—came into view, it was not of these things he was thinking.

For perhaps the tenth time he asked anxiously, "Do you think I'll be seasick, Lena?"

"Is that all you're worried about?" asked Lena, who was pretty worried herself.

G. H. grinned. "That's the first thing. I'll think about the others when I get to them."

He wasn't seasick and *La Savoie* docked on schedule. Nevertheless, every hour counted now. The *Grande Semaine d'Aviation* was to begin in less than a week; all the other contestants were already on the ground. Curtiss inaugurated his stay in France by making another speed record. By taking his plane on the train with him as part of his personal baggage, he broke all records for transporting a piece of machinery from Havre to Rheims.

From the station at Rheims, the small crates containing the

wings and frame, the motor and propellers, were taken in a cart drawn by two big Percherons to the field. Curtiss felt an unexpected emotion as he drove through the ancient city. He had had little time in his hurried life to think of anything but speed and progress. Now he felt the full impact of an old civilization.

He passed through narrow cobbled streets up which men in armor had marched singing; from the windows of the tall stone houses the people had leaned to wave and cheer as the kings of France went by. Dominating the crowding houses of the town was the great Gothic mass of the cathedral, its towers rising against the evening sky.

Then he came to the field of Bethany, where the meet was to be held. The long tribunes stood empty, but ready to hold the throngs that were already gathering. The aerodromes were like wooden tents along the edge of the field, and real tents were pitched in impromptu streets to hold the overflow. Someone told Curtiss that on that very meadow the troops of Joan of Arc had camped when she came at last to see her Dauphin crowned. It stirred him surprisingly.

A reporter hurried up to ask him for his impressions. Looking at the wide stretch of level turf, the tribunes and the hangars and the tents, this prosaic American made an unexpectedly romantic comment. "It's like a medieval tournament," he said.

But the medieval mood did not last long. There was work to be done. Tod Shriver and Ward Fisher started uncrating the aeroplane, and Curtiss hired some French mechanics to help them. Then he must go to Paris to see Mr. Bishop and be presented to James Gordon Bennett.

Mr. Bennett did not think much of America's chances in the meet and, when he met her entry, his hopes fell lower still.

Curtiss, in his store clothes of rusty black, hanging loosely on his gaunt figure, and carrying that chauffeur's cap which he always affected, was not a figure to inspire confidence.

Bennett greeted him cordially, but when he was alone with Bishop he shook his head. He failed to sense the quality of the man through his clothes, and missed the flame of enthusiasm in the hazel eyes under the heavy brows.

"I have grave doubts," Bennett said.

"Curtiss is a good flyer," remarked Bishop. "But you're quite right, he'll never win."

When Messrs. Bennett and Bishop came to Rheims to see the plane, they were even more disturbed. It was such a little thing, looking almost forlorn in the big aerodrome that had been reserved for America's entry.

The "Rheims Machine" was exactly square. Its length over-all was twenty-five feet, and its wing spread the same. The chord of the wings was four and a half feet and they were covered with the same varnished fabric which gave the *Gold Bug* her name. Only the magnificent motor with its V of gleaming cylinders gave a hint of what was to come.

To tell the truth, G. H. himself was little more confident than his backers. Never had he felt so alone; never had he been so conscious of his country upbringing, his lack of sophistication. As he walked down the line of aerodromes peering within, he could see these rich Europeans with their entourages of mechanics and plethora of equipment.

There was busy Blériot, acknowledged to be the greatest flyer in France. He was eager, but serene in the confidence he had earned by the great Channel flight. In his shed were no fewer than five machines and numerous spare motors and parts. Groomed to a fine point was the big monoplane he had built especially for the *Coupe Internationale* with its five-cylinder radial, eighty horsepower E. N. V. motor. That was full thirty horsepower more than Curtiss could allow himself, and in a monoplane! Already men were saying that the single wing was more efficient than the biplane.

Then there was Latham's hangar, which seemed full of planes and parts. There was hardly room in it for the two fully assembled Antoinettes, with their wide-spreading wings and pointed noses on which, like a row of copper cans, were the multiple cylinders of the new inline engine that was rated at thirty-five horsepower, but amazingly developed fifty-five.

In the next aerodrome was young Bunau-Varilla's new Voisin, which his father had just given him on the occasion of his passing his baccalaureate. Curtiss looked at that box kite and was not worried. It had no ailerons, but only the enclosed ends of the wings and the vertical planes between them to give it lateral stability. It would be impossible to maneuver or bank properly on the turns.

In the same hangar was Louis Paulhan, who had but lately learned to fly and now outflew his masters. His Voisin mounted a seven-cylinder Gnome Rotary motor in which the whole engine revolved with the propeller around the crankshaft. This gave the cylinders fine air-cooling, but so great was the loss of efficiency in spinning that mass of metal that though the motor was rated at fifty horsepower, it delivered only thirty-five.

In another shed Tissandier and Lefébvre kept their Wrights. Lefébvre's was a cut-down model built in France. It was faster than the conventional Wright, but not, Curtiss thought, a menace. However, the Wright machines had the great advantage of not having to drag a lot of landing gear through the air; they were still launched from the monorail trolley and landed on their curved wooden runners.

One more aerodrome held Curtiss' interest as he walked slowly down the line, sniffing with intense pleasure the exciting aroma of gasoline, varnish, and burned castor oil. This was the one where the English flyers, Farman and Cockburn, kept their machines.

Henry Farman, G. H. saw, had designed an enormous biplane. Compared with it, his own ship would look like a yacht alongside a liner. Its wings, stretching all across the hangar, towered above him, and the single-surface elevation rudder jutted high out in front, while the broad, boxed tail extended far to the rear. The landing gear was a massive structure of struts and skids from which two pairs of wheels were underslung on thick rubber bands.

The huge Farmans were powered by Gnome Rotaries; only thirty-five horsepower to drive that mass of wood and fabric and wire through the air. They might fly a long time, Curtiss thought, but they certainly were not fast.

Back in the American hangar Tod Shriver asked, "Well, now that you've looked them over, what do you think of our chances?"

"Not good," said G. H. "We can throw out the European biplanes—they're slower than cold oil—and I think we can beat the Wright machines, but Latham has a beautiful ship, clean and powerful—there is no telling what he can do. And Blériot! That's a sweet motor he has there, if it runs as good as it looks. I think he is faster than we are. Yes sir! Blériot is the man to beat."

"And you're the man to beat him," said Tod Shriver loyally.

They got the American plane ready in time to make two short flights on August 19. Then it began to rain. For two days the low clouds seemed to scrape the tops of the poplar

trees, and the quiet, determined rain of France turned the
roads into furrows of mud and the field into a green morass.
The promoters of the meet were frantic. Riches or ruin hung
on the turn of the wind.

August 22 . . .

That Sunday morning a French reporter roused himself and
stumbled out to the field. It was still raining hard, but standing
patiently in the downpour was a queue of people waiting for
the grounds to open. Inside, workmen, who had been at it all
night, were putting the last touches on the great tribunes and
the promenade.

Around the aeroplanes there was already some activity.
Latham was jovially overseeing work on his several machines.
Blériot, almost lost in an enormous raincoat, was chatting with
Anzani, who designed his motors. But the American aero-
drome was dark.

The reporter reconnoitered. He tried to look through the
closed doors with no success. Then he peered through the
window of the little wooden room that was built onto the
side of the hangar. In the dim gray light he saw three men
sleeping there on cots. Curtiss was nearest the window. His
face looked somehow strained, intent. And the reporter recorded that even in sleep the American's fists were clenched
with determination.

A little later in the morning the solid clouds began to break,
and the sun shot out a tentative ray. A tremendous crowd of
people surged toward the field as the specials from Paris began
to arrive. Before ten the tribunes were filled and estimates of
the crowd ran to a hundred thousand. How Captain Baldwin's
eyes would have sparkled at a "gate" like that!

But the ground was in dreadful shape. Everywhere stout

farmers' teams could be seen dragging heavy, underpowered automobiles out of mud holes. And there was a wind. It was no great hurricane, hardly more than a breeze, in fact—perhaps twelve or fifteen miles an hour in the gusts. But nobody dared risk it.

So the band played furiously, the food vendors did a roaring trade in the packed tribunes, and the notables, the ambassadors and cabinet ministers, the generals and admirals, noblemen, millionaires, sportsmen, all the forgotten *grand monde* of the last decade of peace, wandered down the flag-lined promenade to meet the famous *hommes oiseaux* in the aerodromes. It was a very splendid pageant. The women wore princess gowns and huge cartwheel hats, which looked either like circular flowerbeds or aviaries of birds of paradise. The gentlemen mostly affected gray toppers and monocles.

Courtlandt Bishop arrived early at the American hangar.

"If you will let me," he said to Curtiss, "I shall do the honors here, and present you to the distinguished visitors."

G. H., still in his store clothes and chauffeur's cap, looked frightened.

"Can't you just show them the machine and leave me out of it?" he asked.

"I'm afraid not," said Mr. Bishop. "You see, they would be disappointed."

"They will be anyhow," said Curtiss.

Then they began to come: Ambassador Andrew D. White, Sir John French, M. Millerand, Mr. Lloyd George, and a bewildering array of Vanderbilts, Goulds, Astors, and American ladies with fancy foreign names. Curtiss greeted them awkwardly. They murmured good wishes, looked disparagingly at his little plane, and moved on to more glamorous quarters, while he suffered and wished he were working on his machine.

As the morning dragged on with never a plane off the ground, the people began to get restless. It was a very fine mass picnic, but as an air meet it came close to being a total loss. Then, just before noon, the self-taught Lefébvre decided to take a chance.

There was a commotion in front of the Frenchman's aerodrome. The big white wings of his Wright machine appeared, being carried by a group of mechanics. It was taken to the center of the course and mounted on its monorail trolley. The mechanics stood around holding the wings to keep the light machine from blowing away as Lefébvre, helmeted and goggled, walked stiffly out and took his place at the controls. Everyone held his breath. Only a Frenchman would dare to fly in such a wind!

Lefébvre raised his hand. The weight began to fall and the wide white wings moved forward. His mechanics ran alongside, steadying the machine until it should be air-borne. Against the fifteen-mile wind it hardly seemed to be moving before it floated free of the car. A wild cheer went up from the huge crowd, most of whom were seeing flight for the first time.

When the result of the flight was posted, Lefébvre had won third place on the French Team for the Gordon Bennett speed classic by flying two miles in 19 minutes 24 seconds at a speed of 6½ miles an hour.

That was all the flying there was until late in the afternoon. The bored crowds were starting homeward, when just before sunset the wind dropped. Hangar doors flew open and the machines came out. Before you could say Jack Robinson in French, six machines were in the air at once for the first time in history, and as they landed, six more took their place.

It was a grand finale, and remote-control victory for the Wrights since Tissandier, de Lambert, and Lefébvre, all flying Wright machines, took first, second and third places in the thirty-kilometer race, which was the main event of the day.

The American entry did not leave the ground. It looked as though Mr. Bishop, in the favorite phrase of the time, "had picked a lemon."

August 23 . . .

There was no wind this day, and a much smaller crowd saw some very fine flying. Herbert Latham starred in his big Antoinette. In flight it was probably the most beautiful aeroplane ever built. The broad wings set at a sharp dihedral and the long, birdlike tail made it look like a mythical flying dragon, and it soared through the air with the grace of a condor.

Latham's own gallant personality added much to this effect of ease. As the French papers put it, "Mr. Herbert Latham flew thirty kilometers in his usual majestic manner, nor did he forget to wave to the ladies each time he passed the tribunes."

After that preliminary flight Latham got down to business and took the *Prix d'Altitude* and the world's record by ascending to the terrific height of 503.79 feet.

This was as daring a performance as any at the meet; not because of the risk involved, but by reason of the psychological hazard. Almost any of the machines present were capable of going higher; many of them later ascended several thousand feet. It was the men themselves who were incapable of attaining altitude. They were then still earth-bound, venturing but a little way into the atmosphere, exploring it foot by foot. To them flying high seemed not safer, as we know it to be, but incredibly dangerous.

Latham landed from his great flight, and the air was full of lesser wings. But still the American did not come out. There were those who said the little biplane was just a gigantic hoax; that it couldn't fly and never would. There were others who thought that the plane was all right, but the aviator had cold feet.

Curtiss said, "I'll fly when I'm ready."

He was, as always, single-minded, never to be swerved from the object in prospect. His mind was concentrated, now, like a narrow beam, on the *Coupe Internationale*. Nothing else mattered.

But that evening he was ready. He had to have some racing practice and he chose to get it in the *Tour de Piste*, the speed trial of one lap which was ten kilometers or 6.21 miles.

The little, golden-winged machine was wheeled out into the sunset, and the loyal Americans sighed their relief.

"At last he's going to fly," they said. "If he can."

They sat back, not hoping greatly.

The motor was cranked and the shining cylinders gave splendid tongue. Curtiss stepped into the pilot's seat. He waved his hand and the little plane shot forward. It hopped into the air and, skimming the ground, shot past the excited tribunes. Then it banked steeply around the first pylon and rapidly diminished into the distance.

The people saw it dip into the hollow toward Vitry, the little valley which was already known as the "graveyard of aeroplanes." It was lost to view, and they thought it was down. Then they saw it again, flitting along like a bat in the twilight. It turned the last corner and roared down the stretch singing a song of power too mighty for its miniature frame.

A thousand stopwatches clicked as it crossed the line. Two thousand eyes bugged out as they read the dials. Curtiss had made the circuit in 8 minutes 35 3/5 seconds, breaking all speed records.

When they told him, he was pleased, but not excited.

"Wait till Blériot tries," he said.

August 24 . . .

The President of France came down in his special train, accompanied by his wife, Madame Fallières, and various members of his Cabinet, most of them young politicians yet to be heard from, but very much to be heard from. Millerand was with him and Briand, Generals Joffre and Foch, others for whom glory and shame waited beyond the seemingly sunny horizon of the future.

It was bad flying weather, a twenty-mile wind, but the French flyers were on their mettle. They had not yet heard about bad morale.

Paulhan took his box-wing Voisin up. With no ailerons to steady it, it swayed and staggered in the puffs, but he managed to wave to the President as he went by the flag-draped box.

And Blériot *tried*. He drove his big eighty-horsepower monoplane around the course in 8 minutes 4 2/5 seconds. The next morning's paper screamed:

BLÉRIOT AGAIN SUPREME

Curtiss' Time Is Beaten

Curtiss said, "It looks bad, but we're not beaten yet."

August 25 . . .

Another windy day and young Prince Albert of Belgium, coming all the way from Brussels, wondered if he would see any flying. He did.

Paulhan was tired of waiting. He decided to try for the *Prix de la Champagne*, the distance contest.

Tipping and bucking, the Voisin bumbled past the pylons, round after round. Ten laps and the crowd began to get excited. Twelve and they were in a frenzy. The Wrights' incredible record of 124 kilometers in 2 hours 20 minutes 23 seconds made at Le Mans in December 1908 was about to fall. One more lap and the crowd cheered wildly. The distance record was broken and a few minutes later the duration record fell too. Paulhan stayed in the air for 2 hours 34 minutes. He landed amidst terrific acclamations.

Curtiss joined the crowd who hurried to offer congratulations. Then he turned to Tod Shriver.

"If it's going to blow the whole time we're here," he said, "we've got to learn to fly in a wind. Bring out the plane."

Tod shook his head. "I don't like it, G. H."

"Neither do I," said Curtiss. "But we've got to do it. Suppose it's blowing the day of the race? Besides, I want to beat Blériot's time."

So the little plane came out and Curtiss drove it hard around the course, through the gusty weather. He broke his own record by twenty-three seconds, but failed to match Blériot's time by over seven seconds.

"We've got to do better," said Curtiss.

August 26 . . .

Curtiss did not do better. Even Latham beat him in the daily *Tour de Piste*. The American biplane made its worst lap of the meeting taking 9 minutes 31 seconds for the ten kilometers. It was a terrible blow to Curtiss. Something had gone wrong.

August 27 . . .

A day of perfect flying weather, but Curtiss never moved from his hangar. He and Shriver and the French mechanics toiled all day and most of the night, overhauling the motor and working on the plane. Tomorrow was the day of the great race. It had to be at its best. And even its best was not good enough. If Curtiss was to win, he must think of something. So he worked and thought, and paid no heed to the excitement out of doors, though there was plenty of excitement.

It was the last day of competition for the distance race. Latham had beaten Paulhan's record.

Now it was Farman's try. The bearded Englishman had not entered any events in the meeting, and apart from a few short practice flights had not been off the ground at all. But he was a secret sort of person and had been working behind closed doors.

At 4:25 in the afternoon the heavy English machine dragged itself into the air. At a height of about thirty feet it started around the course.

Latham, Delagrange, Lefébvre, and others were in the air flying high, wide, and fancy, but Farman stuck to his knitting and the great plane rumbled on. Before the crowd waked up to what was happening he had passed Paulhan's record, was treading on Latham's heels.

The sixteenth lap and all records fell. As he passed the former mark they opened champagne in Farman's hangar. It was a wild celebration to which everyone in the aerodromes was invited. He had won the *Prix de la Champagne* and twenty thousand francs. He would be landing any minute now.

But he flew on and on. The longer he flew the more champagne was consumed. A toast for each new lap. Bottoms up! and the corks popping like 75's.

The sun went down and the dusk closed in. Men climbed the pylons and hung lanterns to their tops. The darkness grew and the searchlights failed to pierce the gloom. Automobiles dashed across the field to train their acetylene headlights on the sky. Nobody knew whether Farman was still flying or not except when he passed the tribunes.

At 7:30 the timers and officials quit according to the rules. Farman's record stood at 3 hours 4 minutes 56 2/5 seconds, and 189 kilometers. Actually he flew for ten minutes longer.

Finally, "a ghostly thing fluttering out of the night," the plane landed.

"I'm so cold," Farman said.

Perched out on the front of his plane in the forty-mile wind of its progress for all those hours, he was virtually congealed. He could not walk, and a big fireman carried him to the warmth and gaiety of his hangar.

Curtiss knocked off long enough to go over and congratulate the Englishman. He smilingly refused a glass of champagne and lingered no more than a moment. Then he went back to work and ponder. He had to think of something.

August 28 . . . The Coupe Internationale d'Aviation.

Curtiss awoke at dawn to look out on an airless day. If only it will stay like this, he thought, conditions will be perfect. But even if they were, he calculated that he couldn't win.

The pattern of the coming race had shaped itself plainly in the days just passed. No other plane was so fast as Curtiss' at its best, except Blériot's, and that was just those seconds faster. Even though he could push his machine a little harder, G. H. knew that Blériot too had a reserve. The thirty-horse-power advantage of the French plane would continue to give it those few precious seconds unless he thought of some racing trick, some new technique, that would enable him to shave the time still further. It seemed almost hopeless.

At ten o'clock there was still no wind, the sun burned in an absolutely cloudless sky. It was so hot and still that the dust of arriving automobiles hung over the roads to settle back and be churned up again. G. H. looked at his watch, which told him that the official hour when a start could be made was at hand. He looked at the sky and made up his mind.

"Take the plane out," he said to Tod.

"Are you going to start?" the mechanic asked.

"I'll run my trial lap," Curtiss said. "If she goes well I'll start."

"Better wait," counseled Tod. "You have till 5:30, and if you go first the others will know what they're shooting for."

"It doesn't matter," answered Curtiss. "We'll all go as fast as we can anyhow, and the weather might change. Let's get it over with."

He smiled grimly. "At least I'll have a nice smooth ride."

So the doors of the hangar were opened, and the first machine on the field that day was the American.

The motor was started and warmed. While his mechanics braced themselves against the wings, Curtiss opened it up and listened critically. Never had it sounded better. He slowed it down and waved the men away. Then he opened the throttle wide and the plane shot forward.

The instant he left the ground, G. H. lost his hope of a nice smooth ride. The apparently still air was literally boiling, and the little plane bucked and pitched like a crazy bronco. Fighting the controls, Curtiss tried vainly to find a reason for this turbulence. No one then knew that, without a wind to iron it out, the air becomes a series of up- and downdrafts caused by the differing temperatures of fields and roads, trees and barren stretches on the earth's surface.

The wildly careening plane was hardly the place to reason this out. G. H. gave it up and concentrated on controlling his machine.

For the first time he kept the engine wide open. In spite of this, he was sure that he was making slow time. It seemed to take forever to get around the course and he mentally resolved that if he got out of this alive, he would not start again for the *Coupe Internationale* or anything else.

At last he saw the finish line ahead and shot downward to land a little way beyond it. Almost as his wheels touched the ground a signal was hoisted that a new record had been made. To his amazement Curtiss learned that his time for the lap was 7 minutes 55 1/5 seconds.

"You've got him," shouted Tod Shriver enthusiastically. "That's nine seconds better than Blériot's best time."

"Blériot will go faster today," said G. H. pessimistically. "It's my opinion that the turbulence of the air helped me. It probably breaks up the partial vacuum which, forming behind the plane, holds it back. But it will also help Blériot. We've got to do still better."

"You will," said the loyal Tod. "Remember how you used to beat better motorcycles by cutting corners?"

"But you can't cut corners in the air," said Curtiss. "Or can you?"

His eyes became speculative and then burned with excitement. He had thought of something.

"Fill her up," he said to Tod. "I'm starting in the *Coupe Internationale*."

"Right now?"

"Right now!"

The *Coupe Internationale* was two laps of the course, twenty kilometers. As he took his seat in the plane once more, G. H. wondered if it could stand the strain that long; he wondered if he could. Perhaps the air would be smoother. Still, if it was, he might not go so fast. Grimly he hoped that conditions had not changed. When he circled for height before making his start he found that they had changed: the air was even rougher.

At forty-five feet, more or less, swooping and rising in the boiling air, he roared across the starting line with the throttle jammed wide, where it was to remain all through the flight. Two hundred thousand eyes followed his course; the packed tribunes were screaming with excitement. He raced for the first pylon, and as he reached it the great crowd moaned aloud. For the little golden plane seemed to rise slightly; then turning on its side, dove into the corner. Just above the ground it leveled off and winged away.

Not one of all those thousand knew what they had seen. They thought it was a near accident and lucky recovery. But Curtiss, in a moment of inspiration, had invented the racing technique which pilots of another age would use as they drove their screaming planes at three hundred miles an hour in the Schneider Cup.

Over the "graveyard" conditions were terrible. The plane bounced so hard that G. H. was flung from his seat; having no safety belt, he stayed with it only by hooking his feet in the frame. On the Vitry side of the course some large birds rose and fled in terror before the plane, swerving aside just in time to let it pass.

Then Curtiss was turning into the stretch again, diving the corner. This time the crowd saw that it was no accident, but still they shuddered at the American's daring. Past the blur of faces in the tribunes he flashed; their cheers sounded like distant surf beyond the roar of his engine.

On toward the first turn of his second lap, and now he thought he detected a skip in the beat of his motor. After his bad race Thursday he had provided a remote control to the carburetor for this contingency and now he twirled the little wheel until the engine sang louder and stronger than ever before.

Back over the "graveyard' Curtiss drove, jockeying the elevation rudder, gripping with his feet. He knew he was going fast now. The last turn seemed to race toward him. He dove into and straightened out in the stretch.

The plane still had some altitude left and Curtiss brought her through in a diving finish, barely skimming above the ground as he crossed the line.

The record signal was flying as he stepped from his plane, and hundreds of people dashed across the field to congratulate him. The time was announced as 15 minutes 50 3/5 seconds. His first lap had been slow; 7 minutes 57 2/5 seconds, but his second had been flown in the remarkable time of 7 minutes 53 1/5 seconds. His speed was calculated at 47.65 miles per hour.

Jubilant Americans rushed up and surrounded the plane, shouting their congratulations. The French were generous with their praise. To them all G. H. said, "Don't congratulate me yet. I made a fast run, but I haven't won by a long shot."

All the rest of that day he felt like a prisoner awaiting judgment. Every second of the race ran through his mind again and again. He knew that he had given his best, and yet a hundred things occurred to him that he might have done to gain a fifth of a second here, a fraction of that there. If only he had another chance he knew he could better his time. But he had made his run; he must win or lose by that.

Meanwhile, Blériot, too, was sweating. He had expected an easy victory. Now he knew he must work for it. He put a new four-bladed propeller on his plane and at two o'clock ran a trial lap. The big monoplane raced around the course faster than ever before. As it landed on that windless field, it made two great kangaroo leaps, before settling on the turf. Blériot jumped out.

"What was my time?" he demanded anxiously.

"Seven minutes fifty-eight and one-fifth seconds," was the answer.

"Not fast enough," muttered Blériot.

He stood looking at his machine, pondering.

The wily Santos-Dumont, veteran of the air through his long experience with dirigibles, came up.

"Put back your two-bladed propeller," he said.

"Do you think I should?" asked Blériot. "The machine never went faster."

"You cannot lose, for with this one you lose anyway," said the South American.

So the monoplane was wheeled back to its hangar. All afternoon they worked on it, changing the propeller, tuning the motor to its ultimate perfection.

The crowd grew restless. They wanted to see their own champion fly. They were desperately afraid that he might not take off. Five o'clock came and an angry buzz went up from the tribunes. The people had misunderstood the conditions of the race, and thinking that the deadline had passed, imagined that the French entry had defaulted.

"Five-thirty," shouted men through megaphones. "They have until five-thirty to start."

A few minutes after five both Blériot and Latham came upon the field. Engines were started, warmed, and tested. Almost together the white monoplanes of France took off. Blériot was first across the line with the Antoinette close behind, like a gigantic dragonfly chasing an enormous mosquito.

But the smaller plane sped swiftly away from its pursuer to be lost from view in the hollow.

Then, almost before the crowd began to look for it, it was in sight, coming fast. The white wings tilted sharply for the corner and they could see Blériot, imperturbably working his controls. Then it flashed down the stretch, and the thunder of cheering was like the roar of a river in flood, for Blériot had exactly equaled his rival's fastest lap. All he had to do was to keep this pace to win.

G. H. in his hangar gave up hope as the French machine fled away on the final round. The frantic crowd kept cheering as the slow minutes passed. Then the sound died down as the seconds ticked away and Blériot did not come. Something was wrong.

At last he appeared flying up the far side of the course. To the waiting Frenchmen the hands of their stopwatches seemed to race around the dials; the plane appeared to lag in the air.

It banked the corner and gathered a last burst of speed. The crowd cheered loyally as it crossed the line, but the heart was gone from the sound.

Cortlandt Bishop clicked the stem of his watch and stared almost unbelieving at its face.

"America wins!" he shouted and ran to the judges' stand. Tod Shriver ran after him, clutching his watch. Before they reached the judges, Blériot's time was announced: 15 minutes 56 1/5 seconds. Curtiss had won by 5 2/5 seconds.

Back ran Bishop to drag G. H. protesting from the shed. He marched him to the flagpole. As they reached it, the Stars and Stripes moved jerkily up the staff, limp in the airless heat, glorious in the bright slanting sunshine. Everyone stood very still as the band played the *Star-Spangled Banner*.

As the last notes died away, bedlam broke loose. Every American in that great crowd tried to reach Curtiss' hand, and the gendarmes had their work cut out. Ambassador and Mrs. White were among the first. Then came Mrs. Theodore Roosevelt and her sons, Archie and Quentin.

"Bully for you," said Quentin, in imitation of his famous father, and everyone laughed.

Blériot came bursting through the crowd and, flinging his arms around the embarrassed American, kissed him on both cheeks. Then the great French sportsman climbed back into his machine and started in the *Tour de Piste*.

He did the single lap in 7 minutes 47 2/5 seconds, smashing the record by 5 2/5 seconds. But the Gordon Bennett Cup belonged to America.

On Monday night there was a grand banquet at the Hotel de Ville. Five hundred people gathered to honor the farm boy from America. Curtiss came in with his great French rival. M. Blériot wore his arm in a sling and there was a bandage on his face. On the last day of the meet his big racing plane had crashed in the "graveyard" and disappeared in a column of black smoke from which the gallant Frenchman emerged, fortunately, without serious damage.

Curtiss wore an air of acute embarrassment. This, to him, was the worst ordeal of all. When his turn came to speak he muttered unhappily and sat down as quickly as was decent.

In front of him was the great trophy he had won. He stared at it, unbelieving still. In massive silver it represented a mountain on which a man stood balanced lightly as though about to leap into the sky. Above the figure's head was an exquisitely wrought model of the first Wright machine.

Curtiss smiled a little grimly as he savored the irony of that.

For cables had told him, that even as he was driving his machine in the *Coupe Internationale*, on the day, almost the hour of victory, the Wrights had served the first papers of their suit against him for infringing their patents. Beyond the brilliance of this moment, when all the world seemed eager to do him honor, G. H. saw a future dark with trouble.

CHAPTER EIGHTEEN

THE LEGAL JUNGLE

IT SEEMS TO BE a law inherent in its nature that the art of aviation shall move forward not by the methodical progression of earth-bound science, but in a series of splendid leaps followed by periods of comparative quiescence. The meet at Rheims furnished the first of these spectacular impulses which loosed the forces of aviation. The world suddenly realized that flight was no longer a mystical abstraction, but a present, practical fact.

Curtiss, arriving in Paris, found himself the most sought-after man in Europe. The whole Continent was aeroplane-mad, and people from St. Petersburg to Constantinople clamored to see the great American fly. Offers backed by cash poured in upon Curtiss. He could have spent a year touring from one lucrative engagement to another. And, judging by the messages that kept the cables hot, America was in the same state of mind.

But there were other cables less agreeable. The Wrights had obtained an injunction forbidding the Herring-Curtiss Company to sell, exhibit, or even to manufacture aeroplanes. Curtiss knew he must return to defend himself in his own country.

So he refused all European engagements with the single exception of the meet of the Royal Italian Aero Club at

Brescia. Thither he journeyed in the second week of September, with Cortlandt Bishop, his two mechanics, and the little golden aeroplane.

There was no Gordon Bennett Cup to be gained at Brescia, but Curtiss lived up to his new reputation by winning the Grand Passenger-Carrying Race of 50 kilometers, worth seven thousand dollars.

Far more important than that was one brief, unofficial flight he made. It lasted no more than ten minutes, but its effects echoed onward through the years.

The tiny plane staggered into the air that sunny afternoon carrying its first passenger. The man was sitting insecurely on the lower wing. His hands grappled the bracing wires for very life, but his burning eyes roamed wide over the blue water and the cypress-covered hills as Gabriele d'Annunzio, who was to become the poet-pilot and hero of all Italy, essayed for the first time the element he was to claim for his own.

From Brescia Curtiss started home. Throughout the voyage he was driven by a mixture of eagerness and dread. There was so much he had learned, so many things to do.

He was burning to translate the lessons of Rheims into accomplished fact. In many ways his plane had proved itself better than Europe's best. His double-acting ailerons, for instance, were far in advance of any other form of lateral control.

The aeroplane expert of *L'Auto*, in an article rating the aerodynamic efficiency of the different planes at the meet, put Curtiss' in first place, and (a small consolation to a harassed man) the Wrights in last.

But in spite of the dramatic manner in which his theories of design had been justified, Curtiss felt no complacency. New ideas were seething in his mind and he was impatient to try them out. And striking at his eagerness was the dread thought that perhaps he might not be permitted to do so.

"Forbidden to manufacture aircraft." Did that mean that he could no longer experiment, that he was estopped forever from putting his genius at the service of the science to which his whole being was now devoted? He flamed with an intolerable sense of injustice.

We, who are able to view calmly the embittered issue, can see the right on both sides. The Wrights had been the first to fly. Their wing-warping device was the basic patent on which they relied to gather the fruits of their long years of patient experimentation and personal peril. They regarded the aileron as an imitation and a quibble.

But Curtiss was no pick-brain, no conscious thief of other men's ideas. He implicitly believed that his aileron was a completely new conception. It was certainly much better than the Wright method, for it permitted a simple, rigid-wing construction which was cheaper to build, stronger and more efficient than those built to flex for maintenance of lateral balance. Whether or not it was basic has never been settled, for the ultimate decision of the courts was lost eight years later in America's necessities of war. That Curtiss passionately believed it to be basic is unquestionable.

The roaring welcome in New York, the gold medal of the Aero Club, the banquets and poems and paeans in the papers meant little or nothing to Curtiss. His single-purpose mind was focused on the vital issue: Would he be able to build aeroplanes?

Lena met him in New York and gave him words of comfort. Judge Monroe C. Wheeler, his true friend and legal adviser, was sure they would win. But it would take a long time; the immediate future was a blank.

It is probable that Curtiss' only happy hours at this time were on the day of his triumphant return to Hammondsport. When the New York train pulled into Bath at five o'clock on a drizzling afternoon, a special, chartered by his home-town friends, was waiting in the station. There were Harry and Martha Genung, Leo Masson, Tank Waters, and dozens of others very dear to him.

After the inevitable speeches the special train got under way. It was seven o'clock and the rain was slashing down when they pulled into Hammondsport. Every inhabitant who was not on the train was at the station, and each of them must shake Curtiss by the hand. The rain whipping across the platform could not dim the warmth of that welcome.

When the last little boy had felt the touch of his hero's hand, the whole crowd escorted G. H. and Lena to an old-fashioned buggy, which was waiting outside the station. They crawled into the dampness under its inadequate top, and all the men and boys struggled for a place at the shafts or the long towing ropes.

With torches flaring and sputtering and the local band tooting valiantly, the people of Hammondsport hauled the carriage up through the mud and pouring water. They passed under a limp triumphal arch bearing the single word CURTISS, and on to where the House on the Hill blazed with the lights of welcome.

The whole crowd poured in for a great impromptu reception. The champagne bottles banged and the wine fizzed into any vessel that would hold it, from long-stemmed glasses to teacups. G. H., feeling warm and happy at last, made one of his sincere, awkward little speeches, and everyone cheered and cheered again.

The next day the bad news began to pour in, and it kept

on coming. G. H. figured he had had too much good fortune, now the luck had turned, and Old Man Percentage was catching up. One blow fell after another. The Army canceled its forty-thousand-dollar contract for a plane to be built by the Herring-Curtiss Company. The partners themselves fell into dispute, and the whole company into which Curtiss had put such high hopes and all his money began to disintegrate. Herring refused to turn over the patents on which Curtiss had relied to fight the Wrights, and he added to the confusion by suing Curtiss to force him to give to the company the prize money he had won at such personal risk.

Suit and countersuit rent the ranks of the embattled Hammondsporters.

Even Curtiss' own element, the air, forsook him. He was scheduled to make an exhibition flight at the great Hudson-Fulton Celebration in New York. High winds kept him grounded for days. He finally left that city under something of a cloud, to keep an engagement in St. Louis. The weather promptly changed and the Wrights, who showed signs of coming out of their scientific shell, made a triumphant flight over the flag-dressed warships in the Hudson from Governor's Island to Grant's Tomb and back.

The rest of the winter resolved itself into a race between Curtiss trying to make exhibition flights and the Wrights slapping on injunctions. The way the embittered brothers saw it, nobody could fly in America for profit without their permission. Louis Paulhan bought a couple of Farmans to replace his obsolete Voisin and came gaily over to fulfill a rich contract. He should have risked his neck in the old machine without lateral control, for the first time he hopped into the air the Wrights cracked down. The Little Mechanic stayed long enough to smash the world's altitude record to smithereens, by taking his heavy plane a mile up in the sky. Then he fled back to France considerably wiser and a great deal sadder.

Thus, with a veritable blizzard of injunctions, the Wrights tried to snow their opposition under. But they couldn't stop the wildcat flying that was springing up all over the country, no dam of legal foolscap could halt the flood of young Americans who were enthusiastically hurling themselves into the air.

Curtiss gave exhibitions at St. Louis and Chicago, and then went back to Hammondsport. On his arrival he found that he had a flying school on his hands; a group of eager young men had arrived seeking instruction. The two most likely pupils were Bud Mars of the Aeronautical Society and a little daredevil named Charlie Hamilton. Mars was willing enough to wait to be shown, but not Hamilton. One day he found the new plane, which had been built in Curtiss' absence, standing unguarded in a field, and helped himself. For nearly half an hour Hamilton flew all over the valley, while Henry Kleckler, Harry Genung, and the others from the factory wrung their hands in agony, not over Charlie's probable fate, but at the prospect of losing their new plane.

Curtiss arrived at the field in time to see the young scapegrace set the plane down in an almost perfect landing.

"He may never have flown before," said G. H., "but he's a pilot now."

Charles K. Hamilton thus became the first Curtiss exhibition pilot, and he was the most reckless of them all.

A tiny man with the build of a jockey, he had brilliant red hair and his pale blue eyes looked out from a face so emaciated that it seemed more like a skull. For Charlie was a victim of tuberculosis. It mattered nothing to him if he lost his life, because there was so little left to lose. In fact, he lived and flew as though the one thing he was afraid of was dying in bed, so, of course, in the end, he did.

On the last day of the old year, Justice Coman of Utica vacated the injunction against Curtiss. But G. H. had little time to enjoy his new freedom for, on January 3, 1910, Justice Hazel of Buffalo handed down an even worse decision which virtually made Curtiss a criminal every time he took to the air.

The Wrights' patent, which was admittedly badly drawn, made the conjoint use of the rudder with the wing-warping a basic element. Therefore, the Wright contention had to be that the Curtiss planes also used the rudder in balancing. Curtiss and all his witnesses swore that his ailerons produced no turning movement and operated entirely independently of the rudder.

When Curtiss heard of Judge Hazel's decision, he was with Bud Mars and Charlie Hamilton, flying in the first American aviation meet at Los Angeles. There was, he figured, a way of proving his point beyond the whisper of a doubt. He sealed the rudder on one of his planes, and Hamilton made a successful straightaway flight in it before thousands of people.

G. H. naïvely supposed that this would settle the matter, but the injunction remained in force.

In addition to his legal troubles, the newspapers, who had praised Curtiss so loudly, put on a campaign of vilification. The New York reporters had never forgiven his failure to fly at the Hudson-Fulton Celebration. They now treated him as a charlatan and a pirate of the air, who sought to steal the gleanings of other men's brains.

The controversy so begun raged with unbelievable bitterness for many years, and even today, when the names of Curtiss and Wright are linked in the greatest aviation company in the world, the easiest way to start a fist-fight in aeronautical circles is to bring up the subject.

With the storm roaring around his head, Curtiss returned dejectedly to Hammondsport, where he became even more completely bogged down in the legal morass. Scuppered by the Wright injunction, the Herring-Curtiss Company slid rapidly beneath the financial waves. In a last effort to save it, G. H. borrowed funds on his personal notes and gave them to the company to meet its payroll.

It was no use. An aeroplane company which can neither manufacture nor exhibit aeroplanes is obviously doomed. On April 1, 1910, the Herring-Curtiss Company went into bankruptcy. Fortunately, it did not own the physical properties, the little factory and scant machinery at Hammondsport. These were all that Curtiss had left.

So G. H. stood alone with no capital and with only a few loyal friends. Against him was a million-dollar combination. For the Wrights were no longer brothers, but a corporation. In November a great company had taken over their interests, and its board of directors boasted such names as Morton F. Plant, August Belmont, Allan A. Ryan, and Howard Gould. These were men who put their trust in trusts, and it seemed to them that they could monopolize the aviation industry of America without even bothering to buy up the outsiders. Once involved, the Wrights had to go along whether they liked it or not.

In so desperate a situation Curtiss resolved on a measure of desperation. Sinking his pride, he went to Dayton to ask for terms. Late one evening, in the parlor of their little house, he met the famous Wright brothers and their sister Kathryn, who had brought them up and been secretary, financier, business manager, and mother to them. The brothers were firm. They

solemnly announced their terms: twenty per cent royalty on
every penny taken in for exhibitions; twenty per cent on the
retail price of every plane sold—a thousand dollars on a five-
thousand-dollar machine.

Stunned, Curtiss muttered, "I'll think it over," and stumbled
out of the house. Trying to realize what it meant, he paced the
deserted streets of Dayton under the old gas lamps. It was, he
reckoned, the end. No one could pay such a royalty and survive financially.

He came to a drugstore, which was still open, and turned in
to telephone Judge Wheeler.

When he heard the terms the judge was shocked into silence
for a moment. Then he said, so vehemently that the receiver
squealed in protest, "Don't accept, G. H. If you do, you're
through. Don't even go back there. Come home!"

So G. H. went home.

Though, in the days that followed, Curtiss was often at the
point of despair, he never lost his passionate belief in the future
of flying. Indeed, his enthusiasm carried him past present actu-
alities into the realm beyond the horizon of time. He saw so
clearly what could be accomplished that he confused it with
what had been done. The sport planes of another generation
were already taking off in his imagination, the aerial armadas of
the war-after-next were maneuvering in the back of his brain.

Two newspaper interviews which he gave in the spring of
1910 show clearly the truth of his vision and the unexpected
impracticality of the dreamer who inhabited his apparently
prosaic person.

In the first he referred to aeroplanes as "the automobiles of
the air," and in the second he said, "By the time the next great
war breaks out, battleships will be useless. A swarm of light,

swift aeroplanes will replace the ships as the easiest machines of terror. Airships will swarm over the navies dropping a poison in the shape of picric-acid bombs.

"I hardly subscribe to the preparations we will make to defend our country. I don't believe we are going about it the right way. . . . It is as sure as death and taxes that the airship will supersede the battleship."

Curtiss was one war ahead of himself when he said that, but the world is surely catching up with him.

However clear his vision of the future, Curtiss could see no way out for the present. The lawsuits had become so numerous that Charlie Hamilton cracked, "A man has to have ten years in law school before he has a chance of becoming an aviator."

With his prestige vanishing, his activities forcibly restrained and his financial position desperate, G. H., as always, turned to Judge Wheeler for advice.

"I can't sell planes," he said. "I can't even build them, nor show them. What can I do?"

"They've got us sewed up pretty tight right now," the judge admitted, "but I've got it fixed so that if we post a ten-thousand-dollar bond we can go ahead."

"Where can I get ten thousand dollars?" G. H. demanded. "I haven't any money left and I couldn't borrow ten cents."

"You can still compete for prizes," Wheeler pointed out.

"I see," said Curtiss thoughtfully.

What he saw was the ten-thousand-dollar prize which the New York *World* had hung up for the first aeroplane to fly from Albany to New York. It was the exact sum he needed; it looked like the pointing finger of destiny. And yet—

No one knew better than he the dangers that beset such an adventure. However far afield his imagination might carry him when he was just talking, he was keenly aware of the present limitations of the aeroplane. He thought of his light machine tossed in a vortex of winds sweeping around the corners of the Catskills. He reviewed the long river route between the jagged mountains with no possible landing place for many miles except the treacherous surface of the water. One major hazard was man-made, the Poughkeepsie Bridge. Should he go over or under it?

He figured gasoline and oil consumption, the probabilities of engine failure, elementary precautions. He came at last to the conclusion that under the most favorable circumstances it could be done. If his luck came back to him, it could be done.

So he walked into his factory one day and said in the casual way that always masked his determination:

"Well, boys, I'm going to fly from Albany to New York."

CHAPTER NINETEEN

FROM ALBANY—

THE ENGINEER OF THE "Times Special" sat in the cab of the fastest engine the New York Central owned and cursed all aviators generally and Glenn Curtiss in particular. For three mornings now he had been routed out of bed at 3:00 A.M., gotten up steam, and waited until eight or nine o'clock. Then word had come that there would be no flight. Personally he thought that the whole business was a fake and that aeroplanes were silly things anyhow.

His opinion was shared by several million people. Ever since Thursday the whole Hudson River Valley and New York City had been on the qui vive for the great flight from Albany to New York, and so far nothing whatever had happened. The press were getting particularly disagreeable. They had forgotten all about Rheims and the Gordon Bennett Cup, but they had not forgotten Curtiss' fiasco at the Hudson-Fulton Celebration. So the reporters said all the things in print that the engineer was thinking.

Curtiss appeared totally unaffected by the storm of criticism that intensified each time he postponed the flight. Each morning he came out to his plane with the dawn at five o'clock. He read the weather reports, felt the fatal south wind blowing hard, and curtly announced, "No flight today."

To the excited questions of the reporters, he answered, "No comment."

"That guy's made of ice," said one.

"Yeah, no feeling at all. I don't think he ever expected to fly; just out for notoriety."

But G. H. was more troubled than he had ever been before. Whatever the reporters and the public might think, he had a tremendous stake in making this flight. He had risked sorely needed cash in the preliminary experimentation.

From the moment he had announced his intention of trying for the *World's* prize, all the energies of his organization had been bent toward its accomplishment, and Curtiss' own mind had, as it always did, narrowed to the single purpose. He needed that ten thousand dollars desperately. Perhaps even more he needed the favorable publicity success would bring him. He was not indifferent to the hostile attitude of the public toward him; on the contrary, he was deeply hurt. But his creed, his pride, and his inarticulate nature forbade any effort to change it, other than the gesture of showing them.

There had not been much time for preparation. The new plane, named the *Albany Flyer*, with a smaller motor than the Rheims Machine, had been hastily assembled. He flew it at Hammondsport and then, as an elementary precaution for a flight over water with no landing field on either side, he devised a system of flotation, worked it out and tried it. Two pontoons were lashed to the landing gear just above the wheels, and a slanted planing board was set between them to keep the plane from nosing over. Early in the week he took off at Hammondsport. The first question as to whether the plane would fly at all was answered affirmatively. She handled clumsily and rose a trifle sluggishly, but she did fly.

In the air above Lake Keuka he posed the problem to himself as to whether to try a water landing. On the one hand he would, with luck, not need to on the Hudson flight and the essay might wreck the plane and all his hopes. On the other, he felt that he should make the first attempt, not as an impromptu measure of desperation, but deliberately in his home waters. Besides, there was his consuming ambition to fly off water; this, obviously, was the first step.

So he headed over for the shore of the lake, where the water at least was shallow. Gingerly he babied the plane down, until she was skimming barely above the surface. Now he throttled the motor and, feeling her sag in the air, pulled back on his control. The planing board hit with a bump as though on solid ground, the machine bounced along, and a sheet of spray rose to blind him. Then she settled, stopping with a drag that pulled him forward on his slippery seat. The spray subsided and motion ceased. The *Albany Flyer* floated, graceful and unhurt, on the calm surface of the lake, and incidentally to his ultimate purpose, Curtiss had set another milepost in the progress of aviation. For the first time a plane had landed on water.

Immediately he packed the *Flyer* up for her trip to Albany. Time pressed hard. One day to ride down the Hudson on a Day Line boat, talking to the captain all the way, trying to find out, what no man really knew, about the air currents that blew off the Catskills. One day more to pick a landing field for the refueling stop—halfway it should be—near Poughkeepsie. But the country there was all tilted this way and that, with trees and boulders making additional hazards.

"Stop—there's a piece of fine flat lawn."

The car drove through high iron gates, on one of them a sign:

STATE ASYLUM FOR THE INSANE

The superintendent was a genial man who liked a joke. "Sure you can land here. Most of you flying-machine inventors end up here anyway."

But they found a farm at Camelot, three miles out, that was better, and Farmer Gill agreed to raise a flag to mark the spot.

Curtiss was ready Thursday and so were the reporters and the notables and the special train.

But the weather was not. The south wind blew as though it meant to blow forever, and time was even shorter now. For down at Governor's Island, Charlie Hamilton, with a plane he had bought from Curtiss and fixed up on his own, had announced that he would start Tuesday and "do it easy." He probably would, too, with the luck of fools. Others were making ready. If Curtiss did not go, three or four aircraft would start during the next week.

G. H., as usual, got up at four on Sunday, May 29. He went out to the Rensselaer flats, where his plane was housed in a tent. The south wind was still blowing, but very gently; the weather reports were good.

Curtiss stood irresolute.

"I hate to go on Sunday," he said. "It will offend so many people, but I guess I've got to."

He ordered the plane made ready and went back to his hotel. "Lena . . . Lena! Wake up. I'm going," he shouted.

Lena rolled over and looked at him with sleepy anxious eyes. "Must you, Glenn?" she asked. "Is it really a good day?"

"As good as can be," said Glenn. "Get dressed and get aboard the train. I'll start at seven."

Lena had been against the flight. While there was time for argument she had protested violently, but when the decision was made she backed her husband with everything she had. Nothing in the world could have kept her off that special train.

Curtiss dressed as warmly as he could. Though it was a pleasant summer day, he knew that sitting on the edge of a wing splitting a sixty-mile gale was chilly work. Over everything else he wore a high pair of rubber waders, not to keep dry, but because they were the warmest thing in the way of a flying suit that the times afforded. At the last moment Tod Shriver produced a cork life preserver and anxiously buckled it on his beloved chief.

"What do I want with that thing?" demanded Curtiss. "I can swim."

"You might get knocked silly. Wear it for me, G. H."

"All right."

At 7:02 they started the motor, and a flag went up on the tallest building in Albany. The engineer, with all his passengers aboard, saw it, and opened his throttle so wide that the drivers spun and the train went off with a jerk. One minute later Curtiss opened his throttle and the little plane leaped off the mud flats of Rensselaer Island.

He took her up to what he figured was seven hundred feet— it's hard to guess exactly with no altimeter—and scanned the East Shore tracks. There came the special roaring out from between the hills, the line of her smoke flat along the roofs of the cars. He dove toward it and, holding level alongside, saw the flutter of hands and handkerchiefs. Then he was moving past, outdistancing the train!

He pulled out over the river and up to seven hundred again. While he climbed the train caught up, but, as he leveled, the plane again pulled ahead. That meant he must be doing better than sixty at this stage. He noted how hard his coatsleeve fluttered in the wind; that indication must serve until someone invented an air speedometer.

The air was quiet here above the water between the low hills near Albany; the treacherous mountains were still far ahead. G. H. worked the foot pump that shot oil to the motor, and then had leisure to contemplate. The river below looked singu-

larly uninviting, yet, if he had a forced landing, there it must
be. He wished he had a real water plane; that's what was
needed for a flight like this. He thought of his failure with the
Loon and figured on how to make it good. Sitting there seven
hundred feet above the Hudson, he worked out the details in
his mind: a single float set at a planing angle like the board
beneath his feet. But that would be unstable, the wings would
tilt into the water and be torn off. Small pontoons then, placed
at the wing tips, just big enough to float them when she heeled.
He could see the new ship in his mind, knew his fingers could
trace the plans as soon as he landed, if he ever did land with
the doubtful river below him and the inhospitable shores on
either hand.

Abruptly his attention came back to his present situation. A
wire was loose and vibrating. It was the main support of the
elevation rudder and should it go, as it surely would if it continued to oscillate long, why the bamboo outrigger would
crumple and the plane fall like a broken kite. Anxiously he
peered ahead. There was the long line of the bridge and
Poughkeepsie just beyond. Carefully he watched its smoking
chimneys to judge the direction of the wind.

Three miles more, a little over three minutes since he had
slowed the motor to ease the strain on the wire. He searched
the eastern shore, wondering if he could find the farm at
Camelot again—things looked so different from the air.

Curtiss swung inland, circling the field. Landing would be
a tricky business, for there was but one place between the trees
and ditches where an attempt might prove successful. There it
was. He glided toward it, and set the *Flyer* down as lightly as
a sparrow.

Curtiss jumped out and looked first to the engine. It was in perfect condition, and as cool as a boardinghouse radiator. By now people were running across the field from the automobiles that lined up along the lane. They surrounded him ten deep; his little plane was lost in the crowd. Then the passengers from the train arrived: Shriver and Kleckler. They cleared a space for him and went over the plane. They fixed the wire with a quick home-made repair.

He was all ready to go on again, except for gasoline and oil. The supply he had ordered had not arrived. The garageman did not believe in working on Sunday!

"What shall we do?" demanded Henry.

"Get some," answered G. H.

"What do you need?" asked a motorist, who remains anonymous to history.

"Gasoline."

"Take some of mine. Siphon it out of the tank."

So they did, and it was all right. The aeroplane motors then were not such dainty feeders as they are now, and there was no such thing as aviation gas. Curtiss decided to take a chance that his oil would last. Somehow they cleared a lane for him through the crowd and he lifted the plane into the air.

Here began the dangerous part of the flight. Above Poughkeepsie there had been no landing place on shore, but at least the hills were low, they did not play tricks with the wind. Now the mountains closed in on the river, towering thousands of feet on either hand. Far below their summits Curtiss drove his plane down the narrow winding lane of silver. The river captain whom he had consulted had warned him of the treacherous air currents off the highlands, but the reality was far worse than his frightened expectation. The little box kite of a plane was tossed from wave to wave of air as though the giants

of the river had found a shuttlecock to play with. Beacon
Mountain tossed him up and hurled him down. Then up again
and Storm King loomed angrily ahead.

Curtiss braced himself for battle as he swept past the shoulder
of the mountain, and it was well he did. The vast breath of
the Storm King blasted his plane out of control. Down it fell,
nose down and sidewise at the same time. Then the wind
caught it up and tossed it helpless in an aerial maelstrom. G. H.
was almost thrown out; he clung by his toes as he had at
Rheims, but this was a thousand times worse. He thought it was
the end.

He made the final move of desperation, pushed the control
forward hard. The plane dove straight for the water, but by
its added speed Curtiss regained control. He pulled out at forty
feet, and considered whether to climb again. The air might be
smoother here; it could hardly be worse.

So it proved to be. Skimming just above the surface, with
the mountains almost shutting out the sky, Curtiss threaded
his way through that tremendous gorge.

Past Peekskill the river widened out, and the battle with the
air was won. But as one anxiety faded, another hastened to
replace it. Curtiss noticed that the oil gauge was nearly dry.
He figured that he had pumped too enthusiastically at first;
now it was questionable if his oil would hold out until he
crossed the line into the city limits. So he was faced with a critical decision. He could land on the water, tow the machine
ashore and hope to get off again, or he could chance it and keep
on. Either way he stood to lose the prize so nearly within his
grasp.

He looked ahead and through the crystal morning saw the
Metropolitan Tower seeming to beckon him onward. So he

held on, and with his oil tank practically empty crossed the line of the Harlem River.

Now came the question of where to land. They were waiting for him with flags and bands on the parade ground at Governor's Island, but he could never make that. He circled and saw a green field just beyond the Harlem that he thought would do. He steered toward it and set his plane for landing. The ground flew sharply up in front as though it would hit him in the face, for the field was a steep hillside. He hauled back full on the controls; the *Flyer's* nose lifted and her wheels made contact at just the right angle.

She rolled a little way, stopped, and started sliding backward. Curtiss jumped out and held her by main strength until two boys came running across the field to relieve him. They put rocks behind the wheels and braced themselves and against the wings, and promised to stay there while Curtiss hurried to the nearest house to telephone the *World* that he had arrived.

The prize was safely won. By landing within the city limits, Curtiss had fulfilled the conditions and the ten thousand dollars was as surely his as though he had landed in Central Park. But there yet remained something to be done. He had not forgotten his failure at the Hudson-Fulton Celebration, or the way the people of New York had thought about him then. He was determined to revise that feeling. Further, he knew that hundreds of thousands of people had stood all that morning before the bulletin boards and news tickers watching the progress of his flight. However needless the added risk, G. H. decided to keep his appointment with the people of New York.

Again a motorist helped him out; oil this time and gasoline, too. There was a little green plateau at the top of the hill. It was not nearly large enough for a normal take-off, but the ground dropped steeply on the windward side. Curtiss thought he could get up sufficient speed to catch the plane in the air as it jumped over the edge.

The crowd helped to shove the plane up to the plateau. His mechanics, who had arrived on the panting train, started the motor and braced themselves against the wings. When the engine was revving full, they let go. The *Flyer* leaped forward, and the edge of the cliff came toward Curtiss at fearful speed. The plane went over and dropped with the sickening feeling of a too fast elevator. G. H. let her fall for an instant, then caught her with the elevating rudder and soared out over the Hudson.

As he banked to the south again, the realization of what that take-off meant came to him. If a plane could get off from that tiny hilltop, it could take off from any fair-sized raised platform. It could take off from *the deck of a battleship*.

Down the broad river he flew in the noon sunshine. A hundred boats greeted him with whistles he could not hear for the noise of his motor, but he could see the white steam at their stacks. Riverside Drive was black with people, and he could see others like swarming bees on the tops of the tall buildings. All New York was cheering him on the last thrilling lap of his hundred-and-fifty-mile flight.

A hundred and fifty miles across country, between mountains, over cities. Less than a year ago he had won a leg on the *Scientific American* Trophy by flying twenty-four miles in a circle. Less than two years ago the *June Bug* had fluttered the measured kilometer of the first leg. This last leg was, in truth, encased in seven-times-seven-league boots.

The gusts from the towers of Manhattan tossed Curtiss about, but it was a children's game compared with the giants of the river. Liberty held up her torch to him, and there was Governor's Island waiting in the bay. He never saw a lovelier sight than the flat, sandy parade ground that was his journey's end.

Then he was down and the bands were playing and the people crowding around. He couldn't hear the music or the congratulations for the humming in his ears. So he nodded and smiled and tried to make sense for the reporters. Then the ferry and the ride through the cheering streets to the *World* Building, where the biggest crowd of all roared itself hoarse. Lena met him there with, "Glenn, you did splendidly."

Preoccupied, he answered, "You bet."

It wasn't conceit, just the logical acknowledgment of an obvious fact.

He had indeed done well.

CHAPTER TWENTY

WINGS FOR THE NAVY

IN FIVE HOURS ON that Sunday morning the whole attitude of the people of America toward Curtiss changed. He was up on a higher pedestal than he had been after the Gordon Bennett Cup. Forgotten were the diatribes and the phrases about flying pirates who couldn't even fly. He had made the greatest flight ever attempted: more than a hundred and fifty miles across country in two hours and forty-six minutes of flying time, at an average speed of fifty-four miles per hour. Nothing like it had been done in Europe or anywhere else. America once more took the lead in the air, and America was grateful.

The newspapers, which yesterday had attacked him, yelled his praises in their biggest type; the people who had whispered and sneered crowded up to shake his hand. There were banquets and speeches and cheering crowds. There was the *Scientific American* Trophy, his now to keep. But through all the din Curtiss remained unimpressed. Like all men who have felt the fickleness of popular favor, he mentally had his fingers crossed. But if the acclamations mattered little to him, one thing meant a great deal: the check for ten thousand dollars.

When G. H.'s fingers touched that slip of blue paper, he smiled at last and his eyes glowed with exaltation. This meant something; it meant he could go on.

The ten-thousand-dollar bond was posted, and now quickly to work before some fresh obstacle arose to cross Curtiss' plans.

But first he must have money, for the till was just as empty as ever. It was easy to get now via the exhibition route. The whole country was screaming to see Curtiss fly.

First then a trip to Atlantic City to gather in the five-thousand-dollar prize offered for a fifty-mile flight over the ocean. That was a cinch; just circling a five-mile course above the quiet sea with no tricky air currents to bother him, while beyond the white line of the breakers stood black masses of cheering people. It took less than an hour.

Another flight over Lake Erie, sixty miles from Cleveland to Cedar Point, was more difficult; but Curtiss made it, and flew back the next day in the rain.

Then to stage air meets, with a flying troupe for the sake of diversity. The material was ready to hand. Jack McCurdy had come back to Hammondsport; Bud Mars and Charles F. Willard were there, and a youngster named Eugene B. Ely wanted to take lessons, and after less than an hour in the air became the most skillful of them all.

Curtiss took his aerial circus to Pittsburgh and cleaned up. Then he staged a meet at the Sheepshead Bay Race Track. His new publicity man, Jerome Fanciulli, thought up all sorts of ballyhoo for that. Jack McCurdy received the first wireless message ever sent to a plane on the opening day of the meet, and on another the members of the team took their wives up.

"Is it safe, Glenn?" asked Lena nervously.

"As long as you're with me," answered Glenn. "But promise me you'll never fly with anyone else."

"I promise," Lena said.

Sheepshead Bay was G. H.'s last appearance as an exhibition flyer. He disliked the cheap publicity, but most of all he hated the interruption of his serious work. So he organized the Curtiss Exhibition Company, made Fanciulli its manager, and with a heartfelt sigh of relief, retired from the profession of aerial acrobat to the relative obscurity of scientific accomplishment. This does not mean that he stopped flying. For years he personally tested each new invention; there was no one he could trust so well, and he would risk no life but his own with an untried machine.

There was, however, one more interruption before he could settle down to his main object. This was the Aviation Meet at Belmont Park in October 1910, the return engagement for the Gordon Bennett Cup.

To defend his trophy, Curtiss forsook biplanes and designed a single-surface racer, which was the fastest plane in the world. It was rather like one of his biplanes with the top wing left off, for the motor was mounted high above the single plane and drove a pusher propeller. The Rheims Machine had won at 47.65 miles per hour a year before; the new plane could do over 80 miles per hour.

But the racer never raced. The Aero Club was not fond of Curtiss any more. Even Cortlandt Bishop had turned against him, because of what he considered the Hammondsporter's stupid insistence on exhibition flying. Mr. Bishop did not realize the financial necessity that drove G. H. to a distasteful task. So Curtiss was ignored and the American team consisted of Walter Brookins in the "Baby Wright," John Moissant in a Blériot, and McCurdy in a conventional Curtiss.

The only one of them who stood a chance was Brookins— the Wright racer was really fast. But the engine stopped on the first round of the course, and the little plane dropped like a dead duck in front of the great stands at Belmont and rolled up the homestretch wrapping its tail around its wings. When the dust blew away, Brookins was miraculously intact, but Claude Grahame-White of England, flying a Blériot, had the

Gordon Bennett Cup. Curtiss immediately returned to Hammondsport to resume work on his greatest contribution to aeronautics.

From the moment he landed at Governor's Island, Curtiss had been under the strongest compulsion to fly from water. What had been a dream was now almost an obsession, since he had seen how it could be done. Adding to his determination was the fact that now, when the serious scientists had given way to stunt flyers, the death toll of aviation was rising fast— much too fast. People no longer went to meets to see men fly, but to see them killed. Aviation was becoming just a question of thrills. Curtiss did not want it that way.

He figured that the only method of stopping the aerial Roman holiday was to make flying safe, and the way to do that was to enable men to fly from water.

Then, too, there was his almost mystical belief in the future of naval aviation. Again and again in his newspaper interviews he stressed the helplessness of ships, slow-moving with cumbersome guns, beneath a darting aeroplane. There were many who said that a plane could no more bother a battleship than a mosquito could stop a soldier. But G. H. knew that a mosquito's sting may also be deadly; and, when he thought of what easy targets those boats beneath him in the Hudson would have been, he resolved that America's line of battle should never wallow defenseless under aerial assault, if by his vision he could save them.

So he drew plans for hydroplane floats to be constructed at his factory, and wrote to the Secretary of the Navy, offering to teach without charge any officers who might be sent to him. This was a shrewd move, for even governments can seldom resist getting something for nothing; and, if he could catch a few young officers, he knew he could light the flame of their enthusiasm at his own.

The Secretary bit; and, eventually, Lieutenants Theodore G. Ellyson and John H. Towers were designated to look things over. "Spuds" Ellyson was a happy, freckle-faced, red-headed boy, who loved hot weather, candy, and potatoes—especially potatoes. Jack Towers was a reserved young man with the straight, strong features of a young knight and a tremendous sense of responsibility. They both came to love G. H. and developed an enthusiasm for naval aviation which matched his own.

Government interest in naval aviation was further demonstrated when Captain W. Irving Chambers of the Bureau of Equipment wrote to the Wrights requesting them to attempt to launch one of their planes from a ship. The Wrights wrote back that it was too risky.

Meanwhile Curtiss decided to try it on his own. In conjunction with his new friends on the *World*, he arranged with the Hamburg-America Line to build a launching platform on their liner *Pennsylvania*. Jack McCurdy was to sail out to sea on her and attempt to fly back. This trial never came off because Jack's plane was damaged before the ship sailed.

However, the Navy saw that Curtiss was in earnest and offered him the cruiser *Birmingham* for the experiment. She was sent to Newport News, where a sloping platform was built on her bow according to Curtiss' specifications. Eugene Ely was exhibiting in Baltimore at the time, and his nearness to the scene and his beautiful precision-flying made him the logical choice for the trial.

The Navy set November 13, 1910, as the day for the experiment. With Ely's plane lashed securely to the clumsy platform on her bow, the *Birmingham* steamed out to an anchorage in Hampton Roads. Then Gene and his nervous wife, and the admirals, staff officers, and reporters sat down to wait on the weather.

It was a discouraging day. Heavy clouds rolled in from the ocean, dumping showers of rain on the ship; gusts of wind made the aeroplane shiver in its lashings. Instead of improving, the weather got worse. Toward afternoon a heavy fog began to roll in between the capes.

"Well, I guess that settles it," said one of the older officers, almost with relief.

"It does," agreed Gene Ely. "I'll take off now."

Quickly the tarpaulins were stripped off and the plane backed up until its tail touched the front turret. Ely climbed in and the new sixty-horsepower engine was started. After warming it briefly, he opened the throttle wide while sailors strained against the quivering wings.

Ely took one look at the gray, choppy waves, saw the first strands of the advancing fog whip by the masts. Then he signaled, "Let go."

The little plane shot down the sharply sloping boards. She fell, rather than flew, off the bow, dropping so far that the wheels kissed the wave tops, and skittered over the water like a rising duck. Then she lifted, fighting the gusts, and disappeared swiftly into the mists.

That was the first step, or rather hop, in getting the Navy into the air. It impressed the department into officially accepting Curtiss' offer to train personnel, and Lieutenants Ellyson and Towers were ordered to report for instruction. The Secretary of War accepted a similar invitation.

But as for any concrete expression of faith, such as the purchase of an aeroplane, there was still nothing doing. Captain Chambers was enthusiastic, but the Navy High Command took as much showing as a Missouri mule. "This is all very well,"

was the gist of their comment, "but we can't just sling planes
out over the sea and never get them back. If they could be
landed on a deck now—but, of course, that's impossible."

Curtiss didn't think so, and in San Francisco Bay on January 18, 1911, the full cycle was accomplished.

The cruiser *Pennsylvania* was the scene of the final experiment, and Ely was again the guinea pig. This time the platform
was built on the stern of the big warship. It was one hundred
and twenty feet long from its sharply sloping overhang to the
base of the after turret. Hugh A. Robinson, an old circus man,
designed the arresting gear. It was adapted from one which he
had used to stop his automobile after a loop-the-loop act in the
circus. Twenty-one ropes were stretched across the platform
and raised a few inches above it, by a strip of wood down each
side. At each end of each rope was a fifty-pound bag of sand.
This is essentially the same arresting gear as is used on the great
carriers today, except that the ropes are now steel cables and,
instead of sandbags, the drag is provided by hydraulic cylinders
below the flight deck.

Ely's aeroplane was fitted with three U-shaped hooks, one
behind the front wheel, one under the center, and another at
the tail. Though Curtiss supervised the arrangements, Robinson
had never seen the hooks and Ely had never seen the arresting
gear until hooks and ropes met on the deck of the *Pennsylvania*.

In the end it was a near thing. The *Pennsylvania* was crowded
that morning. Admiral Barry of the Pacific fleet, with his officers and distinguished guests and poor Mrs. Ely, who loved
Gene so much and spent her whole life waiting to see him
killed, stood on the after turret. From the fighting tops, smoke-
stacks, and all parts of the superstructure sailors hung like
swarming bees.

Ely over at the San Francisco Aviation Meet at Camp Selfridge was late getting off; his motor was giving trouble. The tension on the cruiser rose second by second. At the hour set for the trial, she had been lying just right, with her head to the wind. As they waited, the tide changed and the great mass of steel swung inexorably around until the light breeze came over the port quarter.

"Why doesn't he come?" asked Mrs. Ely. "Can't you swing the ship, Admiral, so it will head right?"

"No, Ma'am, there's nothing we can do."

"Then he'll have to land down wind."

"I'm afraid so," said the admiral gravely.

At last they saw the plane, skimming like a gnat just above the surface of the water. It flew close by the *Pennsylvania* and banked steeply astern, one wing almost touching the water. Then it was coming straight for the stern, lower than the level of the deck.

At precisely the right moment Ely cut the engine and pulled back on the elevating rudder. The plane rose slightly and seemed about to make contact. Then the updraft blowing over the end of the platform bounced it six feet into the air. A groan ran through the ship as the plane flew straight at the crowded turret. But the air dropped it just in time. Missing the first ten ropes, the hooks caught the eleventh, and, gathering in the rest, brought the plane up just two feet short of the steel barbette.

When, forty-five minutes later, Ely took off and winged safely back to shore, the aircraft carriers of the future were as good as launched.

Back in December, Curtiss had decided to transfer his operations to the West Coast for the winter, for, with his new obligations to the Army and Navy and his intense determination to fly from water, he could not afford to have his activities literally frozen for four months.

While he was looking for a site for his camp, the Spreckels Company offered him North Island, near San Diego. The moment he saw the place G. H. said, "This is it."

The island was an absolutely barren waste about four miles long by two wide, covered with rank scrub and populated by enough jack rabbits to make an Australian feel perfectly at home. There were two abandoned buildings on it, a dilapidated cottage and a ruined boxing arena. But it was as flat as a folded opera hat, and its golden beaches running down to the shallow water of Spanish Bight were just the ticket for handling hydro-aeroplanes.

They fixed the cottage up as living quarters for the men. G. H. and Lena stayed at the Coronado Beach Hotel—that is, Lena stayed there and her husband came over when he could tear himself away. The Aero Club of San Diego contributed two hangars, and a tent was pitched on the beach for the hydros. Rough runways were cleared through the undergrowth.

It was here that Curtiss was joined by Hugh Robinson, who soon became his right-hand man on the Coast. As a flyer, Hugh was a natural; he already had had some experience with a monoplane of his own design that didn't fly so well. In addition, he was mighty handy at devising contraptions as evidenced by his arresting gear for the shore-to-ship experiment.

As soon as they were installed on the island, Damon Merrill arrived from Hammondsport with an assortment of fish-shaped floats, and experiments began.

G. H. was sitting at the controls of his new experimental machine. It was the regulation exhibition job with a single-surface elevating rudder and the powerful new sixty-horse-power motor. But it rode on the surface of San Diego Bay on one of those fish-shaped floats. Mechanics knee-deep in water cranked up the engine. Curtiss opened the throttle and plowed off across Spanish Bight.

The plane handled badly on the water, for the float alternately skittered and dove. Nevertheless, after getting the feel of it, Curtiss decided to try a take-off.

Heading into the wind, he opened the engine wide, and the plane plunged forward. Soon it was tearing along at forty-five miles per hour, with great sheets of spray flying over it; G. H. was almost blinded by the stinging drops. Now he judged he had flying speed, and pulled back on the control. The bow rose, but the stern remained glued to the water. He knew something of the sensation of a fly trying to take off from flypaper.

G. H. tried every trick he knew to break the grip of the water. He rocked the plane and rolled it, he skidded it about with the rudder. Nothing did any good.

At last he was forced to return unhappily to the dock.

"This float's no good," he said grimly. "We'll have to try another."

They tried another and still another; forty or fifty variations on the floats from Hammondsport. The plane was hauled out of the water a dozen times a day. To make it easier to drag it over the soft sand, they improvised a dolly out of two beer barrels with an iron pipe as an axle. The dolly worked well, but the floats didn't work at all.

Finally Curtiss developed a design for converting one of the other machines into a tractor biplane with the engine and propeller in front and all the controls behind.

"If we can't push ourselves off," he said, "perhaps we can pull ourselves out."

He had also designed a new pontoon.

"Where can we get this float built?" he asked Hugh Robinson.

"I know a feller called Gillmore, who has a little boat works in San Diego," said Hugh. "He could do the job."

They took the drawings to William Gillmore, who allowed that he could manage it and made a couple of excellent suggestions of his own. The float was scow-shaped, with an upward curve in front and a down curve behind. It was made of very thin spruce and was 14 feet long by 2 feet wide and 14 feet deep. Underneath were three small steel runners to protect the delicate shell from contact with the bottom.

The float was ready before the tractor plane, so G. H. decided, without much hope, to give it a whirl on the standard machine. It was fastened on by steel bars, and in addition, the plane had as many auxiliary gadgets as a college boy's Ford. There were wooden paddles trailing back at an angle from the wing tips to keep them from dipping in the water, for the narrow pontoon was very unstable. Inflated inner tubes were bunched under the wings as a secondary flotation gear. There was a spray shield and a little planing board in front of the float.

G. H. was pretty pessimistic about the whole thing as he once again headed across Spanish Bight on the morning of January 26, 1911. Robert Bruce's spider had made it on the seventh try, but this was nearer Curtiss' seventieth attempt.

As the plane gained speed, the float rose to the surface of the water. The little waves spanked hard against its thin bottom. Bounce, bounce, bang, bounce. It skipped, it leaped, it danced from wave to wave, and then it danced itself right into the air.

Three times G. H. landed and took off to make sure it was no fluke. Then, his face split by a broad grin, he headed for the beach where the boys were turning handsprings of triumph.

Curtiss didn't know why this particular float had worked, and for the moment he didn't care. It was enough that he had accomplished his ultimate object; for the first time an aeroplane had taken off from and landed safely on water.

For a couple of weeks more he experimented and improved, getting rid of unnecessary gadgets. Then he was ready for the Navy. The Secretary had been kind but distant on the shore-to-ship-to-shore flight. He had pointed out that if they built platforms all over their ships, they wouldn't be much use in battle. The Navy wanted a seaplane. They were going to get it.

One day in February, G. H. telephoned to Captain Pond of the *Pennsylvania*, which was now in San Diego, that he was going to pay him a visit. "Get a crane ready to haul me aboard," he said.

For the attempt he used the new tractor plane. A little before noon, he took off from Spanish Bight and winged out across the sparkling blue water. The wind from the propeller bothered him, so that he couldn't appreciate the scenery nor be too sure where he was going, and he mentally resolved to abandon tractors though he thought he would keep all controls in the rear. He managed to spot the four stacks of the cruiser as she swung at her anchorage, and landed neatly alongside.

He taxied in close, and sailors rigged a sling around the plane. With G. H. clinging to the steel cable above the wings, the machine was hoisted aboard.

After a rollicking lunch at which everybody congratulated everybody else—as well they might—the hydro-aeroplane was lowered over the side, and Curtiss took off with the whole crew, from the captain on the bridge to the black-faced stokers peering through portholes, cheering wildly.

The inertia of the Navy Department finally broke down. They actually ordered an aeroplane.

On January 17, 1911, the day before Ely's landing on the deck of the *Pennsylvania*, the first military flying school in America was opened on North Island. Captain Paul W. Beck and Lieutenants John C. Walker, Jr., and G. E. M. Kelly were chosen by the Army, and Ellyson represented the Navy.

In the school machines a low-power four-cylinder engine was used. For beginners the throttle was soldered so that it could be opened only a little way. The student was then allowed to taxi slowly up and down the runways until he gained familiarity with the controls. As his taxiing improved, he was given more and more throttle until he finally was allowed to make short straight hops. Only after he had demonstrated real skill in these was he allowed to try a turn.

This process of instruction was aptly called "grass-cutting," for the edges of the propellers cut the tall grasses of the inadequately cleared runways, and as the planes bumbled along they looked like mowing machines. The tough grass nicked the wooden blades so badly that Curtiss was obliged to fit them with steel edges at the tips.

All the first students soon became accomplished pilots. Came the day when G. H. turned Ellyson loose on his precious hydro-aeroplane. Spuds took the machine off perfectly, and after an easy flight around the harbor set her lightly down on the water. He taxied in with a broad grin on his freckled face.

"Nothing to it," he declared proudly.

The other boys were not going to let him get away with any such cocky attitude. Before Spuds knew what was happening, they dragged him out of the plane and heaved him into the waters of Spanish Bight.

So began another Navy tradition, and in memory of Spuds, every Naval aviator is ducked after his first solo.

G. H. hadn't been so happy in years as he was at North

Island. He was free from the necessities of giving exhibitions and worrying about commercial matters, and was able to concentrate on the things he really cared for. With all the eager young officers working and playing, and the excitement of perfecting new inventions, it was almost like Aerial Experiment over again. G. H.'s mind was bursting with new ideas.

He had hardly landed from his flight to the *Pennsylvania* before he started work on his next objective, an "amphibious" plane. To begin with, he put wheels under the hydro, but since they were rigidly attached, their drag in the water kept the plane from taking off. With Hugh Robinson and Damon Merrill, G. H. devised a method of mounting the wheels on jointed braces so they could be pulled up out of the way for water or lowered for a ground landing. Thus the first retractable landing gear—all fast planes have them today—made possible the first amphibian.

G. H. took it off from Spanish Bight, pushed down the wheels, and landed it on North Island. He took off again, pulled them up and set down in the bay. Then he had a good idea.

With a delighted grin on his face he took off again and headed for Coronado. He landed on the smooth sand in front of the great Coronado Beach Hotel. People came running in bathing suits to crowd around this aerial curiosity. Lena dashed out of the hotel and pushed through the throng.

"What on earth are you doing, Glenn?" she demanded.

"I just felt like dropping in for lunch with you," he answered.

"Well, what have you got there?"

"That," said Glenn proudly, "is the *Triad*. It goes on land, sea, or in the air."

The *Triad* was the first plane purchased by the United States Navy. Before they took possession, Curtiss had fitted her with a little device he had just figured out, the dual control. At first this was made with two shoulder yokes, but only one steering wheel, which could be shifted from one pilot to the other. Later two wheels were provided set on a Y-shaped control stick.

Some time later, after the Navy had taken over the *Triad*, Ellyson and Towers made an epic flight down Chesapeake Bay from Annapolis to Buckroe Beach, Virginia, 147 miles in 145 minutes. Ellyson's routine report on the landing they made would take the kinks out of an aborigine's hair:

"After two hours' flying, and having covered 147 miles, the oil gauge seemed to be getting low and we decided to land. This we accomplished in a six-foot surf with a 20-mile wind behind us. I ran the machine high on the beach, coming in at full speed just touching the crests of the waves. Much to our surprise the boat was not injured in the least."

During that first fertile stay at North Island, Curtiss made one more tremendous contribution to aquanautics. Though the hydro-aeroplane now took off perfectly if there was any breeze at all to break up the surface of the water, on a dead still day the pontoons would not break free from a glassy sea. This was embarrassing to say the least. G. H. tried various expedients, but all in vain until one day he said to Damon Merrill, "Maybe if we cut the under section away at the rear it would make it easier for the pontoon to break loose from the suction that holds us down."

"As how?" asked Damon.

"Like this," said G. H.

He fished an old envelope out of his pocket and sketched rapidly:

And that, my friends, was the hydroplane step, on which everything from racing outboards to Atlantic Clippers skim over the surface of the water.

CHAPTER TWENTY-ONE

THE 13 TEAM

THE YEAR 1911 WAS the golden age of exhibition flying. In that single year the rich cream was taken right off the top of the financial bottle. Virtually everybody who was willing to pay to see an aeroplane fly had his chance. The Curtiss Exhibition Company alone grossed nearly a million dollars.

But it was a dismal year in the annals of aviation, for with the wild young "birdmen" diving and swooping all over the country, the death toll mounted with terrific speed. But as long as the rich prospect of making a thousand dollars or more a day held, hundreds of reckless young men rushed to fill the gaps. And they had great fun—while they lasted.

The first spectacular flight of 1911 was Jack McCurdy's try for the five-thousand-dollar prize offered by the *Havana Post* for a flight from Key West to Havana. In a Curtiss plane, with United States destroyers strung out underneath, McCurdy set out on the ninety-eight-mile flight early in the morning of January 30. His own vivid words draw a brilliant picture of the scene:

"I rose to one thousand feet and took the course. Ahead of me was a continuous mirage, the sea instead of being a horizontal plane below had the appearance of a huge vertical picture on which the funnel tops of the destroyers appeared like black spots. . . ."

As McCurdy passed over each destroyer in turn, it cracked

on full speed and followed, so he was never out of reach of rescue. And just at the end he needed it. The white buildings and green parks of Havana were in sight and guns on the shell-scarred battlements of Morro Castle were ready to salute him when Jack's motor failed. He coasted down the air to a landing on the silky sea just two miles short of his goal.

The improvised pontoons on his plane worked perfectly; the last destroyer came foaming up, and Jack was brought ashore without even wetting his feet, to give an exhibition flight that afternoon before wildly cheering Cubans at the Havana Aviation Meet. The *Havana Post*, generously refusing to stand on technicalities, paid over the prize.

With the coming of spring, the country went exhibition mad. Both the Wright and Curtiss camps had their exhibition teams, but because of the speed and maneuverability of the Curtiss machines, his company far outstripped their old rivals.

When Curtiss got back to Hammondsport in April, he found his flying school all ready to begin operations. Ellyson and Towers were there ahead of him and, with an enterprising young man named Beckwith Havens, were practicing on an old exhibition plane which they had reconditioned.

As soon as G. H. arrived, the students began to pour in. Charles C. Witmer, who had had instruction at North Island, came on with him, as did Mr. and Mrs. W. C. Atwater. Other young daredevils, eager for gold and glory and hang the consequence, came clamoring for instruction. Most of them thought they could just take a plane and go up, and it was hard to hold them to the prescribed course of four hours of grass-cutting and four hours of short hops. Some of them, like Becky Havens, couldn't be held and were pilots after their first flight.

Link Beachey, Captain Baldwin's young dirigible pilot, was one of the best, and the old captain himself had regretfully forsaken lighter-than-air to get aboard the new bandwagon. He designed an excellent plane with a tubular steel frame. Its wings were covered with red gutta-percha, and he christened it the *Red Devil*. But, though his plane was a success, the captain never liked it. He would say to anyone who would listen, "These things are just toys, but my dirigible was a real ship."

Nor did the captain ever learn to fly a plane well. In spite of his long experience at high altitudes, he simply could not force himself to take one up more than a few feet. One day, at the old Mineola course, he said to Curtiss, "I'm going to go up if it kills me. Just watch my altitude."

G. H. watched while the captain took off and circled low around the flagged poles that were still left over from the *Scientific American* trial. On the second round his plane rose perhaps fifty feet in the air and then landed.

"What went wrong, Uncle Tom?" asked G. H. grinning broadly.

The captain mopped his forehead with the inevitable bandana.

"G. H., I tried," he said. "I shut my eyes and pulled back on that wheel, and I kept going up until I thought I was a thousand feet high. Then I opened one eye and there was the flag on that goldarned fishpole just level with me."

The captain gathered together a group of youngsters and, taking two *Red Devils*, went careering around the Orient. From Japan to China to India and back, his troupe performed to better "gates" than he had ever dreamed of, and he came home a rich man.

Meanwhile, as fast as a student at Hammondsport was pronounced a pilot, he winged away to gather the gold in the invisible hills of the air.

The Curtiss Exhibition Team of 1911 was probably the

greatest aggregation of skillful and daring pilots ever seen. Jack McCurdy and Eugene Ely; Link Beachey, Charlie Walsh, Eugene Godet, Becky Havens, Jimmy Ward, Cromwell Dixon, Charlie Witmer, Hugh Robinson and several others—thirteen of them in all—"The 13 Team."

Between them they covered the whole country, thrilling vast crowds in all the big and little cities, some of which had never seen man fly and even yet didn't believe he could.

The old pilots—those of them who are left—love to tell stories about that frantic summer; of hostile crowds who shouted, "Fake! Fake!" as they trucked their machines through town, and poured out to the fair grounds or the race course to see them *not* fly; and of those same crowds, when they had beheld the miracle of a man with a couple of fragile wings and a smelly motor playing tag with the clouds, carrying the birdmen back to town on their shoulders, with the local band blaring hoarsely and the torches flaring in the prairie nights.

They talk too of the narrow escapes and the impossible conditions, when they were expected to take off from mere patches of green, from baseball diamonds and quarter-mile tracks. Of bad weather when the crowds howled for a flight, and only stout mechanics swinging struts held them back from wrecking the precious planes and tar-and-feathering the flyers.

They'll describe how the planes got wrecked and were patched up again with baling wire and auto tape and a patch of anything handy on the wings, or perhaps a curving branch from a tree to replace a broken rib.

It was a mad scramble for glory and money, but the glory mattered most. The big headlines in the local papers, the pictures and high-sounding nicknames—like Becky Havens' "The Condor of the Clouds"—and the ardent fans.

As the summer wore on they pulled all sorts of publicity

stunts to whip up enthusiasm. They landed in city streets and they staged aerial bombings. Hugh Robinson once bombarded a mock fort with oranges from a bag tied around his neck. He realized that he could get more accuracy by diving straight at the target, and so established his claim to be the inventor of dive bombing. Nearly all the oranges hit their mark, but one went wild and a soldier tried to catch it. It burst from the impact and the doughboy went to the hospital to have the seeds picked out of his face.

Carrying the mail was another popular stunt. The first official air mail was carried three miles from Nassau Boulevard to Mineola in September 1911, by Earle Ovington. After that everybody tried it, for this was clearly recognized as a great function of aviation.

But beyond those publicity stunts was always the pressure for authentic thrills, and the flyers took ever more desperate chances to gratify their public. They swooped up to the clouds and power-dove to within a few feet of the ground. They twisted and racked their fragile machines beyond any intention of the designers. And the crowds howled for more thrills.

It couldn't last and it didn't last, but in that brief summer more young men died in the air than in all the years before. The loss which saddened Curtiss most was that of Lieutenant Kelly, for he was one of that first group of Army flyers who had been such good companions on North Island; and he was not killed stunting, but in the performance of his duty.

Another terrible blow was the death of Gene Ely at Macon, Georgia, in October. To gratify the thrill-mad crowd, Gene did one of his spectacular power dives from one thousand feet. As the plane shot earthward like a falcon diving on its prey, thousands watched for the spectacular last-minute pull out. It never came. Straight as a shell to the target the plane plunged vertically into the ground, literally burying its pilot six feet below the surface of the earth.

Nothing could have been worse for aviation than the terrible accidents of 1911. The public did not stop to think that these were the result of deliberate recklessness, but assumed that aeroplanes were too dangerous to be useful. They rejected the idea of flying as anything but a desperate gamble with life; and, as a consequence, American aviation began to fall farther and farther behind European developments.

Even in 1910 we had slipped, as shown by the fact that at the end of that year there were 353 licensed pilots in France, 46 in Germany, 45 in England, and only 26 in America. In 1911, when the only way to earn money by flying in America was the "Death-Defying Dive," Europe was offering a total of nearly a million dollars for long-distance flights, such as Paris-Madrid, Paris-Rome, and the Circuit European, which encouraged the serious and useful development of the aeroplane.

Then, too, the European governments appropriated millions of dollars for military aviation, and plane builders could look forward to a chance for some return on their investments and labor.

Doctor Bell, returning from a year's trip around the world—with scientific precision he arrived on the exact anniversary of his departure—sadly stated that virtually every great country had surpassed America in the field of aviation.

In contrast to the millions spent abroad, the United States Army bought three aeroplanes—one Wright and two Curtiss in the spring of 1911. The Navy set up a Department of Aeronautics under Captain Chambers, and Congress munificently appropriated twenty-five thousand dollars for the purchase of aeroplanes. At that, the Navy Department did not see how it could spend so large a sum profitably and returned a considerable portion of it to the Treasury.

In spite of government inertia, Curtiss kept on working for naval aviation. All the experiments he made at the request of the government were at his own expense. After he had spent fifteen or twenty thousand dollars conducting the experiments, the Navy would reward him by buying a plane for six thousand dollars which cost seven thousand dollars to build. It was bad finance, but magnificent patriotism. Single-handed Curtiss kept American naval aviation in the lead.

That summer he developed an eighty-horsepower water-cooled V-8 engine, which was the first of his famous O motors. Its direct descendant, the OX-5, was the mainstay of American aviation during World War I.

Curtiss' one aeroplane crash led to another innovation. He took one of the hydros out for a spin. At the take-off he noticed that it acted sluggishly, and as he maneuvered over the lake it flew like a lame duck. G. H. decided to land to see what was the matter. He put the plane into a glide. The glide changed to a dive, which grew steeper and steeper. Frantically he pulled back on the control, with no effect. The plane dove right into the lake.

Some of the boys pulled G. H. sputtering from the water. Just before he hit he had guessed the trouble. The pontoon had sprung a leak and was half full of water, which had all rushed to the forward end when he started his glide.

Without even changing his dripping clothes he drove to the factory and ordered Henry Kleckler to build compartments in all the floats. That was one accident which could not happen again.

With Spuds Ellyson, Curtiss worked out a launching device

to be used for flying a hydro-aeroplane from the deck of a
ship. A steel cable was run down the hillside at Hammondsport
toward the lake and a groove was cut in the float of a hydro
to fit it. Two lighter wires were used to balance the wings. In
September, Spuds took his place at the controls of a plane
balanced precariously on the cable. The engine was started
and the plane screeched down the wires and soared out over
the water.

Late in the year, Ellyson, with the advice of Curtiss and
some naval engineers, designed and tested a true launching
catapult.

Though his labors for the Navy brought him only financial
loss, Curtiss began to receive the honors which were his due.
On June 8, 1911, the Aero Club of America, under authority
of the *Fédération Aéronautique Internationale* granted him
Pilot's License No. 1. After much discussion it had been decided that, since he had made a *public* flight before the
Wrights, he was entitled to this unique distinction.

In December, the invention of the hydro-aeroplane brought
him the Collier Trophy for "the greatest accomplishment in
aviation during the year." And just before the New Year came
he was presented with the Gold Medal of the Aero Club for
"the greatest advance in aviation in 1911."

"It's worth all the trouble and worry, isn't it, Lena?" he
said to her that night as he fondled the golden disk.

"If it is to you, Glenn, it is to me," she answered. "But
couldn't you take things a little bit easier now?"

"No," answered Glenn. "The Navy have asked me to give
them something more, a real boat that flies, and I'm going to."

He looked at the medal again.

"Maybe they'll have to give me another of these next year,"
he said. "It would be kind of fun to have a pair."

CHAPTER TWENTY-TWO

A BOAT THAT FLIES

AT FIRST GLANCE IT would not seem too difficult to adapt a hydro-aeroplane into a flying boat, but Curtiss, as he knew he would, found many problems to solve. In the first attempt the ordinary flat-bottomed pontoon was used. It was coupled close to the wings, and the engine and passengers placed on it. A tail was built up from the stern. It didn't work.

The flat hull would not rise from the water, and the engine got so wet that it would not function properly. So the engine was raised again, the passengers were partially enclosed by a cowling of canvas, and a small lifting surface added at the bow. This didn't work either.

It took all that winter at North Island to get the flying boat to fly. Curtiss was short-handed, for Hugh Robinson was off demonstrating hydros in Europe and Ellyson had injured himself. Towers was on hand, and did much of the test flying. G. H. came to rely heavily on Gillmore, the boat builder from San Diego. In fact, so valuable did he become that Curtiss persuaded him to give up his business and join the Curtiss Company.

The hydroplane step had been discontinued on the pontoons because it made them instable, but something drastic had to be done for the boat.

"We'll try the step," G. H. decided.

The hull was rebuilt accordingly, and vertical surfaces were added above the wings to correct a possible pendulum swing, due to the center of gravity being so far below the center of pressure. With these improvements the boat made a few flukey flights at North Island, but still it could not be depended on to take off. G. H. saw that he would have to figure something out.

When he got back to Hammondsport, he did. Copper vent tubes were run through the hull to the break of the step. These permitted air to flow in and dissipate the vacuum suction which glued the boat to the water. From the lake, whether it was rough or glassy-smooth, the machine now rose every time. The flying boat of the Navy's dreams was an accomplished fact.

Meanwhile, things were going a little better financially for the Curtiss Company. The Army had bought a whole squadron of Curtiss planes, which were sent to the troubled Mexican border, where Major Foulois had already proved the value of aerial reconnaisance by patrolling up and down in the Army's original Wright, now long outdated and rattling with age.

The Navy snapped up the flying boat, but allowed it to remain at Hammondsport for experimental work. Even more encouraging, orders began to come in for hydros from Europe!

Oddly enough, the thing that sold the Europeans on Curtiss hydros was a terrible crash Hugh Robinson had in the harbor at Monte Carlo. Not all his skill in demonstrating his machines or the trophies he won produced results like that almost-fatal mishap.

Robinson had set up a flying school with Louis Paulhan at Juan-Les-Pins on the French Riviera. Business was slow. The Europeans were far from convinced that there was anything to this business of flying over water. Such machines as they had were mostly land planes fitted with pirated adaptations of Curtiss pontoons. Sometimes they got up and more times they didn't, and even when they did, they staggered around in the air like domestic ducks. The aviators would not even come to see what Hugh could do.

Then came the first Hydro-Aeroplane Meet at Monte Carlo. Robinson flew rings around his clumsy competitors and easily carried off the Monte Carlo Cup.

One day when he was making a practice flight, his plane inexplicably went out of control. With the throttle wide open, it dove straight at the deceptively gentle surface of the harbor. At twenty-five feet Hugh gave up fighting the wheel and jumped. He struck the water with such force that it plucked his clothes off as an expert might strip a chicken.

Down he went until, as he said himself, "I heard sweet music and gongs."

But he came up again sufficiently intact to swim ashore. The plane in his descriptive phrase, "looked like a shredded-wheat biscuit."

The Europeans figured that if a man could have a wreck like that and survive, water flying must be a lot safer than over land. Business boomed at Juan-Les-Pins, and orders flashed across the sea to Hammondsport.

G. H., back from the Coast, found that the flying school had more business than it could handle. A variegated group was this Curtiss class of 1912. The students came from all over the map. There were wild young Russian officers in their white uniforms and solemn, bespectacled Japanese. An enterprising young man came from China, and India sent Mohun Sing. Lieutenant Parla of Cuba and Rafael Marti of Puerto Rico arrived, and there were Frenchmen and Germans, a Dutchman and a Polish baron. Nearly all the nations of Europe were represented.

The little country town by Lake Keuka became as cosmopolitan as Shepheard's Hotel in Cairo, and the Hammondsporters loved it. The houses of the wine magnates were wide open to the dashing young students, and with champagne at six dollars a dozen there was no reason for anyone, whether invited out or not, to go thirsty. Most of the flyers boarded at Lulu Mott's big house, where a room and all of Lulu's delicious food that a man could eat cost five dollars a week.

National temperaments were strikingly evident even in this microcosm of the greater world. The Russians, for instance, ran true to Muscovite form. They were hilarious and moody by turn. For a few days they would work with terrific enthusiasm, and for a week they would do nothing at all.

In contrast, the Japanese were horribly in earnest. Aviation in the Mikado's realm had gotten off to a dismal start, which hardly foreshadowed its present efficiency. In 1910, Captain Hino attempted to fly before the Emperor on the parade ground at Tokyo. He reached an altitude of twenty-five feet, lost his head, control of the plane, and a lot of "face." He crashed almost at divinity's feet.

The trouble with the Japanese students was their fanatic fatalism. They didn't mind dying in the least, and they flew that way. The instructors spent a great deal of energy trying to convince them that a live pilot was of more use to the Mikado than a dead one.

Kondo, a civilian Japanese pilot, was killed trying a machine that Charlie Kirkham of Bath had built with a revolutionary control, which consisted of a single stick to operate ailerons and elevating rudder. Poor Kondo got confused and spun in.

In all the years of flying, it was the first fatality at Hammondsport. G. H. was terribly upset, and the whole Curtiss camp was saddened. The Japanese took the death of their

comrade more philosophically. They took his body to Rochester to be cremated and brought the ashes back with them. In
his little bronze vase, poor Kondo waited on the mantelpiece
of their room until they were ready to return to Japan.

Besides the foreigners, a great many Americans came to the
school. There were fresh relays of Army officers, and Lieutenants Bellinger, Callahan and Richardson from the Navy. Ellyson and Towers were there and many more of the alumni, like
Becky Havens and Charlie Hamilton, came back.

G. H. was very pleased with the way things were going.
The men of this new class were not like the professional daredevils of yesteryear. They were learning to fly with the idea
of getting somewhere. He had reason to hope that aviation
was beginning to grow up.

The school was such a success that Curtiss went to Florida
to open a winter school at Palm Beach. It was his first visit to
the extreme South and he loved it.

"Someday," he said, "when time no longer means so much
to me, I'm coming here to live."

He returned North to receive the Gold Medal of the Aero
Club for the second time. He had earned his matching pair.

More than any of his material triumphs, a peculiarly personal thing made the summer of 1912 memorable for G. H.—
Lena gave him a fine, strong baby boy.

"He must be called Glenn," she said.

"Why?" asked her husband. "I never liked my name much."

"But you have made it honored all over the world," said
Lena, and added in her sweet firm way, which G. H. had long
ago learned it was useless to combat; "I want him to be exactly
like his father, my Baby Glenn."

Lena and G. H. and Baby Glenn went out to San Diego.
In his winter quarters at North Island, Curtiss took stock of

the situation. The schools were doing well; government purchases were far below what they should have been, but they were improving. His greatest disappointment was that so far he had not sold a boat or hydro to a single private individual in America.

Back in June he had expressed his hopes that this new, safe way of flying would attract genuine sportsman pilots. In announcing the flying boat he said, "Here is a flying vehicle as nearly absolutely safe as any fast vehicle can be. It rides on the water at fifty miles an hour and flies at more than sixty."

That he was not exaggerating is shown by the astonishing fact that nobody was ever killed by one of those early Curtiss flying boats.

Still they had not caught the fancy of the public, and G. H. set to work to remedy that. The new F boats of 1913 were the most luxurious vehicles that had ever mounted the air. They had V-bottomed hulls of fine mahogany, polished so brightly that a man could shave by his reflection in them. There were softly cushioned seats and the passengers were completely protected from spray. In fact, they were as smart and comfortable as any speedboat of the time. And they brought results.

Harold F. McCormick of International Harvester sent word to G. H. that he was interested, and Curtiss dashed back from the Coast to make the deal. He designed a special job for McCormick to use as a commuter from his country place to Chicago. Charlie Witmer had just returned from delivering an order of hydros to the Russians at Sevastopol in the Crimea, and McCormick hired him as pilot.

Charlie was very glad to get the job. He had been pretty disgusted, for the Curtiss Aeroplane Company were, as usual, short of cash and could not pay him the five thousand dollars they owed him for his services. Grumbling, he settled for twenty-five hundred dollars in cash and twenty-five hundred in stock. He peddled the stock all over camp, finally offering it for two hundred and fifty dollars. There were no takers.

When Charlie returned from his next trip to Russia during World War I, his incredulous eyes read a Stock Exchange quotation on his despised certificates which showed them to be worth seventy-five thousand dollars.

McCormick, with Witmer, flying all over Lake Michigan, was a wonderful advertisement, and real sportsmen began to follow his lead. Jack Vilas, William Thaw, III, Marshall Reid, G. M. Heckscher, George Von Utassy, and J. B. R. Verplanck all ordered boats.

The class of 1913 at Hammondsport was just what Curtiss wanted. In addition to the sportsmen pilots, there was an unusually large complement of Army and Navy flyers. In fact, the Navy erected their own hangar down by the lake, and operated a sort of Inland Naval Base.

The students led a pleasant life. Four hours of practice in the early morning. Then it was time for a late breakfast. Bill Thaw would drive his sporty Fiat back to Lulu Mott's with students hanging on it like monkeys on a tree. During the afternoon there was instruction, for those who were really serious, in the Curtiss engine factory or the aeroplane assembly shed. From 4 P.M. until dark there was more flying and then back to Lulu's for a big dinner of pork chops, fried potatoes, and home-made pie.

After dinner they usually went to Smellie's shooting gallery and bowling alley, or dated delighted Hammondsport girls for a trip to Mrs. Young's dance pavilion way down on the shore of the lake.

The only student fatality which ever marred the idyllic life was that of popular young Fred Gardiner. He was tremendously keen to get his pilot's license and was almost frantic with excitement the day he took his test. Right in the middle of it his plane inexplicably crashed in the lake. An autopsy performed on his body showed that the excitement had been too much for his heart. He was dead before he hit the water.

The boats were coming out of the factory fast now, and various publicity stunts were pulled to show their usefulness, in which G. H. so firmly believed. One gag in particular had a curious sequel.

Doctor Phillias Alden, who had loaned the electrical apparatus for the first motorcycle, was still a red-hot sport. He suggested that he get one of his patients down the lake to phone for him, and that he be taken to the call in a Curtiss boat, thus becoming the first flying doctor. G. H. jumped at the idea and the trial was set for a certain Sunday.

In the morning Doctor Alden arrived, primed for the adventure. G. H. dashed his hopes.

"Look at the weather," he said, pointing to the rain squalls sweeping over the white-capped surface of Lake Keuka. "You can't fly today."

"I thought your boats were good for practically any weather," objected Alden.

"They are, Doc," said G. H. "But it's no use sticking your neck out. Stay for lunch anyhow."

The doctor stayed, and during the meal he was called to the telephone. He came back with a strange light in his eyes.

"Jim Calahan, down the lake, fell off the roof of his barn. Mrs. C. thinks he broke his hip. If I don't reach him quickly, he may die. Get out your boat, G. H. This is the real thing."

Hastily a flying boat was launched in the choppy waves. Hugh Robinson took the controls and Doctor Alden splashed through the shallow water to climb aboard. Off they went through the driving rain, skipping and pounding over the rough water, with sheets of spray making the machine seem more like a submarine than an aeroplane.

Conditions were so bad that Hugh never did dare to take the boat into the air. Nevertheless Doctor Alden reached his patient faster than he could have by any other means, and Jim Calahan was saved to climb on other barns.

Another triumph for Curtiss boats that summer was the Great Lakes Cruise, a thousand-mile race from Chicago to Detroit via Michigan City, Muskegon, Mackinac, Port Huron, and many small intermediate towns. Prizes totaling fifteen thousand dollars were offered and all kinds of seaplanes and flying boats were entered.

Becky Havens and Verplanck were the white hopes of the Curtiss camp, and they justified that confidence by leading all the way, through thunder storms and gales, to win easily.

In September 1913 G. H. and Lena sailed on the *Imperator* with Baby Glenn for a quick swing through Europe. In spite of the success of the flying boat, orders were coming in too slowly. Judge Hazel, undaunted by one reversal in the higher courts, had handed down another of his sweeping decisions in favor of the Wright company. Wilbur had died of typhoid fever in 1911, but Orville carried on the effort to put Curtiss out of business.

Anyone who purchased a plane from the Wright company bought a brass tag, which permitted him to operate under the Wright patents as long as he was a good boy and obeyed the rules. An aeroplane was thrown in. W. Starling Burgess, who started an aeroplane company, testified that his agreement with Wright forbade him even to put Curtiss motors in his machines.

But the adverse decision, which was, of course, appealed, did not trouble G. H. so much as governmental parsimony. The Army and Navy would not buy more than half a dozen planes a year, so he determined to see if he could get some business from the lavish powers of Europe.

If America failed to furnish much money to the struggling Curtiss company, she continued to shower honors on its owner. Late in 1913 Curtiss was given the Langley Medal, inaugurated in 1908 at the suggestion of Doctor Bell, and presented at that time to the Wrights. No achievement in aviation had been deemed worthy of it since then, until it was voted to Curtiss for his invention of the hydro-aeroplane and the flying boat.

CHAPTER TWENTY-THREE

TRANSATLANTIC

WHILE CURTISS WAS STILL in Europe he received a piece of very bad news and made a most fortunate acquaintance. In Russia a cable arrived telling him that Link Beachey had had a peculiar and terrible accident. He had been stunting at Hammondsport for the Hildreth girls, who were watching him from the roof of the Navy hangar. For once he had called it too close. In a terrific power dive he knocked Ruth Hildreth off the roof of the hangar, killing her instantly. Her sister was badly injured and Link was in a critical condition.

The cable decided G. H. to cut short his trip and head straight for home. He did stop in England for a few days to demonstrate his boat. In London he met Captain Ernest Bass, the adventurous son of a rich manufacturer, and Lieutenant John C. Porte. Lieutenant Porte had lately been retired from the Royal Navy, having contracted tuberculosis in the Submarine Service. Although flying was considered anything but healthy, the young officer took it up "for his health." He expected to die anyway and he hated the idea of waiting around for it to happen.

G. H. took his new friends down to Shoreham to see him demonstrate a flying boat. After watching one flight, Porte took the controls and handled the machine with great skill. That evening he was in a state of high enthusiasm.

"Why don't you build one of these things capable of flying

the ocean, and have a go at the ten-thousand-pound prize the *Daily Mail* has put up?" he asked. "I'll fly it for you."

G. H.'s eyes lighted, but he shook his head.

"I'm afraid I can't do it," he said.

"You mean it's impossible to get the distance?" asked Porte.

"No," said Curtiss. "I could build the ship all right, but it would cost an awful lot of money, and I just haven't got it."

"I know Rodman Wanamaker very well," remarked Bass. "I'll bet he'd finance it."

So the great project for a flight across the ocean was born.

Curtiss came home with his head filled with plans, which were soon translated into preliminary drawings. Careful calculations were made as to the weight of fuel and oil which would be necessary to drive the two engines, with which the big flying boat was to be powered, over the 1,140 miles of ocean, which was to be the longest jump—from Newfoundland to the Azores. These motors were to be the latest development of the Curtiss company—the OX. The first one had unexpectedly developed ninety-five horsepower when it was only designed to produce eighty horsepower, so it was referred to as $O \neq$, later corrupted to OX.

Rodman Wanamaker was completely sold on the idea of a transatlantic flight and signed a contract to purchase the *America* for fifty thousand dollars, provided she was able to lift the calculated load from the water. With plans well under way for her construction, G. H. prepared to commute back to Europe to wind up the unfinished business he had left because of the Beachey cable.

If America was a famine for aeroplane builders, Europe was a feast. Appropriations of the great powers for military and naval aviation were as follows: France, $7,400,000; Russia, $5,000,000; Germany, $2,500,000; Great Britain and Italy, each $2,000,000. Besides the publicly announced figures, each of the competing nations in the great armament race had special secret funds which were destined to be used for the same purpose. To meet these stupendous sums our Congress had appropriated $125,000.

In addition to establishing agencies in France, Russia, and England, and securing orders, Curtiss had another purpose in this trip. France had offered a prize of one hundred thousand dollars for an automatically safe aeroplane. G. H. thought that a young friend of his might win it.

Elmer Sperry, Jr., looked like an idealized statue of Abraham Lincoln. He had arrived in Hammondsport in 1913 with a fixed idea which he pursued as unswervingly as though a miniature gyroscope were revolving in his brain. It was the automatic control of an aeroplane by the use of one of those extraordinary pairs of whirling wheels, which refuses to be turned from its set course.

G. H. had helped him in his early experiments, and by December the machine was definitely practicable. So Curtiss invited "Gyro" Sperry to come along.

Sperry demonstrated his machine in a solo flight over Paris in February. Throngs of astounded Parisians moaned in dismay as they saw the young man leave the controls of his machine and climb far out on a wing. But the aeroplane continued to sail steadily on its way a thousand feet above the Champs-Élysées.

It seemed the invariable rule that G. H. returned home to find bad news. The blow he received when he landed late in February was a haymaker. The Court of Appeals had sustained Judge Hazel's decision in favor of the Wright company and made the injunction permanent. It looked like the end of the road.

Orville Wright triumphantly said that the *America* would never fly to Europe because "We have been left in absolute control of the aeroplane business of this country!" and added that, anyhow Curtiss knew that he couldn't build a machine that could cross the ocean and was just out for publicity.

G. H. replied by pointing out that he wouldn't get paid for the *America* unless she lifted the calculated load from the water.

However, things looked very black. Even doughty Judge Wheeler was ready to throw in the towel.

"You'll have to try to reach a settlement with Mr. Wright," he said sadly.

"I've tried before," said Curtiss. "Heaven knows I've tried."

"It's that or perish."

"There's one more court," said G. H.

"Yes, but—"

"We'll carry this to the Supreme Court of the United States," Curtiss said.

This time public opinion was on his side. Editorials appeared in the leading papers favoring him, and messages of sympathy poured in. Henry Ford picked up Curtiss in a public restaurant and offered his assistance. This kindly offer from Mr. Ford not only lightened the desolation in G. H.'s heart, but had a practical result in securing for him the services of Judge Benton R. Crisp, who had successfully defended the Ford interests in the great Selden patent suit.

A little idea that Link Beachey had at this time poured gasoline on the roaring conflagration of controversy. Link was up and around again, though still badly shocked by his catastrophic dive.

"It sure would have saved a lot of trouble if that aerodrome thing of Langley's had flown," he said to Curtiss one day.

G. H. grinned wryly.

"It sure would," he agreed, "but it didn't."

"I was studying up on it while I was in the hospital," Link went on, "and I'm certain it would have if it hadn't cracked up on the catapult. It would be kind of fun to get her out and see."

G. H.'s eyes shot sparks, but he shook his head. "I couldn't suggest it," he said. "Everybody would say I was trying to discredit the Wrights."

"Suppose the Smithsonian came to *you?*" Link persisted.

"That would be different," said Curtiss.

A few weeks later he received a letter from Doctor A. F. Zahm of the Smithsonian Institution, asking if he would be willing to test the Langley aerodrome and offering two thousand dollars partially to defray expenses. The Institution was anxious to vindicate the memory of its greatly maligned member, and both Curtiss and the Board of the Smithsonian genuinely believed that valuable aeronautical data would be obtained by a flying test of the machine.

On a raw day in March, three packing cases arrived at Hammondsport consigned to G. H. Curtiss from the Smithsonian Institution. They were placed in the courtyard of the factory close to where the mighty wings of the *America* were taking shape. G. H. and Henry Kleckler, Harry and Martha Genung, and half the workers in the factory gathered around to witness the uncrating of this almost mythical bird. As the boards were carefully pried off, they revealed a tangled mass of broken wood and rotted oiled silk. It was disappointing at first, but when the men dropped to their knees to examine the wreckage there were exclamations of amazement.

"Will you look at this, G. H.?" said Henry. "Every one of these ribs is hollowed out to make it lighter, and gosh, look at the workmanship on those joints."

"It's the most beautiful piece of work I've ever seen," agreed Curtiss.

"It will cost a fortune to duplicate those pieces," put in Harry.

"It cost seventy thousand dollars and seven years of work to build," G. H. reminded him.

"We can never afford to do it," said Harry.

"We'll have to cut corners," Curtiss said. "The ribs, for instance, can be solid spruce. They won't be as strong or as light, but they'll have to do."

"And we can recover the wings with doped nainsook," said Henry. "This silk was awfully expensive. But that will be heavier, too. Do you think she'll fly, G. H.?"

"I'm betting a lot on it," Curtiss answered.

Eventually the aerodrome was rebuilt. The bitterest controversy of aeronautical history has raged ever since as to just what changes were made. It is charged that the machine was virtually redesigned in the reconstruction. This is definitely not the case. Doctor Zahm and Professor Charles M. Manly, who had been Langley's assistant, superintended the entire operation, and the whole thing was wide open to the public. Anybody interested could come in and see just what was being done. Sworn statements conclusively prove that the only real changes made in the machine were those necessary to launching it from pontoons instead of a catapult. The undertrussing was strengthened just sufficiently to carry the added load. Solid ribs, identical in shape to Langley's, were used instead of those broken in the accident, and the rotted oiled silk was replaced by heavier, less efficient material.

Aerodynamically the machine remained the same. There was no change in design or in the controls, except that standard control levers were put in to avoid confusing pilots who were used to them. The same motor was used, though it had deteriorated due to its immersion in salt water and only developed forty horsepower as compared to fifty-two horsepower in 1903. In all essentials the machine was exactly as it had been built by Langley, except that it was not quite as good as new.

On June 2, 1914, the aerodrome, looking like an enormous, white-winged dragonfly, was launched on Lake Keuka. Curtiss took his place between the pairs of wings. He knew that because of the addition of the pontoons the machine now weighed three hundred and fifty pounds more than before. It seemed almost too much to hope that it would fly.

The ancient motor roared, and G. H. marveled once again at the genius which had contrived that exquisite piece of mechanism so long ago. Even eleven years later few motors were as good. He opened the throttle wide, and the broad white vanes of the propellers Langley had designed revolved madly.

Slowly the aerodrome gathered way. Curtiss faced it toward the wind and held it so. The pontoons rose to the surface of the water; they skimmed it ever more lightly. He pulled the control that raised the great dihedral Pinaud tail. The front pontoons lifted. For a moment yet the rear ones clung to the water. Then with slow stateliness the aerodrome took the air.

Only a few feet up, only a short distance did she fly, but somewhere beyond the ultimate range of man-made wings Professor Langley may have smiled and settled back to rest at last in peace.

Trials with the aerodrome continued throughout that month. Only after numerous flights with the original equipment had conclusively proved the flying ability of the machine, were certain other changes made in order to obtain further data on the performance of Langley's design. A Curtiss eighty-horsepower motor was mounted in place of the Manly engine, and the rudder was slightly enlarged. With the new equipment, the aerodrome made a flight of thirty minutes during which ten miles were covered at an average speed of twenty miles per hour. "Gink" Doherty, the pilot, reported that the machine was so stable in the air that all he had to do was to sit there and steer.

In contrast to the open and public reconstruction of the aerodrome, the building of *America* and her sister ship was carried on in opaque secrecy. A huge shed was erected in the courtyard of the factory. Here the *America's* seventy-two-foot wings took shape under heavy guard.

And those guards were kept busy. The moment the flight was announced, all the big English and American papers and press associations sent their crack reporters to Hammondsport. Public interest was terrific. Every rumor that came out of Hammondsport was headline news, and those reporters were out to get it.

For once Curtiss publicity was cleverly handled. The newspapers were fed just enough material to keep public interest boiling throughout the months of preparation, and all their efforts to get more were foiled.

Once two reporters tried a frontal attack. They marched into Curtiss' office and began a little blackmail.

"If you don't give us a better break," they said, "we'll devote all our considerable talents to making the name of Curtiss a stench in the nose of the public. We'll roast you alive."

It was years since anyone had seen G. H. really mad, but

those young men were treated to that rare spectacle. His long, gaunt form uncoiled from behind the desk like a steel spring, his hazel eyes blazed magnificently.

"Get out of here before I kick you out," he roared, "and if you know what's good for you, don't come back."

They knew what was good for them.

The christening of *America* on June 22, 1914, was the gala climax of the gayest season Hammondsport was ever to know. Besides the great newspapermen, the town was full of aviators, scientists, sportsmen, and the gold braid and ribbons of military dignity. People had gathered from all over the earth.

America, exposed at last to the public view, was placed on a huge dolly by the shore of Lake Keuka. Her wide-spreading wings, covered with bright red silk, dwarfed the men who had built them. Technicians were amazed to see that their under-surfaces were almost flat while the upper were sharply curved— the modern airfoil section was making its first appearance. At the ends of the lower wings were balancing pontoons the shape and size of a baby's bathtub. The thirty-five-foot boat, which was also painted a brilliant red, contained a comfortable en-closed cabin. Two one-hundred-horsepower engines, mounted between the wings, drove pusher propellers.

Just in front of *America's* pointed bow a tripod had been erected from which a bottle of Pleasant Valley champagne flanked by good-luck horseshoes dangled on the end of a cord. Katherine, the lovely daughter of G. H.'s old friend Leo Masson, was to wield the bottle.

The whole town and most of the countryside turned out for the ceremony. There were great flights of oratory concerning the conquest of the skies, and then Katherine, a slender figure in white with a big picture hat, stepped forward to do her part.

With touchingly youthful dignity she recited the poem

which Doctor Zahm of the Smithsonian had written for the occasion. Then she grasped the bottle and gave a mighty heave.

There was a dull thud followed by the merry tinkle of the horseshoes. A slight dent appeared on *America's* bow, but the bottle was adamant. The girl tried again and missed completely; once more, and still the bottle refused to yield.

Katherine now had three strikes on her, and Lieutenant Porte rushed to the rescue. He seized the cord in his left hand and held the bottle against the bow of the ship while his right swung a heavy hammer. There was a satisfactory crash, and a great fountain of golden wine deluged *America*, Katherine, Porte, and all the dignitaries.

The difficulty of christening *America* was but an omen of things to come. The following day, Curtiss, with Porte as his copilot, gave *America* her trial run. A little crowd on the shore watched them climb aboard and saw Henry Kleckler crank the starboard motor. It started with such a surge as to swing the great flying boat right around. Then the port engine was cranked and *America* headed out into the lake. In a mighty counterpoint of power the engines roared in harmony. Bright in the sunshine the red wings raced across the water while pontoons and keel plowed a triple furrow of white in its blue surface.

As the huge plane sped along, the line of white near the wing tips diminished and was gone. Then the wake of the hull lessened until it was no more than a thin line of spray, and now it too vanished as *America* took the air.

Curtiss and Porte returned from the flight filled with enthusiasm. They planned to ship the plane on July 4. By the fifteenth, they said, the flight would start. But when they ran a trial with half the necessary load, their hopes were deflated.

The hull was too narrow to lift sufficiently from the water

for a take-off with the added weight. G. H. met this by
extending planing fins from the hull—a principle now employed by the transatlantic Clippers. She lifted better, but still
would not take off with the full load of twenty-four hundred
pounds.

They added a third engine above the center section, and
now she rose with the greatest load that had ever been taken
into the air, more than twice Doctor Bell's "thousand pounds
of bricks." But this was not enough with the added fuel consumption of the extra engine.

Lieutenant Porte worked and worried himself into a hem-
orrhage, and was whisked off to the Adirondacks for a two-
week rest.

Meanwhile, the last days of peace were slipping through
the fingers of a careless world. June 28—a wild-eyed young
man fired off a pistol somewhere in the Balkans with too
excellent an aim. The people in Hammondsport paid no more
attention than if it had been a popgun.

July 13—Porte was back, and they were really getting somewhere, but the foreign ministers in Europe were writing terribly polite notes.

July 15—*America* took off with the full transatlantic load,
the total weight of the laden plane was over five thousand
pounds.

Supply crews were immediately dispatched to the Azores
and Newfoundland, and reporters raced after them. Jack
Towers was mentioned as copilot to Porte. *America* and her
sister ship, which had been built as a precautionary measure,
were crated for the journey to the sea.

But the kings and emperors of the Old World had started
in their series of frantically affectionate epistles signed "Nicky"
and "George" and "Willie."

August 3—the Kaiser's new 155 mm. howitzers were flattening the forts at Liége, while the Russian hordes swept into East Prussia, and England took up the challenge.

Transatlantic flying was off for the duration, and *America* remained in her crate, until she was called upon for sterner service than a jaunt across the ocean.

CHAPTER TWENTY-FOUR

AERIAL NAVIES

THE OUTBREAK OF WAR brought a tremendous influx of orders to Hammondsport. Up to that time the largest single contract the Curtiss company had ever filled was for ten machines for the United States Army. Now the governments of Europe came clamoring for planes. The Royal Navy bought the two *Americas* and ordered ten more like them. So successful were the first two in the Channel patrol that the British reordered fifty more before the rest were delivered. The French and Russians came begging for land planes and the Italians wanted boats; even neutral Spain placed an order.

A representative of Imperial Germany called on Harry Genung.

"My government will buy your entire output for the next year at your own price," he said.

"But the seas are closed to you," said Harry. "What about delivery?"

"You will deliver them here."

"And what will you do with them?"

The German smiled grimly.

"That's our business," he answered. "You will get your money."

Sensing his determination to destroy the planes, Harry replied, "Not a chance in a million. Good day!"

Meanwhile G. H. was behaving in a typically feckless manner. Completely disregarding the possibilities for enormous profits, he had gone off to the West Coast to conduct experiments with a new plane he had just built for the United States Army.

Earlier in the year Colonel Samuel Reber, head of the United States Army Signal Corps, had called for bids for a two-place tractor biplane for the Army. The specifications required it to carry a useful load of six hundred pounds and have a top speed of seventy miles per hour, a landing speed of forty miles per hour, and be able to climb three thousand feet in ten minutes. The most revolutionary part of the government requirements, however, was the demand for a full set of plans giving exhaustive engineering data including lift, drift, and stress diagrams, and enlarged blueprints of every detail of the machine. It was quite an order for an aeroplane industry which still operated largely by rule of thumb. Curtiss was the only manufacturer who cared to get up plans costing ten thousand dollars and spend Heaven knew how much more for experiments on the chance of selling the government a six-thousand-dollar aeroplane.

With the help of Doctor Zahm, who did the heavy calculating, and Douglas Thomas, a young English expert on the brand-new science of streamlining, Curtiss produced the plans and built the plane. Then he took it to California for trials with the Army.

In all its tests the new biplane far surpassed the specified performance; its top speed, for instance, was eighty miles per hour, and its rate of climb much faster than Army expectations.

JN-1 was the prototype of the famous *Jenny* (JN-4), on which nearly all the pilots of the American and Canadian armies were trained during what was then mistakenly referred to as the "Great War." It was a tractor biplane having a fully enclosed fuselage with two seats arranged in tandem. The power plant was a Curtiss OX motor developing eighty-five horsepower. Its wings were raked backward, and their airfoil section was the same as that developed on *America*. It was a fine, rugged plane of great general utility, and it was suitable for quantity production.

While Curtiss was in California laboring to perfect the *Jenny*, Harry Genung and Lyman Seely, his new sales manager, almost melted the telegraph wires with their frantic appeals for him to return and tend to business. Untold millions were waiting to be gathered in, and Curtiss was not there. But to all their importunities he simply replied, "You attend to it, I'm busy."

Thus, with his customary patriotism, he ignored the splendid prospect of incalculable riches in order satisfactorily to finish this one plane for his own government.

For once virtue had a concrete reward, for when Winston Churchill, First Lord of the Admiralty, saw the plans and performance figures of the JN-1, he made the British government place an order for fourteen million dollars' worth of *Jenny* and *America* boats.

G. H. was not a man to stagger easily, but when he saw that order it left him weak in the head and gone at the knees.

"We can't accept it," wailed Harry Genung. "We haven't got the capital to expand fast enough."

But Curtiss had recovered his nerve.

"We will accept it," he said, "but we'll tell them we need some money down."

In his wire to Seely in London confirming the order, he said, "Must have seventy-five thousand cash in advance."

The reply from the British government nearly knocked him

flat again. They had misunderstood his demand and instead of $75,000 sent him a check for £75,000, over $364,000.

So overnight the Curtiss company jumped from a small industry to Big Business. Regretfully, G. H. saw that Hammondsport could no longer contain his great enterprise. It had neither accommodation for the thousands of new workers nor was its single railroad adequate to move his materials. He had to find new quarters, and find them quickly.

In Buffalo the huge factories, which had housed the Thomas Motor Car Company, stood empty because of the failure of that business. Curtiss looked them over and bought them on the spot. When he had completed the deal, he went back to survey the buildings for the installation of his jigs and machinery. As he stood in the queer desolation of that cavernous barracks, looking at the dusty sunshine streaking across the empty space soon to be filled with the tremendous shapes of growing wings, his mind swung backward through the full cycle, and he saw again an earnest boy laboriously writing a letter to the E. R. Thomas Manufacturing Company ordering one single-cylinder engine "as per cut no. 5 in your catalogue. Money order enclosed."

In the spring of 1915 the Curtiss Aeroplane Company, lock and stock, staff and employees, moved by special trains to Buffalo in a single night. But before they even started, Curtiss knew that his enormous new factory was still too small to meet the phenomenal growth of his business, and modern assembly plants were already under construction near by. The Hammondsport factory was devoted to motors.

While Curtiss was immersed in the herculean labor of filling the orders of the Allies, he never ceased his almost unheeded efforts to spur America onward toward needed measures of protection. In the spring of 1915 he gave a newspaper interview which sounded the note of his despair. "We are no nearer ready," he said, "than if we had never begun. The Army has but twenty planes, ten of them on the Mexican border, and the Navy has only sixteen hydros and no boats. Against this the English alone had one thousand planes at the beginning of the war and have at least two thousand now. We need a minimum of one hundred twin-engine flying boats to patrol the Atlantic coast alone."

But though the armies of Europe were making rapidly increasing use of the aeroplane, the navies of the Old World failed to exploit its possibilities. Perhaps the most amazing omission in all history occurred in the Battle of Jutland. Throughout the whole of one smoky summer day in 1916 the battle fleets of England and Germany fumbled for each other through the haze. By their own accounts of the action, neither Admiral Jellicoe nor Admiral von Scheer knew what force he was up against or exactly where his enemy was. One pair of eyes to see beyond the horizon would have given decisive victory to England, or might have furnished such advantage to the slightly smaller German fleet as to have enabled it to wrest the centuries-old rule of the waves from Britannia.

At the time the battle was fought, the Royal Navy had at least seventy of the new Curtiss flying boats, capable of flying one thousand miles with a full load of bombs and a three-man crew, while Germany had innumerable seaplanes safely stowed in her North Sea ports. And yet not a single aeroplane was on hand from either side to observe, report, and change the course of destiny.*

*The British launched one seaplane from the trader *Engadine,* but it took no part in the battle.

Lighter-than-air was still a factor in that war. Zeppelins bombed London and performed many useful services for the German government. In this country Captain Baldwin was commissioned by the Army to build a big new airship. The DN-1 was completed in 1916. When we entered the war in 1917, the captain was put in charge of all military lighter-than-air craft and shortly afterward commissioned a major in the regular Army. But however much higher his military rank might be, he always retained the unofficial title which he had won himself and by which he was known and loved throughout the world. Major was no promotion for "Captain" Baldwin.

In December 1915 the Curtiss companies were reorganized so that at last G. H. had capital enough to carry forward his great enterprises. This took the form of a contract between Curtiss and the syndicate managers, who were to float the new issue of stock. By the agreement, G. H. sold the Curtiss companies for the sum of four and a half million dollars and fifty per cent of the stock of the new company, which was named the Curtiss Aeroplane and Motor Company.

Not only G. H., but all those men who had shown their faith in him by putting up money to help him through his difficulties or accepting stock of doubtful value for services rendered, now reaped a rich harvest.

But G. H. was no more interested in the financial end of his business when it was bringing in millions than he had been when it was losing thousands. He left all that to Harry Genung and busied himself with designing bigger and better aeroplanes. With the help of William Gillmore, who was in charge of boats at Buffalo, he constructed ever larger and more efficient naval planes. Early in 1917 he developed a scout biplane for the Army, which could travel at one hundred and twenty miles per hour and climb ten thousand feet in ten minutes.

Nor was he any more careful with his money; great wealth could not change his nature. One time, when he was motoring on Long Island, with Lena and the Genungs, Curtiss pulled up at the bank in Mineola.

"Think I'd better cash a check," he remarked.

Lena, Harry, and Martha waited in gleeful anticipation. Almost immediately G. H. slouched out with a sheepish grin on his face.

"They tell me I haven't any money in there," he said. "Say Harry, what bank have I got money in?"

Between gasps of laughter Harry answered, "You've got fifty thousand dollars over at Hempstead."

Ten years after Curtiss' death, Genung, quite by accident, found twelve thousand dollars in a bank in Atlanta, Georgia, which G. H. had deposited there in exhibition days and forgotten all about. He immediately sent a circular letter to banks in all the towns where the Curtiss Team had flown, and uncovered three more forgotten accounts totaling several thousand dollars.

Paradoxically, the entry of America into the war brought peace at last to Curtiss in the contest which embittered so much of his life. The United States government could not afford to have this country's two greatest manufacturers of aircraft locked in a struggle to the death. A representative of the government stated the fact which had been painfully obvious for a long time. "The aeronautical industry," he said, "has long been throttled by the basic Wright patents and dominated by the many Curtiss patents. We see great restrictions on our war program in the continuation of this condition, which has caused the United States to fall from first place to last of all the great nations in the air."

Practically by government decree the old antagonists were

forced to shake hands. The Aircraft Manufacturers Association was formed for the purpose of pooling all aeroplane patents for the use of everyone. The Curtiss company received two million dollars for the use of their patents and the Wright company got three million dollars for theirs. In addition, the Wright-Martin patents were made available to Curtiss, which was considered to be worth another two million dollars to his company. The values placed on the patents were certified to be fair and just by the National Advisory Council for Aeronautics, the Aircraft Production Board, and the Secretaries of the Army and Navy.

The agreement blasted the barriers which had for so long dammed the progress of aviation in America. The way was clear for the tremendous onward surge which once again carried this country to the forefront in the air.

After the settlement, John P. Tarbox, Curtiss' patent attorney, estimated the value of all the patents held by the Curtiss company to be $8,725,000.

As his country flung itself into that first great battle to maintain the rights, ideals, and freedoms to which it is dedicated, Curtiss prepared to play his part in building up its air power. In his first interview after the declaration of war, he outlined a strategic conception of aerial warfare which was virtually a blueprint for a blitzkrieg: "If the German line is to be rolled up before too many American lives pay the cost of an offensive, the German positions must be turned by fleets of aeroplanes so many and so powerful that they can sweep the German flyers from the skies, blind the enemy gunners and cut off their supplies of food and munitions a hundred miles back of the fighting line."

His advice was taken nearly a quarter of a century later—by the Luftwaffe.

In the spring of 1917, Curtiss promised the government to turn out the unheard-of total of thirty-five hundred trainers and combat planes at his Buffalo plant, and he kept his word. In addition, he broke ground for a new factory for experiment and research at Garden City, Long Island. As always, his heart was in creating new designs. He left production in competent hands in Buffalo and, as chief engineer of the Curtiss company, took personal charge of experimentation at Garden City.

To be on the spot, he purchased the modern estate of Gage E. Tarbell on Nassau Boulevard. Lena and he left Hammondsport and went to live in their fine new house, but they never loved it half so well as the House on the Hill.

In January 1918 the Garden City factory was completed. There Curtiss began the simultaneous designing of new, fast fighters for the Army and giant flying boats for the Navy. Then, as now, shipping was the bottleneck of the American war effort. Submarines were taking their tremendous toll, and Admiral Taylor, Chief of Naval Construction, thought he saw a way to beat them. There was just one man in the country who could help him. He sent for Curtiss.

"This business of building aeroplanes and having them sunk on the way over," he told G. H., "is ridiculous. I want a flying boat that will jump right over the U-boats and that can carry the war to them when it gets abroad."

"You shall have it," G. H. said.

Plans for the huge three-engine flying boats were drawn by Curtiss, Henry Kleckler, and William Gillmore, with the assistance of Naval Constructors J. C. Hunsaker, G. C. Westervelt, and H. C. Richardson, and G. H.'s old friend Doctor Zahm. They were built at the Garden City factory and the NC-1 made her trial flight in October 1918.

The Meuse-Argonne offensive knocked the fight out of

Germany, and the war came to its unexpectedly rapid conclusion. The NC-1 was temporarily retired. It looked for a little while as if Curtiss' dream of a transatlantic flight were balked again—this time by peace instead of war.

But once set on a course, G. H. was harder to stop than the irresistible force of the physics books. He refused to give up, and the Navy was just as keen. By December it was settled that the transatlantic flying boats were to have a chance to show their stuff.

CHAPTER TWENTY-FIVE

THE FLIGHT OF THE NC-4

GLENN CURTISS STOOD ON the white sand at Rockaway Point and watched three battleships of the air maneuver on the bright morning surface of the sea. For a while they taxied about at random; then, at a signal from Commander Towers' flagship, NC-3, they swung into formation. Twelve mighty engines shouted a diapason of five thousand horsepower, and the fat gray hulls began to race across the water. They went in V formation, and each boat cut a triple V of white in the calm blue surface.

The ships were heavily laden and, as their speed increased, the spray flew over them, almost hiding their great gray wings behind its iridescent curtain. Then it fell away as they rode up on their steps. Right into the sun they sped, and now their wakes were but a thin line of white, and then the flagship shook herself free. Followed *Four* and then *One*.

As soon as they were all air-borne, Jack Towers set the course. In a broad V they headed toward the east. Curtiss strained his eyes to follow them through the light haze. They dwindled rapidly. Now they were like a flight of ducks, then mosquitoes, gnats, and finally specks dancing in the blue. And then they were gone.

A little wearily G. H. plodded back through the heavy sand. Here his responsibility ended. Success or failure lay in the hands of the eager young men who manned the planes, their skill with the controls and instruments, their intelligence and their courage. He had done his part. The great ships of the air, winging steadily eastward, were as perfect as he could make them. They were the culmination of all the work and thought, the experiment and the risk of the long, full years.

G. H. smiled a twisted smile and admitted to himself that for the first time he felt a little old. In a sense this moment marked the completion of his life's work.

The specifications for the transatlantic flying boats had been decided upon in September 1917. While Gillmore and Lieutenant Commander Richardson experimented with hulls at the model basin of the Washington Navy Yard, Curtiss and his engineers worked out the general design with the aid of the brand-new wind tunnel at the Garden City factory. The great difficulty with a large flying boat was that the hull had to be extended so far to the rear to carry the controls that it became too weak for work in rough water. In the new boats this defect was overcome by building a comparatively short, compact hull and carrying the tail surfaces on three long outriggers arranged as a triangle and heavily braced by wires and cross spars.

As soon as the preliminary plans were completed, Curtiss sent them to Admiral Taylor in Washington. The Construction Department of the Navy examined them with the greatest care and then sent for Curtiss. He found the admiral and his assistants grinning broadly.

"Well, what do you think of them?" asked G. H.

"The plans are magnificent," Taylor said, "but you'll have to change the designation of the model."

"What's the matter with it?" asked Curtiss in bewilderment.

"You refer to it as model DT," answered the admiral, "and

with the present political prejudice against alcohol we can't have the Navy flying around in Delirium Tremens."

"I never thought of that," laughed G. H. "What shall we call 'em?"

"I suggest NC," said Admiral Taylor. "Navy Curtiss."

NC-1 was a biplane with the huge wingspread of one hundred and twenty-six feet, and from her bow to the tip of her boxed-in tail she was seventy feet long. The vertical stabilizers above the upper wings, which had made their appearance on the first flying boat, were used to prevent a pendulum swing. In her comfortable cabin there was accommodation for a six-man crew and she was fully equipped with radio and all the instruments and gadgets which wartime experience could suggest. As originally designed, she was powered by three four-hundred horsepower Liberty engines for which Curtiss had designed the lubricating system. They drove two-bladed tractor propellers.

In December, when the transatlantic flight was mooted, NC-1 was equipped with a fourth motor located in the nacelle behind the center engine, driving a pusher propeller. By adding one thousand pounds of motor weight, her lifting capacity was increased four thousand pounds. Thus rigged she had a total of sixteen hundred horsepower.

NC-2 was delivered shortly afterward. In March, NC-1 lost her wings in a storm at Far Rockaway and she was equipped with the wings from *Two*. Thus the boats which started on the great flight were NC-1, 3, and 4.

The flight was no sporting venture, but a carefully planned scientific expedition carried out with the Navy's typically complete staff work. All through the winter the weathermen were at work assembling and analyzing meteorological data. Sixty destroyers were ordered to form a lifeline of ships stretching from Trepassey Bay in Newfoundland to Ponta Delgada in the Azores, and thence to Lisbon in Portugal and across the Bay of Biscay to Plymouth. Bases, with full equipment for refueling and repairs, were established at all landing points. Nothing was left to chance.

Curtiss' friend and pupil, Commander John H. Towers, who is today Chief of The Bureau of Aeronautics, U.S.N., was placed in command of the expedition and chose NC-3 as his flagship. Pat Bellinger commanded *One* and Lieutenant Commander A. C. Read had *Four*. Each ship carried a crew of five in addition to its captain: a pilot, navigator, radio officer, and two engineers.

Although *Four* was not delivered until April 30, the expedition was ready to start early in May. Orders came from Washington to take off on May 8 (weather permitting).

One and *Three* had an uneventful flight to Halifax and on to Trepassey Bay, but *Four* was forced down at Chatham, Massachusetts, by engine trouble and did not rejoin the fleet until May 15. Commander Read lost no time in refueling, and the following morning reported that he was ready to start.

Late the afternoon of May 16th, Commander Towers ordered the crews aboard their ships. The big flying boats taxied slowly in line down the long narrow bay. The dark mass of spectators along the shore suddenly blossomed with the white of waving handkerchiefs, though the sound of their cheering was lost in the roar of motors. Far down the bay the ships paused for a moment like gigantic gulls resting on the water before a long journey. Then Jack Towers shouted to his pilot, "Let's go!"

"Putty" Read saw the flagship's propellers quicken and the flash of foam at her bow. He shouted an order, and *Four* lunged forward. The spray cataracted over her, then she was up on the step. Straight at the harbor mouth she dashed, and the choppy seas crashed against her hull. *Smash, smash!* It seemed that the heavily laden ship would never rise. *Three* was off the water. Smash, skip, and the silken smoothness of riding on air.

In ten minutes the shoreline had vanished, and the three flying boats were winging across the empty, darkening sea. Putty Read had the sense of illimitable space stretching beyond any horizon known to man. Ahead of him *Three* was coasting up and down the invisible hills of air. He watched her through the gathering gloom until she disappeared.

"Switch on the navigation lights," he ordered, "and send a message requesting *Three* to do the same."

There was no answer to the wireless, something seemed to be wrong. *One* had also disappeared. The night was complete, and they were flying inside a dark sphere, divided equally between the starlit upper half and the black bowl of the sea. Jets of blue flame playing along the open exhaust ports of the motors seemed like witch's fire, but within the cabin the lights on the instrument panels and charts were as cozy as the glow of firelight through a cottage window.

Ahead, a streak of golden fire split the night, a star shell from a destroyer. They roared right over her tiny twinkling lights, and read the illuminated number on her deck. That gave them their position and Putty figured their speed at ninety knots.

Then they were in darkness again until the thin rim of the moon cut through the edge of the horizon. Silvered wings appeared in the sky too close for safety. They veered off, and Putty realized that they had passed *Three*.

They flew on steadily through the moonlit night, checking off the destroyers as regularly as a good watchman making his rounds. The early summer dawn came like a gray wraith across the sea, and Putty saw heavy clouds ahead linked to the ocean by a wall of vapor. They flew for a little in the half-light before plunging into it.

The fog was so thick that they could not see the wing tips; the ship felt as though she were in a steep bank, and the compass whirled aimlessly. There were as yet no proper blind-flying instruments.

Putty shouted to the pilot and gestured upward. The great boat began to climb. At three thousand feet the mist began to thin. Strong light glared through from above, and then they burst forth into bright sunshine under a deep blue sky.

The warmth of the sun and the serenity above gave Putty an illusion of safety, which he knew was far from real. For underneath, the gleaming white billows of fog cut him off from contact with the earth. This was fine as long as they stayed up, but how to find the Islands down below?

They talked by wireless with destroyers buried in the fog and found no help. There was nothing to do but keep on until they got a break.

It seemed to Putty as though they flew for days above that beautiful, deadly field of fog. Actually it was a little over three hours before he saw ahead and to starboard a ragged hole in the gleaming floor. He ordered the pilot to steer for it, and as they passed above he saw the most beautiful sight his eyes ever had or would behold.

Down through that fortunate flaw in the solid vapor, seen as though at the end of a mile long tube, was a white house on a green hill. They had reached the Azores.

NC-4 landed through the fog at Ponta Delgada at 9:25 A.M., New York time, May 17, 1919. *One* and *Three* came down on the open sea; there had been no lucky hole through the fog for them. *One* broke up after her crew had been rescued by a destroyer, but Jack Towers brought *Three* in under her own power, two hundred miles through heavy seas.

The flagship was too badly damaged by that pounding to go on, so it was decided that *Four* should continue alone. There was talk of shifting the commodore's flag to the remaining ship, but Jack Towers generously declared, "Read has earned the glory—let him take her in."

The rest of the voyage was purely routine. *Four* made the flight from the Azores to Lisbon in less than ten hours, and went on to Plymouth in a hop and a skip. For the first time in history the Atlantic had been crossed by air.

It was only eleven years since *Red Wing* had staggered off the ice of Lake Keuka to fly 318 feet 11 inches. What men had not dared even to dream in those days was an accomplished fact.

As Commander Read accepted the cheers of the English people and the tributes of the whole world for his great feat, behind him seemed to stand the tall, smiling figure of the man who had made it possible.

CHAPTER TWENTY-SIX

"WHEN TIME NO LONGER MEANS SO MUCH . . ."

CURTISS NEVER HAD A real vacation until the fall of 1916—the trips to Europe didn't count, for they were entirely devoted to business. After the first two years of the war, the terrific strain of expanding his business a thousandfold cracked even G. H.'s case-hardened constitution and he succumbed to a bad attack of influenza. When his doctors told him that he must get away for a rest, he remembered the sunshine of Florida and headed for Miami like a homing pigeon.

It was a very different place from the great pleasure city of today. There were only two hotels and a little cluster of houses along the Miami River. The beach, where the tall white hotels and the luxurious villas now extend for miles in a Venetian atmosphere of intricate canals, was no more than a mangrove swamp. But it was a fine place to rest.

The only trouble was that G. H. was not yet ready to relax. The first thing he did was to call on Mr. E. G. Sewell, president of the Chamber of Commerce.

"I want you to advise me about getting a nice little tract of land to start a flying school," he said. "It has to be good firm ground."

Mr. Sewell thought it over. "Most of the land outside of town is pretty swampy," he admitted. "Now let's see. I know the man for you—Jimmy Bright. He's got a small dairy farm about eight miles northwest of here. The land is drained and put in grass. Perhaps you could buy a piece from him."

"I'll go to see him," said G. H.

He and Lena motored out over a narrow sandy road the following day. The Bright dairy and cattle ranch was the largest in South Florida, but it wasn't very big at that. A long galvanized iron barn housed a small herd of Holsteins, and the fields around it were sparsely populated by small native cattle. James H. Bright was a wiry little man with bright blue eyes and sandy hair. He was as instinct with the sense of nature as his herds. He was, in fact, a very fine farmer.

Curtiss and Bright liked each other on the spot, and before they parted Jimmy had insisted on lending his new friend a field on the edge of the Everglades for the proposed flying school.

G. H. was busy organizing the school when he received word that Harry Genung had also caught influenza. Long-distance telephoning had always been a favorite habit of Curtiss', and now that he could afford it he indulged himself lavishly. He loved to lie stretched out on his bed, with the receiver cocked on one shoulder, and talk all over the United States. He immediately got his old friend on the wire.

"How are you feeling, Harry?" he asked anxiously.

"They tell me I'm better," croaked Genung, "but I feel awful."

"Tell you what," said G. H. "The minute you're up to traveling, you and Martha come down here at my expense. It's the greatest place ever and we'll have a lot of fun starting this flying school."

Harry came down and they did have fun: fishing and lazing in the sun, with the school to keep them interested. G. H. became an incurable Florida addict.

The next winter found him back in Miami. There were only two things he didn't like about the rapidly growing city.

One was the water, which was so brackish that it was poison to drink and almost useless even for washing; and the other was the fact that, since the entire milkshed consisted of Jimmy Bright's dairy and two smaller establishments virtually everyone drank milk out of cans. When Curtiss didn't like a thing he always did something about it.

He met Bright on Biscayne Boulevard one day and startled the dairyman with an abrupt proposition.

"Something ought to be done about this milk situation," he said. "How about you and me going partners in a really big dairy? You furnish the brains and I'll put up the money."

Jimmy was as good a judge of men as cattle. It didn't take him a minute to accept. Although it started in one direction and ended in another, their association was fantastically fortunate. And it was as harmonious as it was profitable. Jimmy Bright says today, "G. H. was the best partner a man ever had."

The new partners conferred in Curtiss' rooms at the Royal Palm.

"Now the first thing we need," said Curtiss, ablaze with his new enthusiasm, "is a good bull, the best bull in the United States. Where is he?"

"I reckon you'd say it was Rag Apple Korndyke 8th," said Jimmy, "but he would cost a powerful lot of money."

Faintly to G. H.'s brain an echo came back through the years, and he saw a round-eyed schoolboy gazing at a man who would pay a hundred dollars for a rabbit.

"You can't make money without spending it," he said. "We'll buy him."

Rag Apple Korndyke 8th was shipped to Miami by express, insured for fifty thousand dollars. There was a terrific bally-hoo about his arrival, and the Chamber of Commerce met him at the station with a brass band. It was a pretty ridiculous performance in one sense, and yet it symbolized the beginning of the great dairy industry of South Florida.

Rag Apple was, however, no more than a symbol. He did not live long enough to perpetuate his strain. A short time after he died, Jimmy Bright came to Curtiss with a mite of consolation for their loss.

"Anyhow," he said, "that bull was so big his hide fetched the highest price ever paid in Florida."

"How much did you get?" asked G. H.

"Thirty-six dollars," said Jimmy proudly.

The Florida Ranch and Dairy Company was more fortunate in some of its other investments. They purchased ten thousand acres of land near Jimmy's ranch for ten dollars an acre from the Florida East Coast Railway. G. H. got Doctor Bell's son-in-law, Henry Fairchild, down from Washington to analyze the soil and tell them what kind of grass to grow. Jimmy Bright took a trip to Texas and acquired four Brahman bulls which had just arrived from India. He also bought twenty-five carloads of cows. His final and most eccentric purchase was one thousand Angora goats to clear the land.

Those goats proved a most picturesque addition to the Florida scene. They loved to pose on the levees of the canal that ran through the property. A small boat sailing down it would often pass through a mile-long line of goats outlined against the sky.

After the flight of the NC-4, Curtiss virtually retired from the aircraft industry. It was lapsing into a period of stagnation following the great wartime forward surge, and was now purely a matter of finance and administration. G. H. cared for neither of those things.

The Garden City house was sold, and G. H. and Lena came to make their home in Florida.

Harry Genung, too, retired from the Curtiss company and bought a beautiful farm at Auburn, New York. Curtiss did his level best to persuade his old crony to join him in Florida. He even went so far as secretly to build an enormous house near his own new mansion and present it to the Genungs. But Harry declined the lavish gift. He felt that G. H. did not really need him now, and chose to strike out on his own.

The Florida Ranch and Dairy Company prospered amazingly. Curtiss had conceived the idea that the Brahman bulls would be a good cross with the native cattle, and succeeded in increasing their size by thirty-five per cent. The dairy was doing a roaring trade. But it came to a sudden end. It went out of business because it became too valuable.

The Florida land boom struck. Suddenly everyone in the United States wanted to own a lot in Florida. The ranch, on which five years before the plows would often turn up a live alligator buried in the mud, became the town of Hialeah. Single lots on that ten-dollar-an-acre property sold for as much as thirty-five hundred dollars. Once more fantastic wealth poured in on Curtiss and his partners.

G. H. plunged into the new game of real-estate development with his customary zest. He purchased sixty thousand acres of cheap land in the interior, northwest of Palm Beach and transferred his herds thither. Then he went to town with Hialeah.

When Hialeah was about sold out, including Curtiss' own house, he bought the land across the canal and built Miami Springs. He also started Opa Locka, seven miles to the north. The boom collapsed just as the elaborate Moorish Administration Building which he had designed for the latter place was opened, but Curtiss and his friends had made too much money to be severely hurt.

The doldrums of the real-estate business did not becalm Curtiss. He had been too busy to attend to that little matter of Miami's water supply. Now he engaged engineers to come to Miami Springs and prove a well. It gushed out an endless supply of pure spring water, and G. H. presented all the water rights and the work of his engineers to the city of Miami. All the water used there now and at Miami Beach comes from those springs.

Curtiss had a dozen other projects afoot at the same time to keep him busy. He could not see why Florida was not as good a place to make movies as Hollywood, and started a motion-picture studio. He set up the second dog-racing track in the United States at Hialeah, mainly because he was fascinated by the mechanical rabbit. He also took a tremendous interest in the new University of Miami and endowed it lavishly.

Then there was the Aero-Car Company. All the trailers of that time rode perfectly terribly, due to the primitive type of hitch. G. H. devised and patented an absurdly simple contrivance which did away with the jerks and jars. It consisted of a fat rubber-tired wheel laid horizontally in a steel box at the rear of the car. The hitching pole of the trailer passed through it and was thus cushioned against shock forward or back, up, down, or sidewise.

These multifarious activities did not fully occupy G. H. by any means. They were only play to him, and he had plenty of time for sport beside. He hunted and fished, and dashed through the mangrove shallows in a flat-bottomed boat driven by an aeroplane propeller. He took up golf and archery and then combined them into archery-golf.

Lena was right with him in all his sports. She toted a gun

through the swamps of Florida in winter and through the woods of the Adirondacks in the fall. "Baby" Glenn, who was growing up into a fine strong youth with his father's type of mind, came with them on most of their expeditions. The Genungs joined in often, and many of the old pilots came to live at Miami Springs. To each of them Curtiss gave a house and a piece of land. He never forgot anyone who had ever worked with him, and they all adored him.

It is doubtful if ever a man spent ten happier years than did Curtiss. It is amazing that a man who had worked so hard could learn to play so well.

One of his great delights was the beautiful house he planned and built for himself and Lena and Glenn. They named it *Dar Err Aha* which means House of Contentment.

In the spring of 1930 he came north to take part in a ceremony which touched him deeply. On the airport at Albany waited one of the great new Curtiss Condor twenty-passenger planes, the latest development of his company, now merged with their ancient rivals as Curtiss-Wright. It was exactly twenty years to a day since the *Albany Flyer* made the course.

With bands playing and people cheering, Lena and all the notables got into the soundproofed cabin of the great plane. G. H. took the copilot's place, the great six-hundred-horse-power Curtiss Conqueror motors roared, and the Condor sailed into the sky.

As soon as they were in the air, G. H. took over the controls. He had lost little of his skill or that accurate sense of timing which had brought him through so many tight places.

Far below the river, once so dangerous, was but a cerulean thread between the meadows. As he flew south at a hundred and fifty miles an hour, Curtiss picked out the familiar landmarks etched forever in his brain. The crowding mountains below Poughkeepsie had no power over him now. High above their tumultuous blasts the Condor soared in the untroubled air. . . .

The disastrous end of 1929 and the financial confusions of 1930 threw Curtiss' affairs into a tangle. His distaste for commercial matters was heightened by recurrent attacks of chronic appendicitis. He became extremely troubled, but he did know where to turn.

One day that spring he walked into the Genungs' house at Auburn.

"Martha," he said in an appealing voice, "may I borrow Harry for a little while? I'm in a mess. Harry, will you come and straighten things out?"

Martha nodded and Harry said, "Of course, G. H."

That was timing again. Harry had just gotten the tangled strings partially unraveled when the ancient case of Herring vs. Curtiss came up once more for trial in Rochester. Throughout the hot days Curtiss listened again to the stale testimony of the old dispute. Then one morning he collapsed from an acute attack of appendicitis.

The opposition claimed that he was faking, and sent a board of doctors to examine him. It was no fake; Curtiss was very ill.

A special train took him to Buffalo, where an emergency operation was performed at the General Hospital. Curtiss rallied splendidly from the operation. In a few days he was allowed to have visitors. Among the first he called for was Harry Genung.

Harry found his chief looking rested and fit. After a greeting that was constrained because of the tremendous affection and anxiety behind it, he glanced around the big, sunny room.

"Nice room you've got, G. H.," he remarked.

Curtiss' face wore a curious grin.

"Yes," he said. "I like it so well I doubt if I'll ever leave it."

Harry's ruddy cheeks drained white.

"Don't talk like that, G. H.," he pleaded. "You're getting on fine. You'll be out of here in no time."

"Yes?" said Curtiss.

"Of course. Appendicitis is nothing for a young fellow like you. Why, you're only fifty-two."

"I know. But they've been quite some years. We went farther than men have gone in a thousand lifetimes before us. It was fun, Harry. But I think it's over."

"Please, G. H."

"I'm terribly serious, Harry," said Curtiss. "It's—it's one of my hunches. You know, they're always true. Now there are a few things I want you to do for me. Get a pencil and paper."

For over an hour Harry wrote while Curtiss dictated directions which he had evidently thought out with the greatest care. Finally he stopped, and his head dropped wearily on the pillow.

"That's all," he said. "I think that will take care of everyone."

"Yes, G. H."

"And Harry. I want a promise. I've asked a lot of you, I know, but give me this one thing more."

"What is it, G. H.?"

"If anything happens to me, you'll look after Lena and Glenn. Promise me, Harry."

"I promise," said Harry solemnly. "Of course, G. H."

Harry and Martha took Lena back to Hammondsport the next day, Tuesday, for a rest. G. H. was in fine form; all his gloomy forebodings forgotten.

At three o'clock in the morning of Wednesday, July 23, 1930, the telephone jangled its alarm through the quiet House on the Hill. Harry, with his eyes startled from sleep, picked up the receiver.

"I regret to inform you," said a voice whose formality marked its agitation, "that an unsuspected embolism entered Mr. Curtiss' heart. Mr. Curtiss died peacefully, five minutes ago."

They brought G. H. home to Hammondsport to lie in the Pleasant Valley Cemetery over which he had so often flown. For the last time the sleepy little town became the aviation capital of the world, as men gathered there to do honor to its great son; and once again the air was full of wings, as the aeroplanes circled over the fresh grave.

Tributes poured in from every corner of the world. Curtiss' old friends and ancient enemies joined in expressing their sense of his great achievements. Every newspaper in the country carried front-page obituaries, and editorials enumerating the things he had done for aviation and for his country.

But none of them, not even those most lavish in their praise, realized then just how much he had done for America. How could they in that serene summer of 1930, when the peace of the world seemed so secure?

It had always been Curtiss' thesis that the first line of American defense was not the Navy, but Naval Aviation. Hardly anyone accepted that writing until the Japanese crossed the T's with their diving aeroplanes and dotted the i's with bursting bombs.

In the gloomy days that followed Pearl Harbor, while Americans learned of disaster upon catastrophe overtaking their armed forces, they had one sure strength to rely on, one unfailing shield. American Naval Aviation was proven the best in the world. All those who know its history remember that this vital supremacy is due largely to one man. And they will tell you that the full count of America's debt to Glenn Curtiss cannot be reckoned.

INDEX

INDEX

INDEX

About the Author

ALDEN HATCH was born on September 26, 1898. He was educated by private tutors and through correspondence courses from the University of Chicago. His early writing began with short stories for magazines, and then he turned to adult fiction. This was followed by biographies for young people and adults, and special articles on military affairs and politics for national magazines. Mr. Hatch makes his home in Cedarhurst, Long Island.